A TRUE STATESMAN

A TRUE STATESMAN

GEORGE H. W. BUSH
AND THE
'INDISPENSABLE NATION'

ROBIN RENWICK

\Bᵇ\
Biteback Publishing

First published in Great Britain in 2023 by
Biteback Publishing Ltd, London
Copyright © Robin Renwick 2023

Robin Renwick has asserted his right under the Copyright, Designs and Patents Act 1988 to be identified as the author of this work.

ISBN 978-1-78590-784-5

10 9 8 7 6 5 4 3 2 1

A CIP catalogue record for this book is available from the British Library.

Set in Adobe Caslon Pro and Bodoni

Printed and bound in Great Britain by
CPI Group (UK) Ltd, Croydon CR0 4YY

FSC
www.fsc.org
MIX
Paper | Supporting
responsible forestry
FSC® C171272

'If the United States does not lead, there will be no leadership. If the US instead turns inward, there will be a price to be paid later.'

GEORGE H. W. BUSH

CONTENTS

INTRODUCTION

This is an affectionate portrait of a great President, at the time a friend, from whom a great deal could be learned today. George H. W. Bush and his sons were 'One Nation' Republicans seeking to unify rather than divide their country. He was a staunch opponent of the right-wing demagogues within his own party and sought to uphold very high standards in public life, banning his campaign team from making any personal attacks on Bill Clinton, with whom he formed a friendly relationship.

In foreign policy there is, in my opinion, much to be learned from the way in which Bush dealt with the Chinese leadership post-Tiananmen Square and from the extraordinary care, patience and sensitivity with which he dealt with the collapse of the Soviet Union. He had the unique good fortune to find himself dealing with Mikhail Gorbachev as its leader. But without his efforts at every stage to help, to avoid making things more difficult for the Soviet President and, especially, to avoid any American triumphalism, the Gorbachev reform process might well have ended sooner than it did.

There followed the exceptional political courage he displayed in leading the campaign to evict Saddam Hussein. His Secretary of State, James Baker, and Vice-President, Dan Quayle, at one point asked each other if they would have been prepared to risk their presidency to save Kuwait, the answer being almost certainly no.

This book examines his attitude to the dramatically different presidency of his son, George W. Bush, and the extent to which a failure to follow Bush Senior's example in dealing with Russia contributed to the crisis in Ukraine. It was at the point when George W. was pressing for the admission to NATO of Georgia and Ukraine that, as his Secretary of State, Condoleezza Rice, put it, 'Moscow's patience finally snapped.'

Obama's failure to uphold his 'red line' against the use of chemical weapons by the Syrian regime and his handover of the problem to Russia sent an unfortunate message to Vladimir Putin, by then planning his first invasion of Ukraine, as did the weakness of the Western response. According to Moscow sources, Putin also saw as a sign of weakness the United States' chaotic withdrawal from Afghanistan, despite the Russians' own experiences there.

As his record in office shows, George H. W. Bush would have been unlikely to make these mistakes. Nor would he have permitted relations with the United States' traditional allies in the Middle East to reach the low point they are at today.

Yet, as Rice also observed and as the East Europeans warned all along, the fundamental cause of the falling out with Russia rests with Putin and the atavistic Russian desire to recreate a new Russian empire in the 'near abroad'. Ukraine posed no conceivable threat to Russia. Before launching his attempt to destroy the country, Putin was told that it would not be joining NATO. His campaign to discredit and undermine the alliance has succeeded so far only in strengthening it.

A myth has developed that George H. W. Bush advised his son against invading Iraq. In reality, because he too was misled by the intelligence about Saddam's weapons of mass destruction, he never did so, though he had other criticisms of that administration. This book describes the debate under George H. W. Bush's successors as to whether or not the United States should continue to serve as the 'indispensable nation' – as he believed it should – and the manner in which that has been turned on its head by Putin.

After the arguments in favour of doing less in the world by Barack Obama and 'America First' Donald Trump, how is it that Joe Biden, not a particularly strong or pugnacious leader, has now pledged America to defend Taiwan against China, to help thwart Russian aggression in Ukraine and, if necessary, to use force to prevent Iran becoming a military nuclear power? Despite the deep and acrimonious divisions in domestic policy, he has been able to do so with strong bipartisan support. Vertiginous sums in support of Ukraine have been approved in both houses of Congress with scarcely any debate.

In my diplomatic career, I experienced at first hand, over the Falklands and in Bosnia, the validity of George H. W. Bush's core belief in the 'indispensability' of the role the United States has to play in dealing with international crises, most notably in relation to Ukraine today, though also of Churchill's observation that 'the United States can be relied upon to do the right thing in the end, having first exhausted the available alternatives'.

George H. W. Bush was a great believer in personal diplomacy. He would be alarmed by the lack of it today and of private Kissinger-like communications with the United States' adversaries. He also was an exemplar of the difference one man can make, for without him there would have been no liberation of Kuwait.

He was an extraordinarily friendly, gentlemanly and approach-able person, including as President. I experienced many small kindnesses from him, including tiny handwritten notes of thanks whenever we were supporting the US on some issue, leaving me wondering how on earth he had the time to do this. When he invited me to drinks on the White House balcony in summer, he would point out the scorch marks left by Admiral Cockburn and his marines when they burned down the White House and other public buildings in Washington in 1814. I would try in vain to point out that this was in retaliation for the Americans burning down York (now Toronto) in Canada.

There were many other encounters with him, including joining in some of those with his great friend, John Major. The last was at a forlorn dinner in the White House with some of his staff and friends a few days before Bill Clinton's inauguration. None of us could really bear to see him go.

I had by then had a friendly meeting with Bill Clinton and knew the incoming members of his foreign policy team. But it was hardly less painful to have to say goodbye to James Baker, Brent Scowcroft, Dick Cheney, Larry Eagleburger and Bob Gates, knowing how badly we would miss them.

* * *

Anyone writing subsequently about President George H. W. Bush owes an important debt to the exhaustive biography by Jon Meacham, published in the US eight years ago. For those wishing to know more detail about the former President, it is an indispensable resource and I strongly recommend reading it. It includes some quotations from the President's diaries which have been incorporated in this book.

Other indispensable sources are the book George H. W. Bush wrote with Brent Scowcroft, *A World Transformed*, and George W. Bush's *A Portrait of My Father*. I also have relied on conversations at the time about him with James Baker, Brent Scowcroft, Colin Powell and Alan Greenspan. *The Man Who Ran Washington* by Peter Baker and Susan Glasser provides an invaluable perspective from James Baker's point of view.

My thanks are due to the George H. W. Bush Presidential Library, to James Stephens and Olivia Beattie at Biteback Publishing, to Chase Untermeyer and other associates of George H. W. Bush, to Sir John Major and Charles Powell, and to Marie-France Renwick for procuring the illustrations.

CHAPTER ONE

BORN WITH
A SILVER SPOON

The 41st President of the United States was happy to admit that, on 12 June 1924, he was born with a silver spoon in his mouth. His grandfather, Samuel P. Bush, grew up in the Midwest. He owned and ran a steel-making company in Columbus, Ohio. A first-class amateur golfer who competed in the US Seniors tournament, he co-founded the Scioto Country Club, which featured a golf course where Bobby Jones won the US Open in 1926 and a young Jack Nicklaus learned to play.

George Bush's great-grandfather, James Smith Bush, had started the family tradition of studying at Yale, where George's father, Prescott Bush, starred in the golf and baseball teams, sang in the Glee Club and volunteered to join the Connecticut National Guard.

Halfway through his studies, the United States entered the First World War. Reserve Lieutenant Prescott Bush left for France as a field artillery officer in the US forces under the command of General John 'Black Jack' Pershing. When Germany surrendered, he served in the occupation forces there.

After the war, while working in St Louis, Prescott met and married Dorothy, the daughter of George Herbert Walker, who had founded his own investment firm there. Moving his business to New York, George Walker merged it with that of W. Averell Harriman, becoming chairman of the combined company. As it prospered mightily, he acquired a yacht, a Rolls-Royce and numerous properties, including eleven acres of land on the shore, which became known as Walker's Point, in Kennebunkport, Maine, and which served the Bush family as their principal holiday retreat thereafter. An accomplished sportsman and golfer, George Herbert Walker founded the Walker Cup international golf tournament.

Prescott Bush also joined W. A. Harriman, which merged with Brown Brothers to become, as Brown Brothers Harriman, a major force on Wall Street. Averell Harriman, a future Governor of New York and Roosevelt's envoy to Churchill, was a Democrat; Prescott Bush a Republican believer in the principle that 'who governs best governs least'. Following the merger, George Herbert Walker broke away to re-establish his own Wall Street firm, subsequently run by his son, George Herbert Walker Junior.

George H. W. Bush's mother, Dorothy, was renowned to be just as competitive at sports, particularly tennis, as the men in her family. The children grew up in Greenwich, Connecticut. The meticulously brought up George earned two family nicknames, one of which was to haunt him later. The first was 'Have half', as, when given a treat, that is what he would say when offering to share it with his brother or a friend. The other, used as a term of mockery against him later, was 'Poppy'. His father being known as Pop, the child, as Pop Junior, was called Poppy. His political opponents and press critics thereafter would make use of the name as a way of suggesting that he was preppy and effete, though the latter charge was singularly inappropriate in his case.

Along with his elder brother, Prescott Junior, the young George was despatched to the best-known private school in the US, the

Phillips Academy in Andover, Massachusetts. George proved to be in his element there. His academic achievements were not outstanding, but he was chosen by his teammates as captain of the baseball and soccer teams and playing manager of the basketball team. He was elected president of his senior class and described by his tutor as 'markedly a gentleman'. When a Jewish boy, Bruce Gelb, was being harassed, George intervened to stop the bullying. Gelb later served in the Bush administration as director of the US Information Agency.

During the Christmas break of 1941, aged seventeen, George attended a dance at a country club in Greenwich. There he encountered an attractive sixteen-year-old brunette called Barbara Pierce. He wanted to ask her to dance but didn't know how to waltz. They agreed to meet at a Christmas party in Rye, New York. This time, they did manage a dance (not a waltz) and formed an instant attraction. He gave her a kiss which, ever thereafter, she swore was her first.

SHOT DOWN IN THE PACIFIC

By this time, the world had changed. On Sunday 7 December 1941, the Japanese attacked Pearl Harbor, destroying much of the US Pacific fleet and killing 2,400 Americans. The Andover senior year was addressed by Henry Stimson, an alumnus of the college and Roosevelt's Secretary for War. He advised the graduating students to go to university. They would have the opportunity to join the military later. Prescott Bush strongly agreed, urging his son to go to Yale and enlist thereafter. Instead, George enlisted for training as a Navy pilot on the first day he could, 12 June 1942, his eighteenth birthday. His father's permission was required for him to enlist at that age. It was the first time he had seen his father cry.

George elected to be trained as a naval torpedo bomber pilot. It was hard to think of any more dangerous occupation in the campaign against the Japanese in the Pacific. His training commenced on an open cockpit Stearman N2S-3 at the US naval base in Minneapolis. The plane was known to the cadets as the 'Yellow Peril' because it was painted yellow and could prove dangerous to fly; also as the 'Washing Machine', given the number of cadets who did not succeed in their pilot training and were washed out of the programme. George described his first solo flight as 'one of the greatest thrills of my life'.

By the time the commanding officer awarded him his flight wings at the Corpus Christi Naval Air Station in June 1943 he had grown two inches since enlisting, bringing him to 6ft 2in. He was not quite nineteen years old, making him the youngest pilot in the US Navy.

Barbara, meanwhile, was studying at Smith College in Massachusetts. They spent two weeks of his leave together at Walker's Point in Maine, where they decided to get engaged. Though this was supposed to be secret, their attachment was obvious to everyone. In December 1943, before the commissioning of the aircraft carrier USS *San Jacinto* for service in the Pacific, their engagement became official, with George writing to Barbara: 'How lucky our children will be to have a mother like you.' His mother gave her son a star sapphire engagement ring, which he presented to Barbara, who never failed to wear it thereafter. George wrote to his mother that, unlike his crew mates, he intended to remain celibate until he could marry Barbara.

From the deck of the *San Jacinto*, with the aid of a catapult which he 'was mighty glad worked', Bush now was flying the single engine Avenger torpedo bomber, carrying four 500-pound bombs. The carrier sailed through the Panama Canal to Pearl Harbor, where he saw the wreckage of the US battleships destroyed by the Japanese. Following victories in the battles of the Coral Sea and Midway, the US Navy was engaged in the progressive destruction of the Japanese bases across the Pacific. The reality of war hit home for Bush in an encounter with the Japanese forces on Wake Island. The attack was successful, but his roommate and closest friend on the carrier, Jim Wykes, crashed while on patrol. Bush wrote to Wykes's mother: 'We have lost a beloved friend.'

It very nearly was his turn next. As his Avenger took off by catapult from the carrier, the oil pressure failed, obliging him to crash-land the plane tail first on the water. He and the crew climbed out onto the wing, inflated the life raft and paddled away as the bombs exploded beneath them. An accompanying destroyer, the *C. K. Bronson*, scooped Bush and his crewmates up in a cargo net. Not long after, on deck at night, he witnessed an arriving plane missing the tail hook and crashing into the gun mounting and the sailors having to clean up the remains of the pilot and crew.

On 2 September 1944, the pilots on the carrier were briefed for an attack on the radio tower on the heavily fortified island of Chichi Jima. Bush flew with his usual crewman, the radio operator John Delaney, but that day, Lieutenant Ted White asked if, to see the weapons system in action, he could replace the usual gunner, Leo Nadeau. Bush agreed, though White was warned that this could be a rough trip, as they had taken heavy fire over Chichi Jima the day before.

Take-off was at 7.15 a.m., with four Avengers covered by Hellcat fighters flying above them. Bush's plane was third in line to dive towards the target. As they did so, they encountered a barrage of anti-aircraft fire. They were diving through tracer fire with shells exploding all around them. The Avenger lurched as it was hit, the cockpit filled with black smoke and fire ran along the wings.

Struggling to complete the mission, Bush held the plane steady on its 200-mile-an-hour dive, released the bombs, which he believed hit the target and, with the plane on fire, called on his crew to 'hit the silk!' meaning bale out. The other pilots in the squadron heard him give the order. He tilted the plane to try to release the pressure on the crew door, unbuckled his harness, dived out of the cockpit and pulled the rip cord on his parachute.

In doing so, he gashed his head and tore his parachute on the tail of the plane, hitting the sea hard and submerging. Surfacing with his head bleeding and his lungs full of sea water, he struggled to swim away from the enemy shore. Above him he saw Doug West, another Avenger pilot, tip his wings towards an object floating in the water. This was a life raft dropped by one of the other US planes, which had seen his aircraft crash. He climbed in and started paddling with his hands. The planes above him laid down fire to deter the small boats from the island despatched by the Japanese to capture him.

For the next three hours, he kept paddling under a baking sun, refusing to give up, with however little prospect of success, until he saw a black object in the water approaching him. To his amazement and relief, this turned out to be the periscope of an American submarine, the USS *Finback*. The captain of his squadron had alerted the submarine, patrolling to try to rescue pilots who were shot down. He was rescued just before noon. Two sailors hauled him out of his raft with the words 'Welcome aboard, sir.'

During his enforced stay on the submarine, he suffered nightmares about the crash. One of his crewmen had been seen to fall from the plane, but his parachute failed to open; the other had gone down with it. Bush agonised about the loss of his crew and whether he could have done more to save them, writing to his parents that he felt 'so terribly responsible for their fate'.

He wrote anguished letters to their families, telling them how much he wished that he had been able to do more to save them. He received an extraordinary reply from the sister of Jack Delaney, who wrote:

> You mention in your letter that you would like to help me in some way. There is a way, and that is to stop thinking you are in any way responsible for your plane accident and what has happened to your men. I might have thought you were if my brother Jack had not always spoken of you as the best pilot in the squadron.

Quietly religious, he never forgot what had happened to his comrades, wondering how he had been saved when they were not. Forty years later, on being elected President, he invited their sisters to a private meeting with him at the White House.

He spent a month on the submarine before re-joining his squadron. In December, he received a month's leave. He arrived in Rye, New York, on Christmas Eve, to be welcomed at the station by Barbara. They got married forthwith, with Bush in his naval uniform, on 6 January 1945.

After a brief honeymoon on Sea Island in Georgia, Bush returned to his squadron, which was preparing for the invasion of Japan, with the prospect of horrendous casualties. Bush and his comrades were spared the high likelihood of being among them when, conventional bombing having failed, President Truman authorised the dropping of atomic bombs on Hiroshima and Nagasaki. Bush, unsurprisingly, contended ever afterwards that this had been justified.

The Japanese surrendered on 2 September 1945. Bush had logged over 12,000 hours in the air for the Navy, flying fifty-eight combat missions and making 126 carrier landings. He was decorated with the Distinguished Flying Cross and Pacific Campaign Medal. To celebrate the end of the war, his family watched him fly over Walker's Point in his Avenger. On 18 September 1945, over three years after enlisting on his eighteenth birthday, George Bush was discharged from the Navy.

In 2002, he made a return visit to Chichi Jima. Welcomed by the islanders, he encountered one of the Japanese defenders, who mentioned their amazement that the US Navy should have gone to such extraordinary lengths to save a single downed pilot. His heroism in the Second World War did not prevent Bush later, about to announce his candidacy to succeed Ronald Reagan as President, being pilloried in *Newsweek* as a 'wimp' and described on its cover as 'Fighting the "Wimp Factor"'. In response to this disgraceful episode of political journalism, Bush's mild reply was that his combat colleagues hadn't thought so.

CATCHING THE OIL FEVER

In November 1945, George Bush enrolled at Yale. Five members of his family had preceded him there. His eldest son, George Walker Bush, later known as 'W', was born in the New Haven Hospital on 6 July 1946. Yale was to leave a lasting mark on Bush Senior, who cherished its traditions, including the Glee Club and another singing club, the Whiffenpoofs, members of which in later years he would invite to the White House to entertain his guests.

He and the many friends he made there found themselves in a student community still predominantly of the same class, though half his entry had served in the armed forces. He graduated honourably (Phi Beta Kappa, admission to which required high grades). In reality, as he put it, he majored in baseball and minored in economics. He became captain of the baseball team, won a prize for leadership and was a popular figure on campus. Most importantly to him, he followed his father by being inducted into the secret society, Skull and Bones, admission to which was limited to the leading undergraduates of their year.

Though he was accused ever after of being very wealthy, this was not in fact the case. He had wealthy connections, but the family ethos was that the male children, having been given a good education, thereafter must go out and make their own way.

When it came to finding a job, the obvious course was for him to become a banker in the Wall Street firm of his uncle, George Herbert Walker Junior, or at Brown Brothers Harriman, where his father was entrenched. But his war service had reinforced a strongly independent streak in his character. Commuting between Greenwich and New York with a deskbound job did not appeal to him. A friend of his father, Neil Mallon, head of Dresser Industries, which was the main supplier of drilling equipment to the oil industry, told him to 'head out to Texas and those oilfields'.

He realised that this would be hard on Barbara but felt that he had 'hit the proverbial jackpot' in marrying her. Taking a job with a Dresser subsidiary, they moved with their small son to a town Barbara had never heard of called Odessa, Texas. They rented initially half an apartment connected by a common bathroom, only to find that the other tenants, mother and daughter, were prostitutes, with the bathroom frequently occupied by their clients.

Bush's ambition 'to learn the oil business and make money'

caused him to gravitate to the boom town of Midland, Texas. The small house he bought there in what was then still a small, hot and dusty town of 20,000 people, plagued by sandstorms, cost $7,500.

Having caught the 'oil fever', Bush now took a much bolder step, deciding to join a friend, John Overbey, who was one of the myriad small independent operators buying percentages of potential royalty rights from landowners and small tracts of land from the bigger oil companies, which the independents then would drill at their own expense. The challenge was to find investors for their development company, in which they were helped by the US tax code, which, to encourage exploration, allowed all unsuccessful drilling to be written off against taxes.

Turning down a renewed more formal offer of a position with Brown Brothers Harriman, Bush sought funding for his company in New York and Washington and oil leases wherever he could. He was given a head start by investments from his uncle's Wall Street firm, G. H. Walker, which co-owned the New York Mets baseball team. He also was helped by the financier Eugene Meyer, owner of the *Washington Post* and father of Katharine Graham.

In the 1952 election won by Dwight D. Eisenhower, George's father Prescott Bush was elected Senator from Connecticut. He had a major influence on his son, who revered him. At a Republican Party meeting in the course of his campaign, Prescott criticised to his face his fellow Republican, Senator Joseph McCarthy. He mock congratulated him for having created a new word in the English language, 'McCarthyism', before criticising the methods he was using in his campaign against Communism. He was soundly booed, which left him unperturbed, as he had expected to be.

When lobbied one way or the other, Senator Bush would listen to the arguments but flatly refuse to declare in advance which way he would vote. With his son, George H. W., caught in the middle, he resisted pressure from the Texas oil industry to vote in favour of deregulation. In Washington, he became a regular golf partner and confidant of Eisenhower.

George and Barbara's second son, Jeb, was born in Midland in 1953, with the family then suffering a major tragedy, as their three-year-old daughter Robin was diagnosed with leukaemia. She was treated at the Memorial Sloan Kettering Hospital in New York. Barbara decreed that there must be no tears in front of the child, but nothing could be done to save her. George was beyond distraught at her loss, never allowing himself to forget her. Her photo later was kept in his desk in the Oval Office. Asked by a journalist in the 1980 presidential campaign whether, given his privileged upbringing, he had ever experienced any personal difficulty, he might have mentioned being shot down in the Pacific. Instead his reply was: 'Have you had to watch your child die?'

The Bush-Overbey firm was merged with that of the Liedtke brothers to form the Zapata Petroleum Corporation, named after the Marlon Brando film *Viva Zapata*, which was then showing in Midland. The combined capital of the company was $1 million. They had a major oil find on the West Jameson field in Coke County, Texas.

From the time of Zapata becoming a public company in 1955, George Bush at thirty-one years old had made a modest fortune. The partners then agreed to split the company in two, with Bush managing the offshore assets, with new offshore drilling technology, and the Liedtke brothers retaining the far more profitable onshore business. The Bush family moved from Midland to Houston, centre of the offshore oil business, which, due to the risk of losing multi-million-pound drilling rigs to hurricanes, he found far more stressful. At one point a bleeding stomach ulcer caused him to collapse on a business visit to Lloyd's, the company insurers in London. But, influenced by his father's example, George Bush was becoming far more interested in politics.

'RESPONSIBLE CONSERVATISM'

Prescott Bush was fiscally conservative but otherwise on the more liberal side of the Republican Party. In the formal hearings on the conduct of Senator McCarthy, Prescott Bush denounced him for having 'caused dangerous divisions among the American people ... Either you must follow Senator McCarthy blindly ... or in his eyes you must be a Communist.' He was one of twenty-two Republicans in the Senate (out of forty-four) formally to condemn him. His son deplored the fact that anyone who opposed McCarthy found themselves 'subjected through the lunatic fringe to all sorts of abuse'.

For the previous century, politics in Texas had been dominated by conservative southern Democrats. The so-called 'yellow dog' Democrats, it was claimed, would vote for a yellow dog rather than a Republican. This began to change when Eisenhower won the state in the 1952 and 1956 elections. In 1961, George Bush worked on the breakthrough election campaign for the Senate seat vacated by Lyndon Johnson when he became Vice-President, which was won by the Republican candidate, John Tower.

Bush became chairman of the local Harris County branch of the party. This led to a confrontation with the John Birch Society, which he regarded as representing the lunatic fringe of the party. They wanted to withdraw the US from the United Nations, impeach the Chief Justice, Earl Warren, and abolish federal income tax. Bush detested their 'mean humorless philosophy'. He banned his supporters from calling them 'nuts' but, when that didn't work, decided simply to ignore them. He had discovered, he said, that 'jugular politics, going for the opposition's throat' wasn't his style.

In 1964, he ran for the US Senate, laying out his case for 'responsible conservatism'. He won the Republican primary, but Democrat voters far outnumbered Republicans in the state and Lyndon Johnson rallied to the support of the Democratic candidate, Ralph Yarborough. Bush still looked and sounded like an East Coast Ivy Leaguer. His campaign manager was appalled at his use in speeches of words like 'profligate', which, Bush was told, no regular Texan would ever use or understand. His Mercedes was replaced by a Chrysler. He had to be dissuaded from campaigning wearing a striped tie. Nevertheless, he won just over a million votes, though he lost the election. Republicans won just one of the 150 seats in the state assembly.

Two years later, he ran for a newly created congressional seat in Houston. Denounced by his opponent as a carpet-bagger, he described himself as 'Texan by choice, not by chance' and there were plenty of new Texans in Houston. Supported in his campaign by Richard Nixon and Gerald Ford, he won the seat with 57 per cent of the votes. The secret of his electoral success on this and later occasions was his likeability. He appeared to be reasonable, devoid of malice and eschewing extremism of any kind. Disliked by conservative ideologues, he did well in terms of his perceived trustworthiness with pretty well everyone else.

When Bush became a Congressman, he sold all his shares in Zapata Offshore and took the then still unusual step of publicly declaring his net worth as $1.3 million. It did not increase much until after he handed over as President. It was not until after he left office that he became more seriously rich, mainly through his speaking engagements.

The family moved to Washington, with George W. away at college. As George Senior freely admitted, his son's behaviour was causing the family a lot of concern at the time. Invited to take Tricia Nixon out on a date, he got drunk, spilling wine. There were plenty of worse episodes, with George W. returning home intoxicated, on one occasion supposedly offering to go 'mano a mano' with his father, and his parents making clear how disappointed they were in him.

In the sharpest of contrasts to his father, George W. found little to like about Yale. He called himself a conservative on the by then liberal campus and was, he felt, looked down upon as coming from Midland, Texas, where he had grown up and gone to school, in stark contrast to his father's upbringing in Greenwich, Connecticut. At Yale, he reacted by becoming, in James Baker's words, a 'delinquent, damn near', notable for his bouts of heavy drinking and being arrested three times.

George W. waited thirty-five years, by which time he was President and at war in Iraq, before returning to Yale to receive an honorary degree. Over 200 members of the Yale faculty signed a protest letter at the award being given to such a 'mediocre man'. In a reference to his earlier escapades, he was, he observed, used to being followed by police with blue lights. To those who had achieved honours, he offered his congratulations. 'And to the C students, I say, you too can be President of the United States.'

George Bush Senior, meanwhile, became a popular and hard-working Congressman. He was the first freshman for decades to be appointed forthwith to the powerful House of Representatives Ways and Means Committee. He also was elected president of the Republican freshman class.

In 1968, Congress voted on the Fair Housing Act, which outlawed racial segregation in selling or renting residential property. Bush's congressional district was 90 per cent white and strongly opposed to the bill. Influenced by having witnessed black and white Americans fighting together in Vietnam, Bush alone among the Texas representatives (twelve Democrats and one Republican) voted for it, overcoming an initially hostile local reaction by explaining why he had done so.

That year, he was re-elected from his district unopposed. Developing a consistent Bush theme, he urged an inclusive attitude to the Hispanic population. Mexican Americans are 'essentially law-abiding and family-oriented and yet seem to be forgotten', he told the *Wall Street Journal*. He also said that it was 'too late' to hide behind states' rights in matters of race.

In the Republican Party primaries, he surfaced as a Nixon loyalist, supporting him against Ronald Reagan. He was regarded by the Nixon camp as the coming man for the Republicans in Texas. He was mentioned by the *New York Times* in a list of possible moderate outsider candidates for the vice-presidency but was too junior to be seriously considered at the time.

Before deciding whether to run again for the Senate following his first, unsuccessful, bid, he consulted Lyndon Johnson, with whom he was on friendly terms. Johnson told him that the difference between being a member of the Senate and being a member of the House was 'the difference between chicken salad and chicken shit'!

So in 1970, with Richard Nixon now President, Bush decided to try again for the Senate. His chances looked good against the liberal Democrat incumbent, Yarborough, and the Nixon White House contributed to his Senate campaign. But the odds worsened dramatically when the Democratic Party primary was won by Lloyd Bentsen, a decorated Second World War pilot, also a former

Congressman from Texas and a well-known business executive in Houston. With Bush now running against a right-wing Democrat, the *Dallas Morning News* could not see 'two cents' worth of difference in their basic political philosophies'. Bentsen was on his way to becoming an iconic figure in Texas. Bush lost to him in quite a close race.

Bush had given up his seat in the House of Representatives to run for the Senate. Summoned to the White House to discuss becoming an assistant to the President, Bush suggested to Nixon that instead he should be appointed US Ambassador to the United Nations, an idea that had been suggested to him by a well-connected friend, Charles Bartlett. This, he argued, also would enable him to act as a badly needed spokesman for the Nixon administration in solidly Democratic New York. The appointment came with a seat in the Cabinet.

The *New York Times* observed that nothing in his record qualified him for it. But he threw himself into his new post in classic George Bush style, trying to establish close relationships with the other key UN Ambassadors, demonstrating a belief in personal diplomacy that was just as much in evidence when he became President. For these purposes, he and Barbara made the most of the palatial ambassadorial apartment in the Waldorf Astoria hotel.

The burning issue at the time was whether the Taiwanese authorities or the Communist government should represent China at the UN. On behalf of the Nixon administration, Bush campaigned for dual representation. This position was undercut when the President despatched Henry Kissinger, then the national security advisor, to prepare for the historic Nixon visit to China. The dual representation battle was lost by fifty-nine votes to fifty-five, with several of those who had undertaken to vote for it changing their minds as news of the Kissinger mission broke.

Bush insisted on accompanying the Taiwanese representative as he was obliged to walk out of the UN General Assembly, to a chorus of hisses and boos. He also had to use the US veto for what was then only the second time against a resolution condemning Israeli retaliation for the killing by Black September terrorists of eleven Israeli athletes at the Munich Olympic Games.

When a journalist included him in a list of the most 'overrated' people in New York, Bush's reaction was to throw a party for all the others on the list, including Arthur Ochs Sulzberger, owner of the *New York Times*.

'RESIGNATION IS NOW BEST FOR THIS COUNTRY'

Following Nixon's landslide victory in the 1972 presidential election, in which he won every state except Massachusetts, Bush was asked by Nixon to take over from Senator Bob Dole as chairman of the Republican National Committee. He had reservations about doing so, as he felt that this was 'not a noble calling like affairs of state'. He feared that it would plunge him into the kind of partisan politics he disliked, but as the offer came from the President, he had to accept.

During the election campaign, five men had been arrested breaking into the Democratic Party headquarters at the Watergate Building in Washington. There ensued an increasingly desperate White House cover-up, with Nixon eventually firing the special prosecutor appointed to investigate and his Attorney General resigning. Bush wanted to believe the President's denials of any direct involvement, though tape recordings from the Oval Office showed Nixon complaining that Bush had been weak in supporting him.

Bush was sincere in his belief in Nixon's protestations of inno-
cence but did not trust the White House staff. 'This job', he wrote
in his diary, 'is no fun at all.' In July 1974, he wrote an agonised letter
to his sons noting Nixon's qualities but deploring his insecurity,
poor judgement and disregard for Congress and the amoral way
in which he had talked on the released White House tapes. On 5
August 1974, the 'smoking gun' tape was published, showing that
Nixon had been lying all the time.

On the following day, Bush told Nixon's chief of staff, Alexander
Haig, that the President would not have the votes to survive impeachment. On 7 August, he wrote privately to Nixon that 'I now
firmly feel resignation is best for this country, best for this President'. If he did so, history would accord his achievements a lasting
respect. Bush was criticised for having delayed until this point telling Nixon to resign, but it is difficult to see what else he could have
done in the absence earlier of firm proof. On the following day,
Nixon announced his intention to resign.

ENVOY TO CHINA

As Gerald Ford took over as President, Bush was interviewed by
him as a possible Vice-President, but ultimately the choice fell on
Nelson Rockefeller. Bush was asked by Ford if he wished to be Ambassador to the UK or France. He asked about becoming the White
House chief of staff. Instead he was steered towards becoming the
head of the US liaison office in Beijing. Kissinger, by now Secretary
of State, warned him that from time to time there would be some
substantive work, 'but for the most part you will be bored to death'.
A few weeks later, Donald Rumsfeld, another up and coming star
of the Republican Party, was appointed White House chief of staff.

Bush did everything he could to learn about China and, despite his defence of Taiwan, already had befriended the Foreign Minister, Qiao Guanhua, from their time together at the UN. But, unsurprisingly, he found that all matters of real importance to do with China were dealt with by Kissinger as Secretary of State. A visit by President Ford gave him the opportunity to meet the by now ailing Mao Zedong and, more importantly, the future leader, Deng Xiaoping. He and Barbara became renowned in Beijing for exploring the capital on bicycles. When he returned to Beijing as President in 1989, the Chinese leaders welcomed him with the gift of a bicycle.

The easy-going George Bush did not have any personal enemies in his party, but he did have a dangerous rival in the hyper-ambitious Donald Rumsfeld, who also had hoped to become Ford's Vice-President. Eight years younger than Bush, Rumsfeld had served as a Congressman from Illinois since the age of thirty. Also a former Navy pilot, he had helped Ford in taking over as President and served briefly as the US Ambassador to NATO. As White House chief of staff, he engineered his own designation as Defense Secretary and advised Ford on other key appointments.

'YOU HAVE GIVEN HIM A POST THAT IS NOT CONSIDERED TO BE VERY GOOD'

In Beijing, Bush was astonished to receive a telegram from Kissinger saying that Ford wanted to appoint him head of the CIA. Barbara was appalled. The CIA had been engulfed in a tidal wave of criticism from Congress and the media, as it was discovered to have been involved in a raft of illegal activities, including the monitoring of anti-war activists and other dissident groups. Congress was conducting its own investigation through the Church Committee, led by Senator Frank Church. Bush understood that, as the CIA director was supposed to be non-political, the post was a 'graveyard' in political terms. Even Deng Xiaoping told the visiting Ford, 'You have given him a post that is not considered to be very good!' 'You're talking like my wife,' Bush replied. He told Kissinger that he would not have selected 'this controversial position' if the choice had been his. Nevertheless, he accepted the post offered by the President, as he felt bound to do.

There could hardly have been a less promising time to do so. The Church Committee had revealed details of assassination plots against Fidel Castro and Patrice Lumumba. Congress cut off funding for the help the administration had been giving to the anti-Communist leader Jonas Savimbi in the Angolan civil war. The agency then was accused of involvement in the overthrow and death of President Allende in Chile. Leaks from the congressional inquiry led to the assassination of the CIA head of station in Greece. Frank Church and other Democratic Senators questioned how Bush could possibly be non-political as head of the agency.

As Nelson Rockefeller was distrusted by the conservative wing of the Republican Party, he had been persuaded by Ford not to stand again for the vice-presidency ahead of the 1976 election. Bush was known to be one of the hopefuls on the list of potential Republican vice-presidential candidates, having presented himself to Ford as someone who might be acceptable to both wings of the party. When, in his hearings before the Senate committee, Bush was asked to confirm that he would not be a candidate for the Republican vice-presidential nomination in 1976, he declined to do so. Instead, to secure Senate approval for his appointment at the CIA, Ford himself promised that Bush would not be his vice-presidential nominee.

Ford tried to persuade Bush that this was not on Rumsfeld's advice, a conversation followed immediately by the head of Ford's campaign telling Bush, 'Rummy just got your ass!'

Having secured Senate approval as CIA director, Bush saw it as his task to seek to restore morale in the agency and enable it to carry on with what he considered to the important work it had to do around the world. He was furious about the many leaks from Congress that were damaging its ability to do so. He found a solid ally in Ford's national security advisor, Brent Scowcroft. In one year, he was summoned to answer questions in Congress fifty-five times. As the leaks had revealed that a number of American overseas correspondents had been helping the agency for many years, Bush promised to protect the integrity of the press by ending this practice.

Despite his reservations about being appointed to the post, Bush loved working at the agency. Barbara disliked this period in her life more than any other, in part because her husband did not feel free to talk even to her about his work with the CIA and probably also because of the amount of time he spent with his 'office wife'. For Bush took with him to the agency Jennifer Fitzgerald, who also had worked with him in Beijing. An attractive 42-year-old divorcee, she became extremely close to him as his scheduler and gatekeeper, often accompanying him on business journeys. However, he knew that 'she could be difficult' and was not popular; James Baker could not stand her and nor could Barbara.

Their closeness led to rumours in the CIA headquarters in Langley that they might be having an affair, for which no evidence has ever been produced. This did not prevent the press having fun at their expense by writing that Fitzgerald had served 'in a variety of positions under' Bush. When he became Vice-President, she continued to serve for two years as his scheduler, then as head of his congressional office. When he was elected President, she was moved to the State Department as deputy chief of protocol, where she insisted on an inflated salary. An arch-critic of Bush, Ann Devroy of the *Washington Post* spent two months investigating rumours of the supposed affair, only to report that she could find nothing to confirm them. When Ann Devroy was hospitalised with cancer, disregarding her hostile articles about him, Bush arranged for her to be treated at the M. D. Anderson Cancer Center in Houston.

George W., like his mother, was less forgiving of Bush Senior's detractors, referring to another incessant critic, Maureen Dowd, who loved calling his father 'Poppy' and thought a lot worse of his son, as 'the cobra'.

In the event, Ford chose a more senior Republican than either Bush or Rumsfeld, Senator Bob Dole, as his running mate in the 1976 presidential election. During the campaign, Jimmy Carter asked for briefings from the CIA. These were provided to him by Bush personally. When Ford narrowly lost the election, Bush offered his resignation but, having grown to love the role, indicated to Carter that he might be persuaded to stay on. Carter was not interested, thereby saving Bush's political career. If he had served in the Carter administration, his chances of ever becoming the Republican candidate for the presidency would have been zero.

'TEAM B'

Extremely popular within the agency for restoring morale and defending it in Congress, Bush had to deal with fierce criticism from the right that détente had led the agency to be far too complacent about Soviet intentions and their development of ever more powerful inter-continental ballistic missiles. To counter this criticism, Ford and Bush commissioned an alternative assessment by a 'Team B', incorporating several of the leading critics. The Soviet expert Richard Pipes and Reagan's future (successful) arms control negotiator Paul Nitze tackled head on the agency's comforting assessment that the Soviets were not aiming for superiority but 'sought only strategic parity' with the US. Essentially, they won the argument about Soviet intentions, with Bush declaring that a new National Intelligence Estimate 'presents a starker appreciation of Soviet strategic capabilities and objectives'. There followed under Carter the Soviet invasion of Afghanistan and admission by Gorbachev that the Soviet Union had indeed been seeking military superiority.

CHAPTER TWO

'COULDN'T FIGURE OUT WHAT THE HELL TO DO'

Following his resignation from the CIA, Bush went back to Houston 'and couldn't figure out what the hell to do'. When, to his dismay, his aunt, Mary Walker, felt obliged to sell Walker's Point, he persuaded her to give him time to raise the money to buy it, his finances having suffered during his years of public service. He found a base at the First International Bank in Houston, joined some other corporate boards and accepted innumerable speaking engagements. He turned down an offer from Ross Perot to run his oil business in Houston.

His son George W. narrowly lost an election for a Texas seat in Congress. But, to the huge relief of his parents, his wild days were over. He had graduated from Harvard Business School, married Laura Welch, whom his parents adored, and given up drinking. He was starting to make his way in business in Midland and clearly was going to try again in politics.

In their earlier life in Houston, the Bushes had become close friends with James and Mary Baker. James Baker, a graduate of Princeton who had served in the Marine Corps, was a fast-rising figure as a lawyer in Houston. His family were just as patrician as the Bushes. Baker Botts were the leading law firm in Houston, but the youthful Baker had to work for a rival firm because of Baker Botts's anti-nepotism policy. It was not until after he had served as Secretary of State that he was able to end up working for the family firm.

Baker's approach to wooing his wife ('I have the screaming "A" bomb hots for you,' he told Mary) would never have been that of George H. W. with Barbara, but the two families became firm friends. George and Barbara Bush then helped him through a major tragedy, as Mary died of cancer before she or Baker was forty. The two families enjoyed playing touch rugby together, but so competitively that it seemed more like the real thing. As Bush and Baker both were tennis enthusiasts, they teamed up to win the doubles tournament twice at the Houston Country Club, Baker being the better player. Baker had tried but failed to get himself elected Attorney General of Texas. Six years younger than Bush, Baker saw himself as the junior of the two, sometimes calling his friend 'jefe' (chief).

What George Bush really wanted to do next, he decided, was to try to run for President, regardless of the fact that, at this time, no one would have given him the slightest chance of succeeding in doing so. All but forgotten, except by party insiders, he had no obvious constituency and no national name recognition. In straw polls, his name did not figure on the shortlist of favourites for Republicans likely to run against Carter in 1980, which then included Reagan, Dole, John Connally and Howard Baker. It was to be found under an asterisk, indicating 'some votes also for', in a group of rank outsiders. Bush's response was to offer to hold a party for the other 'asterisks'.

THE FUND FOR LIMITED GOVERNMENT

Pretty well his first call about his improbable ambition was to his closest friend, James Baker. Helped by Bush's recommendation, Baker had served as Under-Secretary for Commerce in the Ford administration. He had helped Ford to win the 1976 Republican nomination for President against Reagan and had managed Ford's electoral campaign against Jimmy Carter. He checked that Ford, who might be running himself, did not object to him helping Bush. Ford had no objection but thought they would have quite a struggle. Baker thereupon agreed to be chairman of the Bush/Baker Fund for Limited Government.

The Republican Party at this time fell into two main camps. Ronald Reagan, former Governor of California, had taken over the leadership of the conservatives from Barry Goldwater. Discussing the vice-presidency with Gerald Ford, Bush had presented himself as an arch-centrist, acceptable to both wings of the party. In reality, he was far more comfortable with and more highly regarded by the pragmatists, who saw governing as more a matter of stewardship than of offering a new vision for the country.

This suited Bush's character and experience and his speaking style. For he freely admitted that he was no great orator and he distrusted oratorical flourishes anyway. In addition to which, he quite frequently misspoke. Ann Richards, the redoubtable Democratic Governor of Texas, was later to describe him as having been born 'with a silver foot in his mouth'.

But what Bush remained very good indeed at was projecting his likeability. He had a horror of ever appearing arrogant or self-satisfied. He sought to project in reasonable terms his commitment to limited government and states' rights and opposition to Democratic spending plans. He was an effective critic of Carter's perceived fee-bleness in foreign policy. On no issue could he be regarded as being at the extreme end of any spectrum. Nor did he ever make any personal attacks on his opponents.

Having learned from Carter's example the make-or-break im-portance of the two earliest primary contests, in the Iowa caucuses and New Hampshire, he launched an invasion of Iowa. He appeared there far more frequently than any other candidate, attending a host of local events, making a good impression when he did so. Very effective in supporting him was Barbara Bush, who, making brief speeches of her own, had a positive impact in all his campaigns. Their sons Jeb and Neil also joined in.

This was retail politics with a vengeance, and it paid off. When the polls closed in Iowa, to general surprise, Bush emerged ahead of the favourite, Ronald Reagan, with 30 per cent of the votes, trans-forming overnight the asterisk into a frontrunner.

Given his upbringing in New England, he felt confident about his chances in New Hampshire. He then suffered a Reagan ambush. For a debate two days before the vote, the organisers had decided to invite only the two frontrunners, but the other candidates also showed up, demanding to be heard. Reagan insisted that they too should be allowed to speak, pointing out that he was paying for the debate. Bush should immediately have agreed that the others should participate. Having failed to do so, he was left looking com-pletely discomfited. Reagan won 50 per cent of the votes, with Bush coming second. Bob Dole and the Texas former Governor John Connally then dropped out of the race.

'A PRESIDENT WE WON'T HAVE TO TRAIN'

Bush would not give up. His campaign slogan was 'A President we won't have to train'. He annoyed the Reagan camp by labelling his opponent's plan to cut taxes while still balancing the budget as 'voodoo economics'. He also kept suggesting that he was 'the right age' to be President (fifty-six) and, by implication, that Reagan at nearly seventy was too old. But Reagan then swept Texas. Bush won in Michigan, but Reagan soon needed only to win his home state of California to secure the nomination.

Baker urged an extremely reluctant Bush to concede before he did irreparable damage to his political prospects. Bush, after quite an argument, withdrew, endorsing Reagan and expecting nothing from the victor. From extremely unpromising beginnings, he had put up a surprisingly strong performance.

The Republican National Convention in Detroit awaited Reagan's decision about his running mate. The frontrunner, by a long way, was the former President Gerald Ford. If he could be persuaded to accept the role, this was regarded as the 'dream ticket' against Carter. Though pressed by some of his advisers to consider choosing Bush, Reagan had been irritated by the 'voodoo economics' charge, by suggestions that he was too far right to win and by Bush harping on about the age difference between them.

Ford still was reluctant, but Henry Kissinger and Alan Greenspan discussed with him the possibility of Ford as Vice-President having a substantial role in policy. For the Reagan team, Bill Casey suggested that Ford could expect to have a major role on the budget and foreign and defence matters. In a crucial TV interview with Walter Cronkite close to the climax of the convention, Ford said that if he went back to Washington, it would not be as a figurehead Vice-President. Cronkite asked whether Reagan would be taking on 'something like a co-presidency?' As far as Reagan, watching, was concerned, 'that did it'.

Meanwhile, Bush delivered his speech to the conference and went to bed with no reason whatever to believe that he would be chosen. Reagan called his close adviser Stu Spencer, who earlier had told him that he should choose Bush. Spencer believed that pragmatism always prevailed with Reagan and proved to be right, and he was nothing if not decisive. As Bush put it, 'I thought we were done, out of it.' Then, out of the blue, at 11.37 p.m. the phone rang. It was Reagan saying that he wanted to tell the convention the next day that he had chosen George Bush to be his running mate. Reagan checked that Bush had no problems with the party platform. Bush confirmed that he didn't. Reagan then went over to address the convention at a quarter past midnight, including his plans for Bush. Dining at the 21 Club in New York, George W. Bush was astonished to see the news flash up on a TV screen.

'WE'RE GOING TO WORK OUR TAILS OFF FOR YOU'

The Bushes met the Reagans for coffee the next morning. Barbara Bush told Reagan, 'You're not going to be sorry. We're going to work our tails off for you.'

Bush was asked how he could support a programme that did not endorse the Equal Rights Amendment and envisaged a constitutional amendment to ban abortion, which he had opposed in the campaign. He said that the real issues were the economy and foreign affairs. He agreed with Reagan on the desirability of tax cuts.

Privately, he regarded the position on abortion as the party's sop to the religious right. He was in principle against abortion but certainly never intended to ban it. He did not believe that Reagan planned to do so either and proved to be right about that. Barbara Bush, for her part, declared that she supported the Equal Rights Amendment and was pro-choice on abortion. The *New York Times* pronounced favourably that 'Reagan's second choice is not second rate … He is a serious, able and likeable man.'

Bush settled immediately into the role of a loyal and highly supportive deputy to Reagan, which seemed to suit him both politically and temperamentally. At a meeting in San Francisco, Reagan's closest associate, Caspar 'Cap' Weinberger, told Barbara that 'lots of top Reagan people were not sure about GB and had questioned his loyalty. Now they were thrilled with the choice.'

In August 1980, Bush made visits to Japan and China. He reassured the Chinese government that, despite Reagan's pro-Taiwan remarks (and sentiments), there was no intention to depart from the official US policy of recognising only one China, a position upheld by Reagan at a press conference after Bush's return. Bush by this time was observing that Reagan 'is such a nice fellow', in contrast to his feelings about Nixon.

The presidential race between Reagan and Carter was depicted by the press as neck and neck throughout the autumn, with almost everyone giving Carter the advantage. Opinion polls were not yet highly developed and proved mostly wrong. In the sole debate, Carter was expected to win hands down in terms of his grasp of policy. As the debate opened, Reagan walked across the stage to shake a disconcerted Carter's hand. What was needed, he said, was to revive the economy and stand up to the Soviet Union. As Carter tried to enmesh him in complicated rebuttals, a far more relaxed Reagan observed, 'There you go again, Mr President.' Addressing the TV audience, Reagan asked, 'Are you better off than you were four years ago?' A lot of them felt that they weren't. Bush's main contribution to the campaign was to keep asserting that Reagan 'is a decent, compassionate man'.

Reagan won the election by a landslide, defeating Carter by ten percentage points and winning almost every state in the Union. Before the election, Bush had said that, in government, if he won Reagan's confidence, he would have plenty to do. If not, he would be going to a lot of funerals. Asked about this after the result, Reagan said, 'He's not going to be going to a lot of funerals.'

Bush wrote a sympathetic letter to his Democratic counterpart, Walter Mondale. He wrote to Reagan that he would never do anything to embarrass him politically. He had strong views on issues and people, 'but once you decide a matter, that's it for me, and you'll see no leaks in Evans and Novak' – nor elsewhere.

'NOT WORTH A BUCKET OF WARM SPIT'

It was John Nance Garner, Vice-President for eight years to Franklin Roosevelt, who, finding that he had no influence, warned Lyndon Johnson that the office was not worth a bucket of warm spit and that accepting it was 'the worst damn fool mistake' he ever made. George Bush aimed to make more of it than that and Reagan supported him, but he was to find that the role had its own peculiar difficulties.

Before they took office, the ground rules for Bush's role vis-à-vis the President were set out in a memo from Reagan's long-term associate Ed Meese. These were that Reagan and Bush should have a weekly lunch, with no staff and no agenda. Bush would be invited to all presidential meetings. He would receive a copy of all memos going to the President. His office would be in the West Wing. As Bush observed, he could not have asked for anything more.

A further positive development was in store. Ed Meese had expected to be appointed White House chief of staff. But Meese was famously disorganised. It was said that any document that went into his briefcase was never seen again. Meese was told that he was to serve as Counselor to the President. To general astonishment, Reagan appointed James Baker as his chief of staff. His office in the West Wing was next to that of Bush, and Baker had influenced the memo about the Vice-President's role.

* * *

George Bush saw his role as being to offer Reagan advice, but only in private, while being determined never to allow any distance between them to appear in public. Inevitably, this led him to be portrayed in sections of the media as a servile nonentity while, at the same time, extreme conservatives in the Republican Party suspected him and Baker of conspiring to stop Reagan being Reagan. None of which affected the respect by now he was feeling for Reagan, who, he said, was 'unthreatened by people or events, a superb person'.

This mutual respect did not, however, extend to Nancy Reagan and Barbara Bush, who, before long, could not stand one another. As Bush himself put it, 'Nancy and Barbara just did not have a pleasant personal relationship.' The fault was primarily that of Nancy Reagan, concerned that the Bushes should be as invisible as possible and alarmed that the down-to-earth Barbara Bush appeared to be more popular than her. But beneath the benevolent grandmother image, Barbara Bush had strong views about everything. She was far less tolerant of his Democratic opponents and press critics than her more easy-going husband. She was notoriously bad at pretending to be pleasant to people she didn't like. The list of those ranged from Nancy Reagan and her glitzy friends from California to, later, the Clintons. The Reagans socialised with their pals from the West Coast; the Bushes with an entirely different group of friends in or visiting Washington.

But when it came to business, this didn't matter. The Reagan team of Meese and Mike Deaver, plus Baker, recommended that Bush should be put in charge of the senior-level national security crisis management group.

The Secretary of State, Al Haig, infuriated by this, made the first of his several threats to resign, but White House sources (probably Baker) said that Reagan felt more comfortable with the calmer and less ego-driven Bush. At Reagan's seventieth birthday party, he told Barbara Bush that he wanted to be sure that his deputy was doing enough. In case the awful should happen, 'George should know everything.'

On 30 March 1981, it very nearly did, as the deranged John Hinckley shot Reagan outside the Washington Hilton Hotel, the deflected bullet missing his heart by an inch. Bush was on Air Force Two about to land in Austin, Texas. Alerted from Washington by Al Haig, he flew straight back to the Andrews Air Force Base outside Washington. Rushed to hospital, where, although in dire straits, he tried to joke to the doctors that 'I hope you are all Republicans', Reagan was undergoing emergency surgery.

The air crew wanted Bush to fly by helicopter from Andrews to land on the South Lawn of the White House, a plan resisted by the secret service on security grounds and vetoed anyway by Bush, who was determined not to appear a 'showboating Vice-President trying to draw attention to himself ... Only the President lands on the South Lawn.' At the White House, a breathless Al Haig had rushed into the Situation Room to say that the Vice-President was returning to Washington. Meanwhile, 'I am in control here.'

Throughout this chaotic day, Bush remained extremely calm. By the time he reached the White House, he had heard from Meese that Reagan was out of surgery, which had been successful. Bush told his colleagues that 'the President is not incapacitated and I am not going to be a substitute President. I'm here to sit in for him while he recuperates. But he's going to call the shots.'

He addressed the country that evening to say that he was 'deeply heartened' by the report from the doctors. Reagan had emerged 'with flying colours'. The US government was functioning effectively. Officials had been fulfilling their functions 'with skill and with care'. The last point was included to partly whitewash Haig, who had wanted to put US forces on heightened alert, vetoed by the Defense Secretary, Cap Weinberger. Bush finished the day by going to see Nancy Reagan, whom he found looking 'tiny and afraid'.

On the following day, Bush convened the Cabinet, sitting in his usual chair, not that of the President. On Capitol Hill, he denied that there was any rift between the President's advisers, then met the Dutch Prime Minister. After briefing Reagan at the hospital a few days later, he told the press that the President was 'fully on top of the situation'.

The press concluded that in this crisis, he had 'struck just the right note' and, in contrast to Haig, he had been an important steadying influence. Bush also felt the episode had helped him with Reagan, as undoubtedly it did.

While recovering from the shooting, the apparent Cold War warrior, Ronald Reagan, decided to send a personal message to the Soviet leader, Leonid Brezhnev. Written on a yellow legal pad, it was a peace offering. He wanted to send a signal to him that 'we were interested in reducing the threat of nuclear annihilation … Should we not be concerned with eliminating the obstacles which prevent our people from achieving their most cherished goals?'

As Reagan observed, this met with an icy reply. 'So much for my first attempt at personal diplomacy.'

Before long, Bush was attending Brezhnev's funeral. He found, he said, that 'something was missing. There was no mention of God.'

Reagan next proposed that instead of the US and its allies deploying new intermediate-range missiles in Europe to match the new Soviet deployment of new weapons threatening Western Europe, there should be agreement to zero missiles in that category on both sides. This proposal was rejected by the Soviets, who were counting on anti-nuclear sentiment in Europe to prevent the deployment of the US Pershing II missiles.

Bush was despatched to Europe to help convince the NATO governments that Reagan was serious about arms reductions. The *Washington Post* thought him to be 'just the right man – positive, experienced, political – to satisfy the allies' craving for a strong and sensible American lead'. He published an offer by Reagan to meet the new Soviet leader, Yuri Andropov, to sign an agreement on zero intermediate-range missiles.

'DO YOU THINK WE CARE LESS THAN OTHERS ABOUT NUCLEAR WAR?'

In Britain, in a meeting at the Guildhall, Bush told Bruce Kent of the Campaign for Nuclear Disarmament, 'Do you think we don't want peace? Do you think we care less than others about nuclear war? We want peace and to keep the peace.' This, he argued, could only be done by maintaining a balance of forces. Margaret Thatcher, faced with a host of anti-nuclear demonstrators at the proposed missile base at Greenham Common, told Reagan that Bush's trip had been very helpful. The missile deployments went ahead in Britain and Germany. The *Washington Post* ran an editorial extravagantly titled 'George Did It'.

In April 1982, Vice-President Bush was dining with the British Ambassador, Sir Nicholas Henderson, on the evening the Argentinians invaded the Falkland Islands. In the struggle for influence that then broke out between the Europeanists and Latin American proponents within the US administration, there was never any doubt where Bush's sympathies lay, though it was the US Defense Secretary, Cap Weinberger, who quietly set about making sure that the British won the war. As Margaret Thatcher observed, without the Sidewinder missiles supplied by the US, the UK could not have retaken the Falklands.

Conscious that he continued to be mistrusted by entrenched right-wing Republicans, Bush agreed to address the American Conservative Union though 'the nuts will never be for me. We might as well recognize it.' Baker, even more so, was under constant attack from right-wingers, who misunderstood their idol Reagan. For although he had strong positions of principle, Bush observed that Reagan was never afraid to compromise, including even to the extent of raising taxes.

By 1983, despite already being the oldest person to hold the office, Reagan was preparing to seek re-election. Bush sent Baker a copy of the *Conservative Digest*, which purported to show that two thirds of conservative leaders wanted Bush replaced on the ticket. Instead Reagan, addressing the Conservative Political Action Conference, took Bush with him and led a standing ovation for him ('Bless his heart,' said Barbara Bush).

The 1984 presidential election campaign against Walter Mondale was a resounding success for Reagan, who ended up winning every state except Minnesota, but not for Bush, who appeared inarticulate and excessively eager to please, at one point declaring that 'I'm for Mr Reagan – blindly'.

The Democrat-leaning press, unable to make any impression on Reagan, went after Bush with a vengeance, with the cartoonist Garry Trudeau and others claiming that his ambition himself to become President after Reagan had caused him to sell his soul. His patrician East Coast origins and supposed wealth again were raked up against him.

Barbara Bush did not help by describing Mondale's running mate, Geraldine Ferraro, as something that 'rhymes with rich'. But her by now well-established grandmotherly public persona, with her defiantly white shock of hair, was helped by her publishing a successful children's book, *C. Fred's Story*, recounting the adventures of the Bushes' pet spaniel. This was followed by *Millie's Book*, about the experiences of C. Fred's successor, Millie, who became a popular feature of the White House during the Bush presidency. When George H. W. became President, Barbara, who hated the addiction to television rather than reading, sponsored a programme to improve literacy, particularly in immigrant communities, helping to spur on George W. Bush's interest in this issue, as well as raising $25 million to renovate the White House.

CHAPTER THREE

RUNNING FOR PRESIDENT

'POLITICS IS NOT A PURE UNDERTAKING'

The moment the election was won, George Bush started planning his own run for President. He knew that he was going to face an uphill battle. After eight years of either party in the White House, the American people normally switched to the other. The last sitting Vice-President to be elected President had been Martin Van Buren in 1836. In the 1986 midterm elections, the Republicans had lost control of both houses of Congress.

Bush was impressed by a memo from Lee Atwater, who hailed from South Carolina and was serving in the Reagan political office. In 1980, the paper noted, Bush had been regarded as a person of substance. He was now being portrayed as no more than a cheerleader for Reagan. 'High irony it is that an Ivy Leaguer with experience in international affairs, domestic politics and private business should be hit with the rap of "lightweight" by the more hostile elements of the press.'

The cigar-chomping, guitar-playing Lee Atwater was a total contrast to Bush. Twenty-seven years younger, he had started in life with no advantages and believed in attack-dog politics. Bush saw him as representing a generation with which he badly needed to connect. George W. Bush moved up to Washington to help. Another important recruit was Roger Ailes, a Nixon and Reagan media adviser and future moving spirit of Fox News. He found Bush a difficult pupil. He tried to improve Bush's speaking style, without much success, and found him dismissive of what he regarded as the 'show business' aura around Reagan.

Bush realised that, for him, politics now was going to get much uglier. He already had experienced a foretaste of this but was unprepared for the attack on him by the conservative commentator George Will in January 1986. Will described him as traipsing from one conservative venue to another while emitting 'the sound of a lapdog'. The more dyed-in-the-wool conservatives did not trust him – not without reason, since, as he observed, he was never of one extreme or the other. Nevertheless, he had been drifting to the right as he sought to bolster his chances of succeeding Reagan.

Genuinely against abortion in principle, he now supported a constitutional amendment to ban it, though he never had any intention of enacting one. He was committed to tax cuts, though the Reagan tax cuts had increased the budget deficit. Asked by the religious right if he was 'born again', his reply was: 'I think I would ask for a definition.'

Donald Rumsfeld had been thinking of running for the Republican nomination but instead endorsed the main right-wing candidate, Bob Dole.

For Reagan's second term, James Baker swapped jobs with the Treasury Secretary, Donald Regan. Baker, predictably, won applause in his new role. He attracted Margaret Thatcher's ire for his success in the Plaza and Louvre accords in persuading (in her view, bamboozling) his European counterparts to take action to hold down the value of the soaring dollar, but it manifestly was in US interests for him to do so. Donald Regan was a great deal less successful as White House chief of staff.

A MURKY AFFAIR

In November 1986, a Lebanese journal reported that the United States had sold arms to Iran in an attempt to secure Iranian help in freeing several Americans, including a CIA agent being held hostage in Lebanon by the radical Islamist movement Hezbollah. This clearly was a violation of US policy, which was not to negotiate with terrorists. Iran had been designated a state sponsor of terrorism, and Hezbollah, controlled by Iran, had its own terrorist record.

The policy, which had been reaffirmed by a task force chaired by Bush, had been overturned by Reagan himself, because of his concern to do all he could to get the hostages freed. The idea of engaging with the Iranians to try to do so had come originally from the Israelis.

In July 1985, the then national security advisor, Robert 'Bud' Mc-Farlane, and Don Regan, as the White House chief of staff, briefed Reagan, who was recovering from surgery at the Bethesda Naval Hospital, about the Israeli-originated plan to sell arms to Iran to seek their help in releasing the hostages. In August 1985, the US made via Israel the first shipment of arms to Iran, followed by further shipments that year and in 1986.

The national security staff were prime movers in this murky affair. But it was an absolute disgrace for Don Regan, as White House chief of staff, to have permitted a decision of this importance to be taken by a President on medication in hospital in the absence of any discussion with the Secretary of State, George Shultz, or the Defense Secretary, Cap Weinberger. This was a mistake James Baker would have been very unlikely to have made. If there had been a proper discussion, the outcome might have been the same, given Reagan's anxiety to free the hostages, but there simply wasn't one.

Bush was aware that, in contravention of its stated policy, the US was seeking to trade arms for hostages, in an attempt to win over supposedly moderate elements in Iran. He recorded in his diary on 5 November 1986: 'I'm one of the few people that know fully the details.' The new national security advisor, Admiral Poindexter, had recorded on 1 February 1986 that the President 'and VP are solid in taking the position that we have to try'.

Bush had been present at a meeting in the Oval Office on 7 January 1986 at which George Shultz and Cap Weinberger had argued fiercely against trading arms for hostages with Iran, though by then, thanks to the national security staff, the sales were already being made. Knowing that the decision had already been taken by Reagan and not wanting to gainsay the President, Bush had remained silent at this meeting.

In July 1986, in the King David Hotel in Jerusalem, at the behest of the National Security Council (NSC) staff, Bush met Amiram Nir, counter-terrorism adviser to the Israeli Prime Minister, Shimon Peres. Nir argued that the objective of the arms sales was, firstly, tactical, to get the hostages out, but also strategic, to establish channels to supposedly moderate elements in Iran.

Not long afterwards, Shultz heard Bush on US television denying that there were any arms sales to Iran. Shultz noted that the 'VP was part of it ... Blows his integrity ... Should be very careful how he plays the loyal lieutenant role now.'

He warned Bush to be more careful in his public statements, triggering a sharp reaction. Did Shultz realise, Bush asked, that there were major strategic objectives with Iran? There was, Shultz recalled, 'considerable tension between us'. But, thereafter, Bush was more careful. Baker subsequently told Shultz that he had saved 'the VP's political life by telling him to be quiet about arms'.

In December 1986, Bush said publicly, 'I was aware of our Iran initiative and I support[ed] the President's decision.' In early 1987, he argued in his diary that his critics within the administration did not know that he had raised the issue over and over again with the President, Don Regan and Poindexter, including his concerns that the Israeli role gave the US little control over the operation. In a bid to 'get everything out, as early as possible', he asked his legal counsel, Boyden Gray, to leak to Bob Woodward at the *Washington Post* the record of his meeting in Israel with Nir.

In August 1987, Bush's performance reached a nadir when he told the *Washington Post* that if he had heard George Shultz and Cap Weinberger express strong opposition to arms sales to Iran, 'then maybe I would have had a stronger view ... But when you don't know something, it's hard to react ... We were not in the loop.'

Weinberger rang Shultz: 'That's terrible. He was on the other side. It's on the record. Why did he say that?' Shultz was as disgusted as Weinberger.

On 24 November 1986, the Attorney General, Ed Meese, arranged a meeting at which, as Bush later put it, he 'laid a real bombshell on me'. An out-of-control, gung-ho US Marine lieutenant colonel on the NSC staff, Oliver North, had used the proceeds of the arms sales to Iran to fund the insurgency by the anti-Communist Contras in Nicaragua, despite a congressional prohibition on US military aid to them. Bush, this time truthfully, told Meese that he knew absolutely nothing about this. The subsequent inquiry found no evidence that either Bush or his staff were aware of the diversion of funds to the Contras.

Bush had been undone by his determination at any cost to show loyalty to the President. But this had been compounded by his dissembling thereafter. The Iran–Contra special counsel, the more hostile Lawrence Walsh, found that Bush was not liable in respect of either side of the scandal, but he was scathing about Bush's claim to have been 'not in the loop' about the arms-for-hostages venture in Iran.

As Bush, well before this, had concluded: 'Politics is not a pure undertaking.'

'THESE ARE SERIOUS PEOPLE, AMONG THE BEST WE HAVE'

Nevertheless, at the end of 1986, there was some cheer, as the veteran columnist Scotty Reston wrote in the *New York Times* of George and Barbara Bush: 'These are serious people, among the best we have, with the gifts of intelligence and friendship and compassion. Quietly, he could make a real difference in the next two years.'

There followed a campaign, led by Nancy Reagan, to get rid of the White House chief of staff, Don Regan. She held Regan partly responsible for the Iran–Contra fiasco. Egged on by Lee Atwater, Bush agreed that a change was needed and told Reagan so, but he proved reluctant. Nancy Reagan insisted that Bush should arrange a meeting for the President to ask Regan to stand down. As this leaked, Regan was forced to make a hurried and undignified departure, which Bush had sought to avoid. Bush felt that this would backfire against Nancy Reagan, as it did when Don Regan published a memoir detailing the extent to which she was guided by her astrologer.

On the Democratic Party side, the initial frontrunner was Gary Hart, who Bush thought would be a tough opponent for him. He felt that Michael Dukakis's liberal ideas would not travel well outside Massachusetts. When Hart was knocked out by stories about his womanising, Bush told his diary: 'I am rooting for Hart. I think the journalists have gone way too far this time.'

The rumours immediately revived allegations in the Democratic-leaning press of a relationship between Bush and Jennifer Fitzgerald. When Roger Ailes confronted Bush about the claims, Bush's reply was: 'They haven't got shit.' No evidence of an affair was ever produced.

What undoubtedly was true, however, was that Bush enjoyed the company of attractive women and was flirty and could be touchy-feely with them. This was a source of constant concern to Barbara, who made a huge fuss when he invited an attractive blonde to his swearing-in ceremony as Ambassador to the United Nations, telling her, 'You should NOT have been there!' There followed further press rumours about supposed affairs, infuriating Bush's family. In reality, there was no evidence that he had ever strayed.

'FIGHTING THE WIMP FACTOR'

In October 1987, Bush incautiously agreed to cooperate in a *Newsweek* profile about him. There was no doubt about the Democratic allegiance of *Newsweek*, nor of the reporter, Margaret Warner. Nevertheless, she wrote a generally fair article about Bush, until it got into the hands of her editor, Evan Thomas. Disregarding Warner's objection to the term, it was Thomas who wrote that, as a candidate for President, Bush suffered from a potentially crippling factor: 'that he isn't strong enough or tough enough for the challenges of the Oval Office. That he is … a wimp.' This was accompanied by a picture of Bush on the cover, with the headline: 'Fighting the "Wimp Factor"'.

Several of Thomas's colleagues squirmed to me about this episode, for which, after Bush's leadership in the Gulf War, he later made a fulsome apology. Her far more forgiving husband might have overlooked this, but Barbara Bush sought to ensure that Katharine Graham, the owner of *Newsweek*, hardly ever was admitted to the White House throughout the Bush presidency.

As the campaign for the Republican nomination got under way, the main challenge to Bush came from Senator Bob Dole, who kept drawing a contrast between growing up the hard way and the relatively privileged existence of his rival. A fellow veteran, Dole had been so badly wounded as an infantryman in the Second World War that he had largely lost the use of his right arm. Highly intelligent and keen to portray himself as tougher than Bush, he was less likeable, with a sometimes waspish element in his character, but he was entitled to feel that life had treated him a lot less kindly than his opponent. As he hailed from neighbouring Kansas and clearly was more 'one of us', he had an advantage against Bush in the Iowa caucuses. Also campaigning hard there was the right-wing evangelist Pat Robertson.

Mikhail Gorbachev arrived in Washington in December 1987 for a summit meeting with Reagan. Bush, who was present, felt confident that he could more than hold his own with Gorbachev. The Soviet Foreign Minister, Eduard Shevardnadze, 'made distinct sounds' that they hoped for Bush to be elected President.

'THE EMPTY CANONS OF RHETORIC'

Bush escorted Gorbachev on his limousine ride back to Andrews Air Force Base. He told Gorbachev that either a Democratic or a Republican President would want to continue the improved relationship, but it was Reagan who would get the new Intermediate-Range Nuclear Forces Treaty through the Senate. He added that he expected to win the Republican nomination and to win the election. In that event, he would want to improve relations still further. Gorbachev should not be concerned about what Mao Zedong had described as the 'empty canons of rhetoric' he would hear during the election campaign, hinting that he might have to sound tougher about the Soviets than he really meant.

Back in Iowa, Bush was under attack from Dole for his role in Iran–Contra. In an effort to help his deputy, Reagan had been persuaded to issue a statement in March 1987 that Bush 'had expressed reservations throughout the process but had supported the decision and the policy'. The White House chief of staff at the time, Don Regan, confirmed that Bush had indeed expressed his reservations.

The editor of the *Des Moines Register* put it to Bush that, 'you seem to be telling the American people, in effect, "Trust me; I did the right thing, but I can't tell you what I did."' Bush's response was that he had answered every question except one, which was 'What did you tell the President?' And he couldn't and wouldn't answer that. A highlight of the campaign was a heated exchange about Iran–Contra between Bush and the CBS anchor Dan Rather, with Bush holding his own against a hostile Rather.

Nevertheless, Dole won the Iowa caucuses and, worse still, Bush came third, behind the evangelist Pat Robertson, an outcome that left Bush feeling like he'd 'been hit in the stomach' and rendering it vital for him to win in New Hampshire. There, he had vital help from the Governor of the State, John Sununu, who told his visitors that success there was about 'see me, touch me, feel me' politics. Public opinion initially favoured Dole, who continued his attacks on Bush. The polling in the crucial southern states looked bad for Bush if Dole won in New Hampshire.

Frustrated that Bush had banned negative ads, Roger Ailes

produced one anyway, describing Dole as 'Senator Straddle', in particular over raising taxes. Finding it 'too harsh', Bush initially wouldn't let him use it, but Barbara Bush weighed in on the side of doing so. With his whole body by now aching from retail politics, Bush pulled off a 38 to 29 per cent victory over Dole. Bush felt heartened by Ronald Reagan's comment on the result: 'I'll sleep better tonight.'

After a lunch at the White House, Bush noted Reagan as saying that Dole had 'a mean side'. About the other contenders, Reagan did not think that Jack Kemp was presidential at all and was concerned about 'some of the extremes' that Pat Robertson brought into the party. Kemp offered to endorse Bush if he was chosen as his running mate. A real estate developer called Donald Trump mentioned his availability to Lee Atwater, an overture that Bush found 'strange and unbelievable'.

'BEING A GENTLEMAN DOESN'T MEAN YOU'RE NOT TOUGH ENOUGH TO SIT DOWN WITH GORBACHEV'

In March 1988, Bush defeated Dole easily in South Carolina and went on to sweep the southern states, with Dole throwing in the towel at the end of the month. After an evening with Richard Nixon, in reaction to the character of the former President, Bush noted in his diary, 'What's wrong with being a gentleman? Being a gentleman doesn't mean you're not tough enough to sit down with Gorbachev.'

The remaining obstacle to be overcome was the Democratic candidate, the Massachusetts Governor, Michael Dukakis. It would, Bush observed, be a classic liberal versus conservative race.

In May 1988, Reagan formally endorsed Bush at a dinner for the

Republican congressional candidates, declaring that he was going to campaign as hard as he could to make George Bush the next President of the United States. Though nothing Reagan had said justified this, a 'gigantic flap' ensued, with the East Coast press contending that his endorsement had been lukewarm. So Reagan had to issue another statement reiterating that he would go all out to make Bush the next President. 'George has been a partner in all we have accomplished and he should be elected.'

Bush felt confident that he was on the right side on the issues, that people did not want to cut defence, 'they want judges who are tougher on crime ... they don't want murderers out of jail' or extreme environmentalists to prevail. But the polls at the time were not showing this. Bush's image was still felt to be fuzzy. A Gallup poll was showing Dukakis sixteen points ahead of Bush.

Within the Bush camp, Roger Ailes felt that they had to 'define' what Dukakis really stood for before the gap became unbridgeable. In the Democratic primary campaign, Al Gore had challenged Dukakis about the furlough (conditional release) programme for convicted criminals in Massachusetts, pointing out that eleven murderers who had been conditionally released had absconded and two of them had committed further murders.

A Bush political adviser, Jim Pinkerton, investigating the programme, found that in the state legislature Dukakis had vetoed a bill with a lot of public support that would have prevented first degree murderers from benefiting from furloughs. The press, notably the *Eagle-Tribune*, had unearthed the case of Willie Horton, a convicted murderer who, while on a weekend pass, had raped a woman twice at gunpoint after pistol whipping and stabbing her fiancé. It transpired that Dukakis also had vetoed a bill requiring public school teachers to lead students in the pledge of allegiance.

While Dukakis, in James Baker's view, was a 'bright, honorable man', it was becoming clear that he was way to the left in terms of US national politics.

'WE ARE DESPERATE'

At the end of May, the Bush team discussed Dukakis at Walker's Point. Bush was worried that attacking his opponent so early could make him look desperate. With Bush trailing in the polls, projecting a fuzzy image and the country appearing reluctant to vote for a Republican presidential third term, Roger Ailes responded, 'We *are* desperate.' Bush concluded that it would be easy to depict Dukakis as what he was – a Massachusetts liberal.

In a speech at the Republican state convention in Texas, Bush developed the argument that Dukakis was outside the American mainstream on economics, criminal justice, foreign policy and culture. 'What it all comes down to is two different visions.' That of Dukakis, he claimed, was formed in Harvard Yard. Bush said that he didn't go to the Kennedy School; instead he went to Texas. 'I didn't go to a symposium on job creation; I started a business.' He was, he declared, a practical man, dedicated to achieving practical results.

Bush now asked Reagan to permit James Baker to leave the Treasury to run his campaign. Reagan was reluctant, feeling that Baker could do more good by keeping the economy on track. Nancy Reagan was even more opposed. In his diary, Bush, bizarrely, blamed this on her dislike of Barbara. But following a further personal appeal, Reagan agreed and Baker left the Treasury to take charge of the Bush campaign. During the Democratic National Convention, Bush and Baker left together for a camping and fishing trip in Wyoming.

At the Democratic convention, Dukakis announced that Bush's old opponent Lloyd Bentsen would be his running mate. Getting to know Bentsen as well as I did later, there is little doubt that he would have been a better President and a far less fragile candidate than Dukakis. The popular Texas Governor, Ann Richards, mocked Bush for at last going after a post he couldn't get appointed to. Arguing that Republicans were for prosperity for the few, not the many, Dukakis emerged from the convention leading Bush by seventeen points in another Gallup poll – 54 to 37 per cent.

'SOMETIMES YOU JUST GET TIRED OF HAVING PEOPLE TELL YOU WHAT TO DO'

Approaching the Republican National Convention in August, Bush was reviewing several candidates for the vice-presidential nomination who clearly would have been better received than the one he alighted on. He did not really want Dole or Jack Kemp, but the list included the highly respected senior Senator from Indiana, Richard Lugar, Senators Al Simpson, John Danforth and John McCain and Governors Carroll Campbell and Lamar Alexander.

But Bush, preoccupied with his lack of connection with the younger generation, became interested in the 41-year-old junior Senator from Indiana, Dan Quayle. Quayle was known to Roger Ailes and Bush's pollster, Bob Teeter, who had worked with him on the campaign to win his Senate seat in Indiana. Ailes made the case for Quayle with an argument he knew would appeal to Bush. As Ailes later recalled, 'Bush had been seen for so long as the junior guy to Reagan that it made sense for Bush's own VP to appear clearly junior.' The youthful Quayle would look good alongside him.

Bush failed to undertake a reality check with either Baker or Atwater; nor did he consult his wife or George W., as he 'wanted it to be a surprise'. Asked years later why he had not consulted Baker or others about the choice of Quayle, Bush said that this was his first opportunity in eight years to make a decision entirely on his own: 'Sometimes you just get tired of having people tell you what to do all the time.'

Just before boarding the plane from Washington to take him to the Republican Party convention in New Orleans, Bush whispered his choice to the by then hard of hearing Reagan, who, registering it was a Senator from Indiana, assumed that it must be the statesmanlike senior Senator, Richard Lugar.

On the plane to New Orleans, all Bush's aides wrote down who they believed his running mate would be. Not one of them got it right. It was only at this point that Bush revealed his decision to Baker. As Bush's mind was made up, Baker did not argue, but he was unhappy not only about the choice, which he thought extremely risky, but about the failure to consult and the fact that he now had to handle the fallout.

After their arrival, the announcement did not go well. Quayle was told just one hour beforehand, Bush recalled, 'then all hell broke loose'. In this first encounter with the press in his new role, Quayle appeared flustered and unprepared (not his fault) and no heavyweight. Yet Bush tried to convince himself that the surprise had worked and the choice was thought to be 'bold, generational and future'.

'I AM A QUIET MAN'

He then needed to make the speech of his life to the Republican National Convention – and he did so, reading from a text brilliantly tailored for him by Reagan's speechwriter, Peggy Noonan. 'I may not be the most eloquent,' he declared, 'but I learned early that eloquence won't draw oil from the ground ... I am a quiet man, but I hear the quiet people others don't. The ones who raise the family, pay the taxes, meet the mortgage ... and their concerns are mine.' He dreamed, he said, of 'a kinder, gentler nation'.

He then pledged never to raise taxes. 'Read my lips,' he declared, 'no new taxes.' The phrase had been suggested by Roger Ailes, who had used it in a previous senatorial campaign. Baker's ally, Richard Darman, tried to get it out of the speech, but Peggy Noonan kept putting it back in, to show that Bush really meant it, which she believed he did.

It was very difficult to resist Peggy Noonan, because she was so good at what she did. Every speech she drafted for Reagan sounded just like Reagan before he even read it. She had produced a speech for Bush which described and defined him far better than he could do for himself.

What happened was a failure by Bush, who knew how serious the budget deficit was. In Reagan's debates with Walter Mondale four years before, Baker had warned Reagan not to say that he would never raise taxes (in fact, he did so, by $50 billion over four years). So Reagan, with much better political instincts than Bush, had said that, for Mondale, 'raising taxes is a first resort. For me, it is a last resort.'

Bush concluded his speech by saying that he had spent over seven years working with the President 'and I have seen what crosses that big desk. I have seen the unexpected crisis that arrives in a cable in a young aide's hand' and others that simmered on for years. 'And so I know that what it all comes down to ... is the man at the desk.' He ended by claiming, 'I am that man.'

The eloquent portrait of himself had all the more effect as he had never made a memorable speech in his life before. The by now very popular Barbara Bush, unusually for a future First Lady, addressed the Republican convention as well.

But the Quayle problem would not go away. Bush told his diary: 'It was my big decision and I blew it, but I'm not about to say that I blew it.' But Bush was referring to the announcement, not his choice.

Yet it still was impossible to justify. Bush had always made a virtue of his caution. Quayle was by no means as limited as the picture painted of him by a generally hostile press. But how could Bush claim that Quayle really was qualified to be second in line for the presidency and competent to take over as President if Bush were incapacitated?

No one was more upset by the choice than his closest friend, James Baker. Not only had he not been consulted, but Baker naturally harboured hopes of becoming Vice-President himself one day, not on this occasion, but possibly at the next election, when Quayle would prove to be an immovable obstacle. The likelihood was discounted as Baker and Bush both came from the same state, but if Baker had replaced Quayle on the ticket four years later, it would have laid to rest all doubts about vice-presidential competence and would have had a badly needed galvanising effect on the 1992 campaign.

As Quayle floundered with the press, Baker asked the key Reagan adviser, Stu Spencer, to help keep him out of trouble. Spencer reported that Quayle didn't want his advice. Baker's response was: 'Just let him hit the buffers a few times. Then maybe he'll listen to us.' But Quayle resented being mentored by Baker and persisted in not listening to advice.

Quayle came under immediate attack for having done his military service with the Indiana National Guard, rather than serving in

Vietnam, though his critics later proved more forgiving about Bill Clinton, who received draft deferments while studying at Oxford, and George W. Bush, who had served as a pilot in the Texas Air National Guard. The problem that, in Quayle's case, never could be overcome was that, consistently, he gave the impression of being a lightweight and not of presidential calibre.

Quayle, however, did have some expertise on defence issues. His interests and those of Bush would have been better served if, when Bush was running for a second term, he had been moved to the Pentagon, but he wasn't.

As Dukakis was majoring against him on environmental issues, Bush took a boat trip around the heavily polluted Boston Harbor. As the boat passed a prison, a reporter called out: 'Anyone there got furloughs?' causing Bush to say jokingly: 'Only one, Willie Horton.' 'Bad boy', no-holds-barred Lee Atwater had told a Republican audience: 'If I can make Willie Horton a household name, we'll win the election.' As usual, he was exaggerating his influence. The press had long since got hold of the story. The July issue of the then hugely influential *Reader's Digest* featured a major article about Horton entitled 'Getting Away with Murder'.

The Bush campaign understood that they needed to be careful about Horton. Baker as chairman and even Roger Ailes did not want a highly effective campaign against Dukakis as being soft on crime being complicated by accusations of racism. A cable TV ad featuring a menacing mugshot of Horton, furiously denounced by Dukakis supporters, was produced by an independent Republican political action group.

As chairman of the Bush campaign, Baker denounced the advertisement, though not until it had been running for three weeks, and the team who made it denied any collusion. The official Bush campaign advertisement showed prisoners moving through a re-volving door: 'While out, many committed other crimes, like kid-napping and rape ... Now Michael Dukakis says he wants to do for America what he's done for Massachusetts.'

'MORE GOOFY THAN PRESIDENTIAL'

By the time both these advertisements were aired, Bush already had closed the gap with Dukakis. To offset his lack of national security credentials, Dukakis, unwisely, was persuaded to be photographed climbing out of a tank. As the diminutive candidate emerged in a helmet too big for him, he was held to be looking 'more goofy than presidential'.

Dukakis observed after the election that he considered the Willie Horton campaign to have been racist but did not regard Bush as such. He did not think that the Horton case had cost him the elec-tion. He had not, he said, believed that the constant 'liberal bashing' would be as effective as it had turned out to be.

In the presidential debate in September, Bush denied that he was questioning Dukakis's patriotism. 'My argument with the Gover-nor is: "Do we want this country to go that far left?"'

Addressing a campaign rally in Illinois, Reagan said that if they wanted to know who was on the side of the little guy, it was George Bush, adding, 'I've seen him keep a cool head in a hot crisis.'

Quayle and Lloyd Bentsen debated each other in October. When Quayle compared his lack of experience to that of John Kennedy, he received a crushing reply: 'I served with Jack Kennedy ... Jack Kennedy was a friend of mine. Senator, you're no Jack Kennedy.'

In mid-October, Dukakis was asked on CNN whether, if his wife were raped and murdered, he would still oppose the death penalty. Dukakis reiterated his view that capital punishment was not a deterrent, but he appeared passionless and remote, defending liberal orthodoxy.

There followed a fresh rumour, again with no evident foundation, about Bush's supposed infidelity. Donna Brazile, a senior member of the Dukakis campaign, demanded to know if Bush would be going to the White House without Barbara. She had to resign as a result of this remark and Dukakis apologised to Bush.

In the last days of the campaign, with the race apparently tightening, Bush was urged to launch fresh attacks on Dukakis as, supposedly, a socialist, which he declined to do, insisting, 'We should stay positive at the end of the campaign.' In response to press charges that this had been an ugly, negative campaign, Bush told his diary: 'I don't know what we could do differently. We had to define this guy.'

Bush won the election comfortably, carrying forty states with 53.4 per cent of the votes and winning several important states, including California, Pennsylvania and others that almost always have voted Democrat since. He won 30 per cent of the Hispanic vote. Bush's success in the election was the more remarkable as, to defeat Dukakis, he had to poll well ahead of the Republican congressional candidates.

But Bush, from the outset, found himself as President with the Democrats firmly in control of both houses of Congress (fifty-five to forty-five in the Senate and 260 to 175 in the House of Representatives). If he had had an ambitious domestic policy agenda, he would not have been able to enact it. Yet, notwithstanding his preoccupation with foreign policy in what Henry Kissinger described as the most tumultuous four-year term since Harry Truman, he did have important domestic policy achievements in the Resolution Trust Corporation, the Americans with Disabilities Act, the Clean Air Act and the 1991 Civil Rights Act.

By some of the dire norms since then, this was not an especially ugly election, but it did encourage a belief in the effectiveness of negative advertising, subsequently adopted by both sides. This was ironic, given the essentially gentlemanly nature of George Bush and his lack of personal enemies, even among his opponents. But faced with what needed to be done to climb to the top of the greasy pole, he did not hesitate to do it.

CHAPTER FOUR

'A KINDER,
GENTLER NATION'

In his inaugural address, on a freezing January morning, George Bush was heartened when a pale sun broke through. He deplored the emergence of 'a certain divisiveness', with a questioning not only of the other side's ideas but of their motives. In his short speech, he had no grand new vision to offer. 'Some see leadership as high drama and the sound of trumpets calling,' he said, but the way he saw his role was rather as one of stewardship, which he was confident he could fulfil.

Once in office, his first act was to announce Baker as Secretary of State. Equally important was the appointment of General Brent Scowcroft as national security advisor. In the pantheon of the most important holders of that post, there were really only two contenders. Henry Kissinger had used the office to such effect that the Secretary of State, William Rogers, could play only a largely negligible secondary role to him. Scowcroft was the opposite, abhorring publicity and seeking to synthesise the quite often conflicting views of the Pentagon, the State Department and other agencies. But this never meant that he did not have strong views himself and no one, not even Baker, was more influential with the President when push came to shove.

I became one of Scowcroft's greatest admirers, but he had plenty of those. He formed a strong bond with Margaret Thatcher's foreign policy adviser Charles Powell, which he described as epitomising the US–UK 'special relationship' at its best.

For Defense Secretary, Bush had nominated his long-term Texas associate John Tower, who had played a leading role in the Republican takeover of Texas. But Tower had made enemies on the Senate Armed Services Committee and had a colourful private life, with an alleged 'love of women and booze'. One of the candidates to replace him was Donald Rumsfeld, vetoed by Bush because Baker didn't like him and Bush worried about his 'game playing', as did Scowcroft.

Bush instead nominated the Republican whip in the House of Representatives, Dick Cheney. Cheney had never served in the armed forces but was to prove his mettle as Defense Secretary in the Gulf War. The downside was that this brought to the fore as the Republican leader in the House the young, bombastic and confrontational Newt Gingrich, a believer in the war of civilisations between liberals and conservatives, who was exactly the kind of Republican politician that Bush abhorred.

Later, Bush and Cheney made the important choice of Colin Powell, the son of immigrants from Jamaica, as chairman of the joint chiefs of staff. A Vietnam veteran, Powell had absorbed the Weinberger doctrine that, for purposes of deterrence, the US needed to have the most powerful military forces on the planet but to use them very sparingly and only if really necessary.

It sometimes was felt of him that he was extremely reluctant to use them at all. He was, initially, a reluctant warrior in the Gulf crisis and, later, an opponent of the US getting involved in the former Yugoslavia. He kept telling me that Sarajevo, with the Serbs shelling it from the surrounding hills, reminded him of Dien Bien Phu, where the French forces had been trapped in Vietnam.

Other appointments, also of the highest quality, were those of Larry Eagleburger, who, with Weinberger, had been Britain's closest ally in the Falklands War, as Baker's deputy, and of Robert Gates as deputy national security advisor, later director of the CIA. In all, without doubt, they represented the strongest US foreign policy team since the era of General Marshall and Dean Acheson.

In contrast to this galaxy of talent in external policy, all with outsize personalities, but with Scowcroft ensuring that they functioned as one team, his domestic policy appointments, several of them personal friends of the President, from the outset appeared less convincing – with two important exceptions: the Treasury Secretary, Nick Brady, and the US trade representative, Carla Hills.

At the heart of this administration lay the extraordinarily close Bush–Baker relationship, a source of fascination to outsiders. Despite his, for good reason, huge self-confidence, Baker ultimately always remained deferential to Bush. The President was aware of Baker's reputation for looking after himself, but that was not Bush's experience of him. Bush occasionally would become exasperated at the deluge of advice he received from his friend, exclaiming, 'If you're so smart, then why aren't you the President of the United States?'

Baker was temperamentally incapable of emulating the kind of retail, pressing-the-flesh politics that had saved the day for Bush in New Hampshire. He was determined to ensure that 'no one ever thought that they could get between me and my President', swallowing his irritation at the choice of Dan Quayle, giving up his position as Secretary of State to try to bolster Bush's chances of re-election and seeing Bush himself fail to do so by not replacing Quayle.

As Secretary of State, Baker seized an early opportunity to demonstrate his abilities as a problem solver. The Reagan administration had fallen completely foul of Congress over its support for the Contras seeking to overthrow the pro-Cuban Sandinista regime in Nicaragua. Baker, who regarded Nicaragua as a sideshow, moved immediately to heal this rift by working out with Congress a bipartisan policy based on no further support for the Contras but a demand for fresh elections in Nicaragua, which, against expectations, the Castro-aligned Sandinistas lost, though they returned to power later.

FIXING THE 'THRIFT' PROBLEM

On his third day in office after his inauguration, the new President was briefed on the crisis caused by the impending collapse of many of the country's savings and loan institutions. These organisations originally were based on the model of UK building societies, though far more numerous – by this stage, nearly 4,000 of them across the US. In the early 1980s, to encourage ordinary Americans to make greater savings, Congress had raised the amount they could invest in these institutions with a government guarantee of their savings, from $10,000 to $100,000. This measure had resulted in massive inflows of new money into these often small, local and potentially fragile 'thrift' companies. Instead of continuing to invest mainly in mortgages for clients they knew, the flood of new money encouraged them to invest in much riskier commercial real estate and other projects. With a slowing economy and higher interest rates, this created huge downside risks, which many of them proved ill-equipped to manage.

Bush at this stage was told that the savings and loan deficit was likely to be around $10 billion. Recognising that the problem could affect tens of millions of American households, Bush told his Treasury Secretary, Nick Brady, a distinguished investment banker, former head of Dillon Read, to lead the effort to fix this nationwide credit crisis 'and fix it fast'.

In February, less than three weeks after the inauguration, Bush sent a message to Congress calling for tighter regulation, increased reserve standards and the creation of the Resolution Trust Corporation to take over the failing credit institutions, all of which was incorporated in the Financial Institutions Reform, Recovery and Enforcement Act passed on 9 August 1989. The final estimate for the multi-year financial effort from government needed to take over, bail out and recapitalise the failing institutions reached the vertiginous sum of $130 billion. Bush's son Neil was a director of one of the failed savings institutions, but so were a host of other reputable businessmen. The problem was not impropriety but an epidemic of over-extension of credit.

'BRADY BONDS'

In the same period, Latin America had become mired in a major debt crisis with no obvious outcome, given the reluctance of the major overseas lending institutions to extend any further credit to several of the affected countries. As President, George Bush regarded it as vitally important for the United States to do all it could to improve the economic circumstances in Latin America. Argentina, Brazil and Mexico, as well as several smaller Latin American countries, were facing an imminent risk of default.

Brady came up with an extremely imaginative solution to the problem. This consisted of coercing the commercial lenders into accepting that they would get back only part of their loans, but these would be recapitalised in the form of US-backed 'Brady bonds'. To qualify for these, the countries concerned were required to undertake to liberalise their economies.

The plan was eagerly embraced by Bush – who joked that, if it proved successful, they could be renamed 'Bush bonds'. The Brady plan succeeded beyond expectations, contributing to a resumption of economic growth in Latin America and providing a model for many further debt relief schemes for developing countries. It was a remarkable achievement, under-appreciated.

It also was Stage 1 in the Bush plan to aid Latin America and tie Mexico and Canada more closely economically to the United States through trade liberalisation, culminating in the negotiation of the North American Free Trade Agreement (NAFTA). Bush's trade representative, Carla Hills, operating at the interface of overseas and domestic policy and with the wholehearted support of the President, made a major contribution to the eventual success of that negotiation.

As George Bush hated to say 'no', the chief enforcers were the White House chief of staff, John Sununu, and Baker's close ally Richard Darman, responsible for the budget. The brilliant but abrasive Sununu claimed to care about the environment but could not stand environmentalists, making clear to me his distrust of Michael Heseltine, then the British Deputy Prime Minister, from that point of view. The exceptionally able but politically tone deaf Darman relentlessly opposed most spending programmes.

'READ MY LIPS'

From the outset of his presidency, Bush found himself wrestling with the intractable problem of what to do about the budget deficit, which had risen to $200 billion or 4 per cent of GDP, figures that appear modest in retrospect but did not do so then, in an era before the Fed had been converted, in dealing with crises, to ultra-low interest rates and printing money. (The US budget deficit in 2020 was $3 trillion and 15 per cent of GDP.) Former Presidents Nixon, Ford and Carter all told Bush that he was going to have to raise taxes, with Nixon saying that Bush had been right about 'voodoo economics'. Basking in high approval ratings at the time, 'if it weren't for the deficit, I'd be feeling pretty good', Bush told his diary.

For the deficit, otherwise, was liable to lead to even tougher economic times. Alan Greenspan, head of the Federal Reserve Board, kept declaring publicly that they would not lower interest rates unless the administration were seen to be tackling the problem. The late Reagan administration economy had been faltering, affected by rising inflation and the cumulative wave of failures of the savings and loan institutions. The federal funds lending rate had reached 10 per cent in 1988, making a major contribution to the recession. Bush told his diary that if he raised taxes, having promised not to, he would be destroyed. He moved subsequently to a conviction that he could not afford to do so 'in my first year'.

With the Democrats firmly in control of Congress, there was strong resistance to expenditure cuts. Nevertheless, as President, Bush resorted to the kind of personal diplomacy that had served him well in his other roles, seeking to cultivate the Democratic congressional leaders, George Mitchell, majority leader of the Senate; Tom Foley, Speaker of the House of Representatives; and Leon Panetta, chair of the House Budget Committee. Foley, who took over as Speaker in June 1989, was interested in a bipartisan agreement. He was used to being accused by some members of his own party of being insufficiently partisan. George Mitchell, though less trusted by Bush, and Leon Panetta also were middle-of-the-road Democrats who recognised that some major spending programmes, and not only defence, needed to be restrained.

Impressed by the Democrats' willingness to support some important caps on expenditure, in May 1990 Bush weakened his position against tax increases by accepting George Mitchell's demand that in discussing a possible budget deal, there must be 'no preconditions', provoking a furious right-wing response. 'The shit', he told his diary, had 'hit the fan'.

A few weeks later there was a further furore when, in response to Foley's willingness to curb expenditure, Bush agreed that there would have to be tax revenue increases. Gingrich and Dan Quayle were appalled, as resistance to tax increases had been a key factor in the Republicans' success in the past three presidential elections.

Roger Ailes also was outraged, telling Bush, 'You are not known for much, but you are known for character.' Bush accepted that his by now regretted 'no new taxes' pledge to the Republican convention meant that agreeing to any would entail not just abandoning a campaign promise but breaking faith in his word. 'It killed me,' he said in retirement, which it did with the more extreme elements in his own party, who had been sceptical about him anyway.

But his ingrained pragmatism having left him with the conviction that he had no real option but to do so, after months of negotiation with the Democrat leaders, he accepted a budget compromise, including increases in taxes on petrol, tobacco and alcohol. It also attempted to require future administrations and Congress to ensure that new appropriations were paid for and not financed by borrowing.

But Newt Gingrich regarded Bush as a 'Connecticut moderate Republican masquerading as a Texan' and not a true conservative.

As Bush observed bitterly, though the Republican leader in the House of Representatives, Gingrich did not regard himself as bound to support the President. He walked out of the meeting on the budget agreement to lead the opposition to it. On 5 October 1990, Republicans in the House joined with Democrats opposed to the spending limits to vote down the compromise, leading to a government shutdown, for which they were held responsible.

The Democrats exploited Bush's weakened position to secure an increase also in income tax, from 28 to 31 per cent, making the breach of the 'read my lips' pledge worse. The revised bill was passed on 5 November 1990, on the eve of the Gulf War.

The fact that the Democrats had agreed to quite significant cuts in expenditure had been a major factor in persuading Bush to change his own position but, with his mind by now on the Middle East, he never got around to explaining this to a national audience. Instead, Bush told Foley that he had 'two years to recover from this grief, and the main thing is to get the job done'.

The expenditure cuts did not help an already weak economy. 1990 started with the Fed lending rate at 8 per cent, falling after the budget agreement far enough to help stimulate a revival in the economy from mid-1992 – not soon enough to help Bush. Most commentators still were describing the economy as mired in recession in the immediate run-up to the presidential election, even though by then it was in fact recovering. Greenspan acknowledged subsequently that the Fed had taken too long to cut interest rates.

Bush had nerved himself to do what he was convinced was necessary for the country. A more political leader would have tried again to defer tax increases. Bill Clinton, to his credit, also followed Greenspan's advice and that of his Treasury Secretary, Lloyd Bentsen, to raise taxes, at a high political cost in the 1992 midterm elections but enabling a further cut in interest rates. It wasn't any wonder that Bush, by now in the midst of the Gulf crisis, told his diary that he preferred working on foreign affairs.

Bush never was comfortable with the rhetorical requirements of the presidency. In stark contrast to his predecessor, and understanding that he was no Reagan, he hardly ever was prepared to take his case to the country and did not attempt to do so about the budget, as George W. Bush, among others, felt that he should have done. But in this respect too, his reluctance did not extend to foreign policy. In the run-up to the Gulf War, he explained his case to the country very effectively.

For Bush politically, the budget outcome was a disaster, dividing the Republican Party. Reagan too had raised taxes, but he had not said, 'read my lips', he wouldn't. With no sustained White House effort made to explain publicly why Bush had felt obliged to abandon the pledge, the dissenters in his party appeared to be expected simply to fall into line. Bush had done what he was convinced was the right thing for his country, which was what mattered to him most, but he also deserved the headline he got in the *New York Times*: 'Read my lips, I lied.'

'A MORE DANGEROUS TYPE OF SOVIET LEADER'

Bush had first met Mikhail Gorbachev at his predecessor Konstantin Chernenko's funeral in March 1985 and had been impressed. 'He was different, totally different, from the types of Soviets we'd been used to.' He reported to Reagan that 'Gorbachev will package the Soviet line for Western consumption much more effectively than any (I repeat any) of his predecessors'. This was why Bush and his key advisers at the time regarded Gorbachev as 'a more dangerous type of Soviet leader'.

In December 1988, Bush met Gorbachev again, saying goodbye
to Reagan, in a brief meeting in New York Harbor, in which Bush
said hardly anything. He wrote to Gorbachev afterwards to say that,
with the President there, that was the nature of the US system. He
would have more to say after his inauguration on 20 January and
much more in a few months' time after the new administration had
concluded its review of overseas policy.

This was the beginning of what Bush described as his 'pause'.
Despite the October 1986 Reagan–Gorbachev summit in Reykja-
vik, the agreement to scrap intermediate-range nuclear missiles,
and the Soviet withdrawal from Afghanistan by February 1989, the
Americans still did not know what to make of Gorbachev, with
Margaret Thatcher, who knew him better, far more positive about
him. Bush's advisers were divided, with Scowcroft, Cheney and
others wondering if Gorbachev was not just a new-style Soviet
leader with the same old objectives – or, as Scowcroft put it, 'the
Brezhnev system, with a new paint job'. Scowcroft's deputy, Robert
Gates, previously of the CIA and soon to be appointed head of the
agency, also was a deep sceptic, as the CIA's view was that there was
indeed more *glasnost* (openness) but *perestroika* (restructuring) was
achieving very little and was likely to fail.

Thatcher agreed with them about Gorbachev's reforms, which
did not address the fundamental problem. Having listened to a long
disquisition from him about *perestroika*, her response was: 'But Mr
Secretary General, you do realise that Communism will never work,
don't you?' This did not prevent her giving him her wholehearted
support. For unlike the US sceptics, from her personal experience
of him, she was well ahead of the Americans in her conviction that
Gorbachev was determined to transform the relationship with the
West, as Bush discovered himself when at last they did meet in

December 1989. In his memoir, Gorbachev expressed his thanks to Thatcher for her help in convincing the US of his sincerity.

What alarmed the Bush team most was Gorbachev's success in captivating Western European opinion when the Soviet Union still was engaged in repression. The Czech regime had just arrested several hundred anti-Soviet demonstrators, including Václav Havel. Baker, who was forging a rapidly deepening relationship with the Soviet Foreign Minister, Eduard Shevardnadze, was more optimistic about Gorbachev's intentions. In their first meeting, in Vienna in March 1989, mystified by the 'pause', Shevardnadze had asked Baker, 'What are you waiting for?'

In April, the US Defense Secretary, Dick Cheney, told CNN that he expected Gorbachev ultimately to fail. He was unlikely to be able to turn the Soviet Union into an efficient modern society and was liable then to be replaced by somebody far more hostile to the West. An infuriated Baker asked Scowcroft to 'dump on Dick with all possible alacrity', causing Bush to declare on the same day that the US wanted to see *perestroika* succeed. But Cheney had blurted out what he, Quayle and others in Washington felt.

Gorbachev kept coming up with arms reduction proposals which appealed to European opinion but would have left intact the huge Soviet superiority in Europe in conventional forces, offset by the US deployment of short-range tactical nuclear weapons in Europe (though the Soviets had larger numbers of tactical nuclear weapons in Europe themselves). Following the 1987 agreement to ban intermediate-range nuclear weapons, the US short-range nuclear weapons were due for modernisation, an idea highly unpopular in Germany, as, given their range, they could only be used on German or Polish soil.

Bush understood that the German Chancellor, Helmut Kohl,

could not afford politically to agree to the modernisation of these weapons, but if they were negotiated away, that would leave the West dangerously exposed. Margaret Thatcher, like the US military, therefore, was opposed to negotiations on short-range nuclear weapons, given the huge disadvantage in conventional forces. Thatcher and the US military were opposed to any cuts in US forces in Europe so long as that imbalance remained. But this left Gorbachev with the initiative and a huge problem in Germany.

'SHE'S NOT A GREAT LISTENER'

Although Bush admired Thatcher as a staunch ally of the United States, as Vice-President he had shared Reagan's opinion that 'she was not a great listener'. He was unimpressed by her suggestion that they should stick to the status quo and leave it to her to deal with Kohl, with whom he knew she had a very fraught relationship.

Bush agonised about this for several weeks with his advisers, with Baker arguing that priority must be given to winning back the initiative from Gorbachev and helping Kohl. In the run-up to the fortieth anniversary NATO meeting in May 1989, Bush decided to propose a 20 per cent cut in the 320,000 US conventional forces in Europe if the Soviets would reduce to the same level. The proposed cut in American forces was opposed by the US chiefs of staff, but Bush overruled them.

Before the summit, Bush invited the French President, François Mitterrand, to stay with him at Walker's Point. George Bush attached great importance to the development of his personal relationships with overseas leaders and devoted a huge proportion of his time to cultivating them. This was despite Henry Kissinger pointing out to him the primacy of deep national interests. No national leader, Kissinger argued, was going to sacrifice his country's interests because he liked another political leader. But Bush believed that, with most of them, his personal diplomacy helped.

Both of them had a point. The Americans, typically, found the French Foreign Ministry, the Quai d'Orsay, almost impossible to deal with. Mitterrand, who appeared clad in polished shoes and a business suit at the Bushes' quite basic holiday resort, was relieved to find Bush alert to the sensitivities in Europe.

In February, to the Americans' dismay, without consultation, Kohl had called for a decision on modernising the US nuclear weapons in Europe to be postponed. Before the NATO meeting, Margaret Thatcher was urging Bush not to give any ground at all. She was still on the same page as the US military. She feared that agreeing to negotiate on short-range nuclear weapons would lead to pressures to get rid of them before the conventional imbalance had been addressed.

Thatcher had been enthused when Bush won the presidential election against Dukakis, whom she regarded as 'an absolute lightweight'. She had always found Bush easy to get on with and, when he was Vice-President, had never failed to meet him whenever she visited Washington. He had done a good job keeping the Reagan administration in touch with European opinion. She had hosted him on many occasions on his visits to Europe. He was one of the most decent, honest and patriotic Americans she had met. 'But', she observed, 'he had never had to think through his beliefs and fight for them when they were hopelessly unfashionable,' as she and Reagan had been obliged to do.

Bush himself had declared that (unlike Reagan) he did not do 'the vision thing'. He did have a core belief, which, like his father, was in limited government, rather than the desire for unlimited government they attributed to their 'progressive' Democrat opponents.

But it was true that he was not a conviction politician to the extent that she was and Reagan had been.

Nor were he and Thatcher the least bit alike in style or temperament. In February 1984, having been invited to spend a weekend with her at Chequers, Bush arrived with his golf clubs, only to find himself embroiled in intense discussions, with no time allowed for golf. It was not by accident that he never invited her to his holiday refuge at Walker's Point, not wanting to suffer the same experience there.

Above all, having regarded him as not quite an equal as Vice-President, Thatcher failed to adjust fast enough to his changed status as President. She always had been deferential to Reagan. When Bush became President, initially, she was not deferential at all. She went on treating him as she had before. It took time for her to realise the extent to which he had changed with the office and, as she put it, that he sometimes was exasperated by her habit of talking non-stop about her favourite issues, when he expected to be leading the discussion himself.

Having, in his words, 'watched Margaret Thatcher wrap Ronald Reagan around her little finger', James Baker was determined that Bush must assert himself. Thatcher underestimated Baker, whom she regarded as a 'fixer' and too 'pragmatic' for her taste. She had distrusted him ever since, as US Treasury Secretary, he had persuaded the other Western Finance Ministers, including her Chancellor, Nigel Lawson, to help to drive down the value of the dollar, which had soared under Reagan, even though, to ease the downward pressure on sterling, she had approved it then. She now believed that Baker was more inclined to listen to German views than hers, which was true, as Germany was the main problem to be managed at the time.

Bush was no less determined to assert himself, having witnessed Reagan in international meetings turn over the discussion to Thatcher, allowing her to speak for both of them. 'Margaret', he observed, 'was never without an opinion, forcefully stated.' She lacked, he found, any lightness of touch or sense of humour. But retaining her support was important and, whatever her misgivings, she did not want a public split with the US either. Bush, furthermore, was as concerned as she was not to enter into negotiations on short-range nuclear forces without prior agreement to deal with the huge Soviet advantage in conventional forces.

Baker's deputy, Larry Eagleburger, and Scowcroft's deputy, Bob Gates, future head of the CIA, were despatched to brief the key allied heads of government on the American proposal to cut conventional forces, getting an enthusiastic reception, except in London. Thatcher, who knew and liked both of them, amused the Americans by referring to them subsequently as 'Tweedledum and Tweedledee'. They found her still resistant to cuts in US forces in Europe, telling them that she was 'very wary'. But, conscious of the realities of power, she also said, 'If the President wants it, of course we will do it.'

Despite this, as they walked together into the NATO meeting, Thatcher still was expressing her reservations to Bush. The summit agreed to mutual reductions in conventional forces to 275,000 on each side, requiring vastly larger cuts by the Soviets. But, sitting next to Bush at dinner, Thatcher continued opposing negotiations on short-range nuclear forces, saying, 'We must not give in on this. You're not going to give in, are you?'

At around midnight, Baker proposed the formulation that once the cuts in conventional forces were under way, the US would enter into negotiations to achieve a partial reduction (not elimination) of short-range land-based nuclear missiles to equal verifiable levels. Bush wondered if Thatcher would accept this, but Baker was confident that she would. By next morning, Thatcher was waxing enthusiastic about the agreement.

It was performances of this kind that led Bush to describe her as his 'anchor to windward'. But it came at a cost. In his account of the NATO meeting, Bush described her as 'principled, very difficult [and] most people were far more down on her than I would have thought possible', with Kohl referring to her as 'that woman'.

In a memo to Thatcher, Charles Powell noted the US 'tilt' towards Germany and France. Her response was that the Americans before long would rediscover who their true friends were.

SUPPORTING HELMUT KOHL

Bush and Baker found themselves dealing with late Thatcher, after a decade as Prime Minister. As she wrote later, the one area of foreign policy in which she experienced 'unambiguous failure' was in her opposition to German reunification. They understood that this view was rooted in traditional British concerns about the balance of power in Europe and her worries that it could prove fatal for Gorbachev, as, in due course, it pretty well did. They were not yet themselves convinced that reunification was inevitable. But in that event, they could not see the point in hand wringing. Their priority must be to ensure that a united Germany ended up in NATO, with all their efforts focused on that goal.

The US offer to negotiate on short-range nuclear forces carried with it an expectation that modernisation would not prove necessary. Mitterrand and Kohl welcomed the initiative. The *New York Times* praised 'the willingness of this deeply cautious man to aggressively seize the moment'. Bush followed this up with an unusually eloquent speech ending with: 'The world has waited long enough ... Let Europe be whole and free.'

Bush went for a cruise down the Rhine with Kohl, whom he described as 'a great big teddy bear'. The British, having witnessed the Chancellor throwing his vast weight about in European Community meetings, had a less cuddly view of him. A reference by Bush to the US and Germany as 'partners in leadership' caused a flurry in the British press. Thatcher took this as a challenge to the 'special relationship' with Britain, though Scowcroft claimed she need not have worried, as the expression had been meant 'only for flourish and encouragement' to the Germans. But in reality, Bush and Baker had decided that they had to give priority to dealing with Germany.

When Bush arrived in London after the NATO meeting, he asked Thatcher if she feared German reunification as a threat to the stability of Western Europe. She said that she did, though she could not say so openly. She worried about the consequences for Gorbachev and the possibility that in response, he would push for a neutral Germany.

But in another important respect, she continued to play a constructive role. When Gorbachev visited Britain in April 1989, he wanted to know why the Bush administration seemed not to want to engage with him. They appeared 'distinctly less friendly' than Reagan. Thatcher replied that Bush would continue most of Reagan's policies, even though his personal style was different. Gorbachev asked if Bush would be acting in the common interest, or only in that of the West. Thatcher said she was convinced that he would act in the common interest.

Thatcher reported to Bush that Gorbachev was looking for reassurance about continuity in US policy, which no doubt Baker could give him in a planned visit to Moscow in May. Gorbachev told her that the Americans seemed to have taken her message to heart, as Baker had arrived in a constructive spirit.

'I WRITE THIS LETTER WITH A HEAVY HEART'

The Chinese leadership had welcomed George Bush's election as President as that of someone they knew already and who understood them better than most other world leaders. They had a short list of foreign leaders whom they regarded as friends of China, led by Richard Nixon and Henry Kissinger, who had led the normalisation of relations with them; Edward Heath, who had recognised Communist China; and the Prime Minister of Singapore, Lee Kuan Yew. George Bush also was on it.

Bush, for his part, needed no convincing of the importance of building a long-term relationship with China. When, shortly after his inauguration, Bush had to attend the funeral of Emperor Hirohito in Tokyo, he added on a visit to Beijing. He was welcomed by Deng Xiaoping and his two senior colleagues, Li Peng and Zhao Ziyang. Bush recalled that in their previous meeting, Deng Xiaoping had described him as a *lao pengyou*, an old friend of China. Bush had assured him that Ronald Reagan would not overturn the United States' 'one China' policy, only for Deng in the course of their meeting to exclaim, 'He did it again!' as an aide informed him that Reagan had again referred to 'two Chinas'. Yet Reagan then had honoured Bush's undertaking about preserving the 'one China' policy.

On this visit, Bush was told by the Chinese President, Yang Shangkun, that China did not intend to have any alliance or military relationship with the Soviet Union, which Bush found reassuring, as Gorbachev was about to visit Beijing. The Chinese leaders observed that Gorbachev was emphasising political reform and democratisation. Their priority was economic reform. The Soviet Union, in their opinion, would have been better advised to do the same.

Vis-à-vis the United States, they would not tolerate any interference in their internal affairs. But they hoped to see the development of their relationship with a 'good friend'.

The by now frail, chain-smoking Deng Xiaoping was optimistic that Bush's personal history would help. There was a deep history of problems with the Soviet Union, which under Khrushchev had deployed a million troops and nuclear weapons on the Chinese border. He complained about the Soviet 'encirclement' of China. Relations might be more normal with Gorbachev, but China would be wary. Yalta had severed Outer Mongolia from China. Bush said that he did not like the Yalta agreement either. Deng's economic reforms should pave the way for a closer US relationship with China.

These positive sentiments were well and truly overturned on 4 June 1989, when Deng Xiaoping unleashed the military to suppress the demonstrations by students and other young Chinese protesters that had been taking place in Tiananmen Square in the heart of Beijing. The protests had embarrassed the regime during Gorbachev's visit and demonstrations had started in several other Chinese cities. Zhao Ziyang, who had tried to talk to the demonstrators, was elbowed aside and the brutal repression by the military equipped with tanks was organised by Li Peng. Li Peng subsequently told Brent Scowcroft that 310 people had been killed, including a few of the military.

Bush found himself immediately facing strident demands from Republicans and Democrats alike and the US media for severe retaliation. But he was not prepared to go down that route. He wanted a measured response and one that would not play into the hands of the hardliners in Beijing. Richard Nixon telephoned him to urge restraint. What had happened was deplorable, he said, 'but take a look at the long haul'. Those were Bush's and Baker's sentiments too. They regarded building a long-term relationship with China as too important to be abandoned.

Nor did Bush believe that imposing general sanctions would help those struggling for human rights in China. It would be more likely to lead to further repression. He did not wish to punish the Chinese people for the sins of their government or to push China back into the arms of the Soviet Union.

He also did not want to disrupt the commercial relationship. However naively in the case of China, he believed that if people had commercial contacts and incentives, 'the move to democracy becomes inevitable'. Despite the outcry, therefore, in Congress and the media for much stronger action, verging on a breach of relations, the sanctions Bush imposed were limited to the Chinese armed forces, suspending military sales and contacts.

Bush's response satisfied almost no one in the US. But knowing the Chinese system as he did, he did not believe that a sharper reaction would have done anything to help the cause of democracy in China. It would have been more likely to have the opposite effect.

The situation was further complicated when a well-known Chinese dissident, Fang Lizhi, sought and was given asylum in the US embassy in Beijing, infuriating the Chinese leadership.

Bush was determined to try to preserve his relationship with Deng Xiaoping. He attempted to telephone him but was unable to get through. He then decided to sit down and write an entirely personal letter to Deng, beginning, 'I write this letter with a heavy heart … in a spirit of genuine friendship,' as someone who believed that a positive relationship between the US and China was in the fundamental interests of both countries. He paid tribute to all that Deng had done for his country, noting that he too had suffered 'reversals' (in fact, imprisonment) in his own pursuit of reform.

Bush was seeking his help in preserving the relationship that they both thought was very important. He respected the differences between their two societies but noted that 'my young country' was founded on the principles of democracy and freedom from arbitrary authority and was bound to react to events accordingly. The world had seen the tolerance initially shown to the demonstrators, then the turmoil and bloodshed at the end. He had resisted stronger action as he did not want to undermine the relationship they had built. He would like to send a special emissary for an entirely private discussion with Deng.

Deng replied quickly, welcoming the idea of an emissary. Nixon, Kissinger and Baker were too high-profile, so the task fell to Scowcroft, accompanied by Baker's deputy, Larry Eagleburger.

Scowcroft knew Deng personally, as he had accompanied President Ford at two meetings with him, when Deng had held a private lunch for the two of them, at which he had railed against the North Vietnamese.

Deng greeted them warmly, saying that the reason he had chosen President Bush as his friend was because he had proved 'rather trustworthy'. Even before the election, he had expressed the hope that Bush would be elected President. But turmoil had broken out in China and the US was now too deeply involved. The relationship was in danger of breaking down. He regarded their mission ('a wise and cool-headed action') as a sign that Bush wanted to preserve it, as did he. But they could never allow foreigners to interfere in their affairs.

Scowcroft said that, despite setbacks, their ties had been steadily deepening. Both sides had benefited, including vis-à-vis the Soviet

Union. Trade had grown to over $10 billion a year. This progress had been disrupted by the events in Tiananmen Square. US reactions to those events were an internal matter for the United States. The US House of Representatives had voted 418 to nil for stronger measures than those taken by the President.

Li Peng concluded the meetings by saying that they would wait to see what the President would now do. Scowcroft reported that the Chinese leadership wanted time and space and no interference from the United States. But he also found them not ill disposed to the Bush administration, albeit very warily. The exchanges had been frank enough for a measure of trust to have been restored. George Bush regarded this as confirming him in his view that he must hold the line against further action against China.

In November, the House of Representatives passed unanimously a bill sponsored by the future Democratic Speaker, Nancy Pelosi, allowing the Chinese students in the US to stay indefinitely until human rights were restored in China. The Chinese government declared that if it became law, they would terminate the student exchange programme. Bush had intended to let those Chinese students who wished to do so to remain anyway, simply by extending their visas. So he vetoed the bill.

There followed a huge struggle to muster the blocking one third minority of votes in the Senate required to prevent the presidential veto being overturned.

Bush wrote another letter to Deng urging that more arrested students should be released and offering a briefing on the outcome of his meeting with Gorbachev in Malta. This was accepted, so Scowcroft and Eagleburger were despatched back to Beijing. The Chinese air defences did not like their unmarked plane but were instructed in time not to shoot it down.

Scowcroft was pilloried in the US media for 'toasting the butchers of Tiananmen Square' when he had to reply to a toast by the Chinese. The Chinese government were impressed by Bush's veto of the Pelosi bill but still were refusing to permit Fang Lizhi to leave China unless the US lifted sanctions. The new leader, Jiang Zemin, who understood that Bush was struggling to improve relations, said that they should not let ideology come between them. The Chinese released some dissidents and suspended some missile sales to the Middle East. Henry Kissinger later helped to get Fang Lizhi released.

There followed further battles with the Democrats in Congress about renewing Most Favoured Nation status for China, which eventually was renewed, once he became President, by Bill Clinton. George Bush left office convinced that he had been right to engage in these politically thankless struggles to preserve the relationship with China.

CHAPTER FIVE

GORBACHEV AND GERMAN REUNIFICATION

'DESTABILISE GORBACHEV AND WE LOSE THE POSSIBILITY OF DEMOCRACY IN THE SOVIET UNION'

Meanwhile, the world was changing faster than anyone could have foreseen. In May 1989, Hungary took down the barbed wire fence separating it from Austria, opening a gateway to the West. In June, the anti-Communist movement Solidarity won the elections in Poland.

The ever-present concern in Bush's mind and those of his team was that either Gorbachev, to preserve his position in Moscow, would revert to repression or that others in Moscow would do so for him. Bush was fully conscious of Margaret Thatcher's warning that 'destabilise Gorbachev and we lose the possibility of democracy in the Soviet Union'.

Visiting Poland in July, Bush urged President Jaruzelski, responsible for prior repression, and the Solidarity leader, Lech Wałęsa, to work together to complete the transition to real democracy in Poland, which he found them disposed to do. Wałęsa described Jaruzelski as a 'radish' – red, i.e. Communist, only on the outside.

There followed a visit with Wałęsa to the home base of Solidarity at the shipyard in Gdańsk, where Bush told a massive crowd that it was Poland's time of destiny. He left convinced that the Poles would work things out between them, but still worried that the Soviets might yet intervene to stop Poland slipping from their grasp.

In Hungary, he found an ebullient atmosphere and the hardline Communist leader, Károly Grósz, being elbowed aside. He got a good reception in pouring rain by tearing up his speech and, in a typical Bush gesture, taking off his raincoat to give it to an elderly woman near the podium. The Prime Minister, Miklós Németh, presented him with a piece of barbed wire from the border fence that had been taken down between Hungary and Austria – literally, a piece of the Iron Curtain.

In both countries, he had urged the need for caution and gradual reform in speeches devoid of any 'hot rhetoric'. 'We had stepped carefully in Poland and Hungary and had avoided aggravating the Soviets, whose military presence still loomed there.'

The missing element in this situation remained a direct relationship with Gorbachev. By July 1989, Bush had told his chief associates that it was time for him to meet Gorbachev. As the new administration by then had formulated its own policies, Scowcroft had dropped his prior opposition to a meeting. Bush had started to believe that further postponement was dangerous. 'We still did not know how much change Gorbachev would allow in the region,' he later wrote, but it was clear the East Europeans would push as hard as they could. The pressures on Gorbachev would be bound to grow as those countries pulled further away and the Soviet security buffer against the West was eroded.

So Bush wrote to Gorbachev suggesting an informal meeting, not one leading to formal new agreements. Gorbachev welcomed the idea of a meeting as early as September, but bizarre difficulties then arose in agreeing the venue, plus some foot dragging by Soviet officials resentful at having been kept waiting. As Gorbachev was due anyway to visit Italy in November, it eventually was agreed to hold the meeting in Malta.

In September, the question arose whether Bush should see Boris Yeltsin, who had resigned from the Soviet politburo to campaign as a Russian nationalist and had become a vociferous critic of Gorbachev's reforms as not going far or fast enough. The fastidious and extremely disciplined Scowcroft had been appalled by the tales of some spectacular episodes of drunkenness during Yeltsin's earlier visit to the US, but he recommended that Bush should 'drop by' at Yeltsin's scheduled meeting with Scowcroft. When Bush did so, emphasising his support for Gorbachev's reforms, Yeltsin pounced on some nearby reporters to give them an impromptu press conference.

There followed a visit to Bush by the Soviet Foreign Minister, Eduard Shevardnadze, who brought some interesting arms control proposals but did not pretend that things were going well for Gorbachev's reforms.

By this time, the turmoil in Eastern Europe had spread to East Germany, which the hardline government of Erich Honecker was struggling to control. Gorbachev was applauded by the protesters when he visited East Berlin and Honecker was replaced.

US suspicions of Gorbachev still endured because he had upstaged Baker by suddenly announcing new arms reduction proposals during their meeting in Moscow, but also because the Soviets were continuing to pour aid into Cuba and Nicaragua. They had withdrawn their troops from Afghanistan but were continuing to prop up a pro-Soviet regime there.

Yet, in August, Lech Wałęsa was permitted to form a Solidarity-led government in Poland. Hungary also was heading for multi-party democracy. But the US Treasury and Darman still were resisting any substantial assistance to Eastern Europe, leaving the administration struggling to persuade the allies to contribute to a multinational assistance effort.

In the run-up to the Malta summit, the three Baltic countries – Lithuania, Estonia and Latvia – were intensifying their efforts to break free from the Soviet Union. This was different from changes of government in countries that never had been part of the Soviet Union. Gorbachev warned that the three republics 'must not think about secession'.

As, by November, the East German government increasingly was losing control, Bush feared that 'the Soviets will be compelled to crack down', which would take things back to square one. If the US mishandled the crisis and made it look too much like an American victory, he feared that repression could be the outcome.

'I'M NOT AN EMOTIONAL KIND OF GUY'

On 9 November 1989, Scowcroft walked into the Oval Office to report that the Berlin Wall was said to have been opened. It was in 1987 that Ronald Reagan, standing at the Brandenburg Gate, had said, 'Mr Gorbachev, tear down this wall!' Now that it was happening, no one could quite believe it.

Bush's reaction, once again, was one of caution. He feared that the crowds could easily get out of control, provoking a violent reaction. His concern was reinforced by a message from Gorbachev, 'urging that we not overreact'. Scowcroft advised that there must be no 'gloating' over what was happening in Berlin.

So, in his meeting with the press Bush deliberately failed to rise to the occasion. Lesley Stahl of CBS News suggested it was 'a sort of great victory' in the East–West conflict, 'but you don't seem elated'. 'I'm not an emotional kind of guy' was Bush's deadpan response.

Gorbachev warned Kohl to stop talking about German reunification. In a message to Bush, he continued to urge him not to overreact. Otherwise, the demonstrations could get out of control with 'unforeseen consequences.' Bush assured Gorbachev that he had no intention of destabilising the situation, though he did support self-determination.

The Democratic Party leader in the Senate, George Mitchell, urged Bush to fly to Berlin to make a statement about the end of Communism. Bush disagreed, convinced that 'sticking it in Gorbachev's eye' was a very bad idea. Instead, he assured Gorbachev that the US had 'no intention of seeking unilateral advantage' from the changes under way in Eastern Europe. Democratic Party leaders criticised him for being 'inadequate to the moment' – for failing, as Bush put it, to 'dance on the wall'.

Peggy Noonan commented subsequently that George Bush had a 'high character'. The fall of the Berlin Wall was a huge moment in history. Yet he told Lesley Stahl that he 'didn't want to rub it in'. What would Reagan have done? He would have made a speech to mark the moment indelibly, thanking the American people for all the efforts they had made to help bring this about. In her view, he had a sense of history, which Bush did not.

But Bush, by nature 'a quiet man', felt that he could help the cause of freedom better by not adding to Gorbachev's problems. By December too, after the long struggle between Václav Havel's supporters and the regime, a non-Communist government had been formed in Czechoslovakia.

As the by now reformist regime in East Germany started looking for economic help from West Germany, Kohl assured both Bush and Gorbachev that he would do nothing to exacerbate the situation there. Scowcroft agreed with Thatcher that if Gorbachev lost East Germany, that could cost him his hold on power. The best course, therefore, in his view, was to go on supporting self-determination for East Germany, which still was Kohl's position at the time.

Baker came up with the principles that, to be acceptable to the US, unification must preserve Germany's position in NATO, be gradual and peaceful and respect existing borders and, to Thatcher's annoyance, that Germany must remain part of 'an increasingly integrated' European Community. A gradual process could help to ease other European countries' concerns. But within the administration, Bush was increasingly outspoken in support of Kohl and unification.

On 23 November 1989, Thatcher arrived for a meeting with Bush at Camp David before his summit with Gorbachev. The British embassy were warning that Thatcher being seen as increasingly isolated in Europe was weakening the 'special relationship'. Charles Powell advised that she must dispel the 'widespread perception that you hanker after President Reagan and don't think Bush is a patch on him'.

'WE CAN'T KEEP IT FROM EVENTUALLY HAPPENING IF THEY WANT IT'

Bush duly asked for Thatcher's advice about Gorbachev, given that she had more experience of dealing with him than anyone else. On Germany, she made clear that she was hostile to the idea of re-unification, not just because of the implications for Gorbachev but for more fundamental reasons. She feared that a united Germany would become dominant in Europe. 'We can't keep it from eventually happening if they want it,' she said, but they should rather concentrate on democratisation in Eastern Europe, including East Germany. Scowcroft agreed at this stage that, with the breath-taking changes in Europe, to add in the most potentially destabilising issue of all – German reunification – would be asking for trouble.

Bush asked what view the US should take on greater European integration. Kohl was telling him that Germany needed to be 'anchored' in the EC and NATO and that he saw German reunification as proceeding hand in hand with European monetary union. Thatcher warned about European protectionism and bureaucratisation.

There was no formal disagreement, except about defence spending, which she wanted to see maintained. Since in reality she was talking about US defence spending, Bush, mildly irritated, said that there was no longer support for high military expenditure.

The meeting was not a success, as Bush intended Camp David meetings to be relaxed and informal and there was nothing relaxed or informal about Thatcher. While Bush sprawled in his chair, periodically rearranging his arms or legs, Thatcher would sit bolt upright in these meetings. In her words, Bush appeared 'distracted and uneasy', the reason being that he had decided firmly, ahead of anyone else in his administration, that the US could not oppose self-determination. He had to support the wishes of the German people. So he must back Kohl on German reunification, provided it was within NATO, whatever the cost to Gorbachev, whom he had not yet met as President. In other respects he had been trying to be protective of Gorbachev, but on this issue he was convinced that he must back Kohl.

On 28 November, with no prior warning, Kohl unveiled a plan for ever-closer cooperation between the two Germanys, culminating in a federal structure. When even Bush remonstrated about this sudden declaration, Kohl said that the process would take several years. Meanwhile, West Germany would remain in NATO and East Germany in the Warsaw Pact.

Scowcroft recorded that Kohl and Bush were the only two leaders at this time who wanted to push for German unity. It was Bush's backing that gave Kohl the confidence repeatedly to accelerate the timetable, as he had promised not to do.

'I AM CAUTIOUS BUT NOT TIMID'

Before their meeting in Malta, Bush was warned by the CIA that Gorbachev's reforms had been enough to disrupt the Soviet system but not enough to give Soviet citizens the benefits of a market economy. Despite all the changes Gorbachev already had made, suspicions about him still lingered among Bush's advisers. Baker, influenced by his relationship with Shevardnadze, was the most optimistic about Gorbachev's intentions. For the CIA, Bob Gates feared that Gorbachev's reforms could easily be overturned. Cheney did not believe that it was yet the moment to relax Cold War-style pressure. Quayle was the most negative of all.

Scowcroft was concerned about the continuing Soviet support for Cuba and the Sandinistas in Nicaragua. They had just sent a shipment of MiG-29 fighters to Cuba. A Nicaraguan aircraft full of missiles and other munitions had just crashed in El Salvador, whose government the Sandinistas were trying to overthrow. Finally, the Bush team, going into the summit meeting, were worried about indications from Moscow that Gorbachev might be looking for signs of tolerance from the US if he had to crack down on the turbulence in Eastern Europe.

Malta was to prove a bizarre choice of venue for the meeting. In Valletta's Grand Harbour, Bush, who was based on the USS *Belknap*, flagship of the Sixth Fleet, was enjoying being shipboard again. But a rough ride on a launch through choppy seas was necessary to get to the first meeting with Gorbachev, held on an impressively refurbished Soviet cruise liner, the *Maxim Gorkiy*.

In his opening statement, Bush ran through the entire US agenda, starting with trade. He wanted to grant Most Favoured Nation status, provided the new Soviet emigration law allowed more mainly Jewish would-be emigrants to leave and divided Soviet families part of whom were living in the United States to reunite. They should negotiate a trade agreement in time for it to be approved at a summit in June 1990.

He then raised Central America, as the most contentious issue between them. The other countries there wanted Cuba and Nicaragua to stop trying to export revolution to them. How could the Soviets continue pouring money into Cuba and still want agricultural credits? Nicaragua had promised Shevardnadze to stop trying to export revolution but still was trying to do so.

Bush added that he wanted to agree a ban on chemical weapons, sign an agreement on conventional forces in Europe and aim for a further strategic nuclear arms reduction agreement.

Gorbachev seemed pleased with the 'looking for cooperation' tone of Bush's remarks. He believed that some in the US felt that their old policies had worked and simply wanted to gather the fruit, but that Bush had a different understanding, more in keeping with the times. In relation to their competition in the developing world, he observed that the US had not entirely abandoned old approaches. 'I cannot say that we have entirely abandoned ours.'

Bush emphasised that the US had not responded to the accelerating changes in Europe with 'flamboyance or arrogance'. He had been called cautious or timid. He *was* cautious, but not timid. He had conducted himself 'in ways not to complicate your life', which was why he had not jumped up and down over the Berlin Wall.

Gorbachev replied that they had seen and appreciated that restraint. There would now be elections in Nicaragua, which did not concern them much. No one could tell Castro what to do. But they did not want rival bridgeheads in Central America.

In a separate discussion, Gorbachev urged Bush to talk to Castro. The US seemed about to intervene in Panama and now in the Philippines (the latter in support of the beleaguered President, Cory Aquino). Some in the Soviet Union were saying that the Brezhnev doctrine had been replaced by the Bush doctrine. What if an East European country asked for Soviet intervention?

But Gorbachev then said that peaceful change was the way. His policy was non-interference. The direction of change in the Soviet Union and Eastern Europe should bring them closer together. But Kohl was in too much of a hurry on the German question. The US should let him know that this could be damaging. Bush said they would do nothing to recklessly speed up reunification. Gorbachev concluded that it was a time of great opportunity but with a need for great responsibility.

By the time the meeting ended, a storm had produced enormous swells in the harbour. The launch carrying Bush and his party had to make a dozen passes before it could tie up alongside the *Belknap* and the dinner planned there for Gorbachev had to be cancelled.

'THE SOVIET UNION WILL UNDER NO CIRCUMSTANCES START A WAR'

Next morning, Gorbachev told Bush that 'the Soviet Union will under no circumstances start a war'. They were ready no longer to regard the United States as an adversary and to state that their relationship was cooperative, though he complained that while the Soviet Union had switched to a defensive military stance, the US and NATO had not yet changed their doctrine. He concluded by handing Bush a coloured map of all US bases and fleets around the world. Bush asked what an American flag against the Panama Canal had to do with encircling the Soviet Union. Gorbachev laughed and said, 'Never mind the Panama Canal.'

Bush said that the US could not be asked to disapprove of German reunification. He understood how sensitive this was and they had conducted themselves with restraint. How did Gorbachev see Europe beyond the status quo? Gorbachev said that all of Europe should grow closer together. In future the Warsaw Pact and NATO should have more of a political than a military stance.

Bush asked directly about the possible use of force in the Baltic states. Gorbachev said that he had been ready to grant greater autonomy, but if the Baltics went for separatism, 'that would be dramatic. I must not create a danger to *perestroika*.' There were millions of Russians living in the Baltics – half the population of Estonia, he claimed, and the majority in Latvia. There were strong feelings in Russia about this. Separatism would bring 'terrible fires'. If the US did not understand this, it would spoil relations more than anything else. Bush warned that if Gorbachev used force in the Baltics, 'that would create a firestorm'. The US would have to respond.

Bush and Scowcroft's takeaway was that Gorbachev was keen to avoid using force if he could. Bush felt that the talks, held 'in a spirit of friendly openness', had established a good relationship between them and reassured Gorbachev that they would not seek to exploit at his expense the changes in Eastern Europe.

On the afternoon of 3 December, they held the first ever joint press conference between a US President and a Soviet leader. Bush declared that, with reform under way in the Soviet Union, they stood at the threshold of 'a brand-new era of US–Soviet relations', which could contribute to overcoming the division of Europe and ending the military confrontation there. Gorbachev sang the praises of 'cautiousness – and I use the favourite word of President Bush'.

*　*　*

Having told Gorbachev that he would do nothing recklessly to accelerate German reunification, over dinner with Kohl before briefing the NATO allies en route back to Washington, to Scowcroft's surprise, Bush told Kohl, 'I will support you.'

As Scowcroft observed, the only two leaders pressing for reunification at this stage were Kohl and Bush. Mitterrand kept telling Thatcher how worried he was by the prospect of a much stronger Germany in Europe and the EC, leading her to believe that he might try to do something to impede it. But he was a far more feline politician than her, concluding that it was inevitable, so it was pointless to resist it.

In the NATO meeting, Mitterrand described the collapse of the Soviet empire as 'the greatest revolution of the past two centuries'. Bush said that his encounter with Gorbachev had given him 'a new level of confidence … to push, push, push' on arms control. Expressing firmly his support for Kohl, he annoyed Thatcher by saying that he felt that the events of their time called for a 'continued, perhaps even intensified, effort by the [EC] to integrate'.

The US planned to remain neutral about monetary union, though the European bureau of the State Department waxed enthusiastic about it and kept warning the UK journalists in Washington about the dangers of Britain being 'left out'. Bush telephoned Thatcher to say that his reference to greater European integration related just to the single market, not political integration, which she did not believe. She saw Bush as aligning himself with Kohl's views on Europe, rather than hers.

In reality, the US was paying lip service to European integration and not much more than that. For while the European bureau of the State Department was singing the praises of monetary union, the Secretary of State, James Baker, was telling me: 'You're not going to join it, are you? You would be crazy to do so.' He regarded it as folly to link sterling to the Deutschmark. How were the Italians and others going to manage when they could no longer devalue? On this subject, he sounded like Thatcher, while Bush reacted with a groan to his encounters with Jacques Delors as the President of the European Commission.

'IN INTERNECINE COMBAT WITHIN THE US GOVERNMENT, HE'S LETHAL'

On his return to Washington, Bush discovered that the Vice-President's staff had been 'seeing a chance to firm him up as the spokesman of the right'. This was not a new development. Two months before, the conservative *Washington Times* had run an article by Morton Kondracke entitled 'Quayle, Baker Square Off', reporting Quayle advisers as questioning Baker's toughness in dealing with the Soviets and suggesting that his support for *perestroika* was 'appeasement'.

Kondracke had warned that portraying Baker as 'a potential softy' was a dangerous game. 'We don't know yet how tough Jim Baker can be with the Russians, but in internecine combat within the US government, he's lethal.' Baker had sent the article to Bush with the comment that they had avoided 'this kind of crap' for nine months. Recalling that he had never played these kind of games under Reagan, Bush was 'thoroughly annoyed about it … I am trying to contain myself.' Yet it never was apparent that he had made his displeasure clear to Quayle.

A more serious distraction took place in mid-December in Panama, where a young US Marine was killed and another beaten up at a military checkpoint. Having started as an ally in the fight against Communism, the Panamanian dictator, Manuel Noriega, had fallen out with the Americans over his involvement in drug trafficking. Bush ordered forthwith an invasion of Panama. Noriega was arrested and charged with drug smuggling. The hyper-cautious President in this case had turned out to be not so cautious after all.

At the end of the year, Bush reflected that 'sometimes you shape events by not making any mistakes'. In the New Year, he noted a comment in the *Baltimore Sun*: 'Bush is competent and confident, well-meaning and well-briefed, but a long way from greatness.' He was, he said, inclined to agree with this assessment.

'I WANT TO DO AS MUCH GOOD AS I CAN, AND AS LITTLE HARM'

With world events demanding his attention, Bush persistently was charged by his opponents with being uninterested in domestic policy and he admitted finding a good many of his forays into that arena an unpleasant experience. An instinctively moderate, centre-right politician, he deplored the increasingly strident partisanship, represented on his own side by Newt Gingrich. He was furious when the Republican National Committee under Lee Atwater launched an attack on the Speaker, Tom Foley – whom Bush regarded as 'a decent fellow, a warm human being' and someone he wanted to work with – claiming that he was secretly gay.

Nor were Bush's achievements in domestic policy as negligible as, subsequently, has been suggested. His objectives were modest. He wanted, he said, to do as much good as he could – and as little harm. Throughout his term, he was dealing with a Congress in which both houses were controlled by the Democrats. Yet he worked with them to set up the Resolution Trust Corporation. He banned the import of most semi-automatic weapons and signed legislation increasing the minimum wage.

In 1990, Bush assured his friend Brian Mulroney, Prime Minister of Canada, that he was determined to take action to deal with the problem of acid rain. In this period, whatever his other preoccupations, he combined with the Democratic leadership in Congress to secure the passage of a new Clean Air Act, setting firm goals and timetables to deal with, particularly, nitrogen oxide and sulphur oxide emissions and the smog affecting several major US cities, including Los Angeles, Houston and Chicago. The Democratic Party leader in the Senate, George Mitchell, described Bush's effort on this issue as 'courageous', given the prior Republican resistance to environmental legislation. An ardent conservationist, who regarded himself as an outdoorsman, Bush found it hard to understand why he was so disliked by environmentalists who wanted much more radical legislation and resented his defence of the Alaska oil pipeline.

Another significant achievement, again with bipartisan support, was the passage, in the same year, of the Americans with Disabilities Act, championed also by Bob Dole, victim of a battlefield injury in the last weeks of the Second World War. It was intended by Bush to help to overcome the difficulties of access, including access to employment, affecting millions of Americans suffering disabilities. When the Democratic Senator Tom Harkin complained that progress on the bill was being held up by the White House chief of staff, John Sununu, Bush instructed the White House counsel, Boyden Gray, to take over the negotiation and 'get it done'.

The domestic legislation he succeeded in getting onto the statute book in 1990 required months of preparation and negotiation, perforce on a bipartisan basis. The accusation of inertia in domestic policy was simply untrue in this period, whatever Bush's limitations in that regard later.

'I DO NOT FEAR THE GHOSTS OF THE PAST'

In February 1990, Bush sought to tackle in his diary the question: who now was the enemy? His answer was that there were all sorts of events that could not be foreseen that required a strong NATO and a strong US presence in Europe. He also started musing about German reunification, on the basis that others could not tell the Germans what to do.

He reflected that while Thatcher and Mitterrand had their reservations about German reunification, he did not. Unlike them, he was not worried about the ghosts of the past. For the Americans, the overriding concern was that this must take place on terms that left Germany in NATO, failing which NATO would lose much of its capability and rationale. If Germany were neutral, with no US troops stationed there, NATO would cease to be credible as a military alliance.

The notion of Germany reunited on a neutralist basis was one they were determined to conjure away. While Kohl never wavered in his determination that a united Germany must remain within NATO, his coalition partner and Foreign Minister, Hans-Dietrich Genscher, was distrusted by the Americans and Thatcher as being far less reliable from that point of view. They suspected, probably correctly, that he would be prepared to settle for neutrality if that were the price of reunification.

Scowcroft saw the US as now running against the clock before Gorbachev left or was forced from the scene. In January 1990, Gorbachev made a visit to Lithuania to try to persuade them not to seek independence.

Despite some resistance from Cheney and Baker, concerned about allied reactions, Bush decided to propose further cuts in US and Soviet conventional forces in Europe to 200,000 on each side. On 27 January 1990, Bush phoned Thatcher, interrupting her in the midst of her seminar about German reunification. Thatcher felt that they were being hustled. She wanted to know if the Soviet forces above that number were to be demobilised or merely withdrawn to the Soviet border. She wanted a coherent view on strategy, taking account of the prospect of German reunification, rather than piecemeal decisions. Bush said that he had to pre-empt congressional moves to cut US forces.

'Tweedledum and Tweedledee', Eagleburger and Gates, were despatched to London to try to mollify Thatcher, who again had been confronted with a fait accompli. She greeted them with, 'Please take your usual chairs.' She accepted the cuts but worried that there could then be German moves to try to get rid also of short-range nuclear weapons, weakening NATO strategy.

Scowcroft felt that 'this staunch ally' had a point. Mitterrand had warned of the danger of Germany embracing neutralism as the best way to achieve reunification, though Bush had confidence in Kohl's assurances that he would not take that route. Eagleburger and Gates were told by Thatcher that they would always be welcome, 'but never again on this subject'.

It was at this point that the British Foreign Secretary, Douglas

Hurd, amused George Bush by explaining that Thatcher was 'a reluctant unifier. Not against, but reluctant.' Bush knew perfectly well that she was fiercely against and would have preferred a more democratic East Germany to have continued separately for several years. But with East Germany collapsing and Gorbachev announcing with its new leader, Hans Modrow, that he now accepted that reunification would take place, she had gloomily to recognise its inevitability. As a euphemism for trying to slow it down, it was agreed that the UK must focus on the framework for 'a transition'.

On 31 January, to try to make reunification more acceptable to the Soviets, Hans-Dietrich Genscher suggested in a speech that NATO should rule out an 'expansion of its territory towards the east, i.e. moving it closer to the Soviet borders'.

On 9 February, Gorbachev acknowledged that the Germans alone would decide whether to unify and accepted James Baker's '2 plus 4' formula for managing the transition. This left the two Germanys in the driving seat, to sort things out between them, though with the four powers with rights in Berlin (the US, the USSR, the UK and France) also nominally involved.

It was in the course of this conversation that Baker sought to reassure Gorbachev that 'not an inch of NATO's present military jurisdiction will spread in an eastern direction'. Gorbachev acknowledged that he could see some advantages in US forces remaining in Europe; he did not want German remilitarisation.

Baker advised Kohl, before Kohl's meeting with Gorbachev on the following day, that any extension of NATO's zone would be unacceptable to Gorbachev but NATO in its current zone might be acceptable. Kohl assured Gorbachev that NATO would not expand its sphere of activity. That night, Kohl walked around Moscow in a state of excitement at Gorbachev's agreement in principle to German reunification and that Germany could choose NATO.

Meanwhile, there were large pro-democracy demonstrations in Moscow. The Communist Party was obliged by Gorbachev to accept the possibility of a multi-party system. Elections were held to what were supposed to be regional parliaments, including a specifically Russian Parliament, giving Yeltsin a Russian nationalist power base.

On 24 February, Thatcher telephoned Bush before his meeting with Kohl. He said that a unified Germany with full NATO membership was the bottom line for him. Thatcher acknowledged Kohl's firmness about NATO but made her usual fuss about the German failure to recognise the Oder–Neisse frontier with Poland, which Bush doubted was a serious problem. She felt that, to help Gorbachev, some Soviet troops should be permitted to stay in East Germany during a transition. Bush was against this, though it was part of the eventual agreement. Bush recalled that her fears about Germany 'came running through'. To Bush's amazement, she even talked about a reformed Soviet Union acting as a counterweight to Germany, whereas US policy was to 'embrace Germany'.

Kohl told Bush that he could not do anything about Thatcher. Germany had been a loyal ally for forty years. Bush raised the issue of the Polish frontier and Kohl did then announce his recognition of the Oder–Neisse line. The pro-reunification party won the election in East Germany, helped by Kohl's offer to exchange the virtually worthless East German currency at one to one with the Deutschmark.

In March, Shevardnadze warned the Americans that the situation in Lithuania was now critical, threatening Gorbachev's position, with an increasing danger that force might have to be used. When, a few days later, Lithuania, under the newly elected President Landsbergis, declared its independence, Gorbachev denounced the move as 'invalid' and vowed to preserve the integrity of the Soviet Union, threatening military measures. Soviet military aircraft started flying low over Lithuanian rooftops.

Attacked in Congress for withholding recognition, Bush was accused of choosing Gorbachev over Lithuania. But the reality was that the only way the Baltic states could achieve independence was with the acquiescence of Moscow. So Bush had to accept being condemned by what Scowcroft described as 'the "feel-good" crowd'.

Shevardnadze told Baker that the Soviets would try to avoid using force. But Gorbachev was under intense pressure from the Soviet military to do so. The head of the Soviet military, Marshal Sergei Akhromeyev, told his American counterpart, Admiral William Crowe, who was visiting Moscow, that the Lithuanians could do what they wanted but the Soviet leadership would not allow a single republic to leave. The public would never accept Gorbachev giving in to Lithuania. Crowe had the impression that Akhromeyev was tired of being overruled.

On 28 March, Margaret Thatcher told Bush that when she spoke to him, Gorbachev was not talking about a peaceful solution in Lithuania. When she pressed him to avoid using force, he was evasive. He had sounded lonely, sombre, pessimistic and felt that he was under attack.

Bush wrote to Gorbachev that the US had no desire to exploit the situation in Lithuania in any way. Gorbachev had told Thatcher that his options were narrowing. But the use of force would undermine the relationship with the West and also his own cause of reform. Bush was urging Landsbergis also to draw back from confrontation.

'I HAD LEARNED TO BE MORE DEFERENTIAL'

By the time of what the British were billing as a 'getting back together' meeting with George Bush in Bermuda on 13 April 1990, Thatcher observed that she had learned to be more deferential. 'I now waited for the President to set out his views before explaining mine.' By this time, the die was cast on German reunification. Whatever her misgivings, it had become futile to argue about it.

The Americans too were looking to make a success of the meeting. On the way there, Bush said that he did not really need to read the briefing book as 'Margaret will do all the talking'. But Scowcroft had reminded him that Thatcher remained 'an indispensable partner'. Britain, in his view, was the only European power unequivocally and reliably committed to the United States' key security and NATO objectives.

Denis Thatcher found himself obliged to play 'the worst game of golf' he had ever experienced with the President and his aides in pouring rain. Margaret Thatcher fared marginally better than Bush at kite flying in a howling gale. But Thatcher having been obliged to temper her position on Germany, they said in their press conference that they had discussed 'just about everything' and agreed on just about everything.

There were two exceptions. Thatcher said that, to help Gorbachev, they should allow some Soviet troops to remain in East Germany for a transitional period. Bush's response was: 'I don't agree. I want the Soviets to go home,' though in the end he accepted what she had suggested.

The other exception was their respective views on Boris Yeltsin. In a meeting in London, Thatcher had found him with more radical ideas about economic reform and the role of the republics than Gorbachev and advocating a multi-party system. She had been impressed. Bush disagreed, with Baker at the time regarding Yeltsin as a 'flake'.

When Shevardnadze visited Washington in April, he delivered quite a positive response from Gorbachev to Bush's message about Lithuania. But otherwise, he was far less forthcoming than usual. The Soviets were hardening their positions on arms control because, he said, there was a feeling that they were making too many concessions.

On 18 April, Gorbachev embargoed oil and gas supplies to Lithuania unless they withdrew their declaration of independence. With Thatcher and Mitterrand, Bush agreed that there would have to be a response. He did not want to stop the arms control negotiations. The obvious course was to suspend the granting to the Soviet Union of Most Favoured Nation status.

'IF YOU WANT TO UNDERMINE THE RELATIONSHIP, THEN YOU SHOULD ENCOURAGE SEPARATISM'

Bush wrote to warn Gorbachev in advance of their planned summit meeting that he would not be able to proceed with a trade agreement unless there was a dialogue with Lithuania, getting a chilly reply. Gorbachev stated that the problem could only be solved without outside interference. 'If you want to undermine the relationship ... then you should encourage separatism,' he wrote, which was not what Bush was trying to do.

By this stage, Kohl was about to warn Gorbachev that, to avoid a mass migration of East Germans after the March 1990 elections there, reunification would have to be accelerated. The East German leaders announced a plan for a neutral confederation of the two Germanys, which was acceptable to Gorbachev but not to Bush or Kohl.

Before Kohl's planned meeting with Gorbachev, Bush wrote to Kohl agreeing that unification could be accelerated. Rowing back on Baker's assertion that there would be no eastward advance of NATO's jurisdiction, he specified that a united Germany must remain within NATO but there could be a 'special military status' for the former territory of East Germany. This meant no US troops there, but, for the Americans, it also meant the phased withdrawal of the Soviet forces in East Germany and that all of Germany would be in NATO and subject to the NATO mutual defence guarantee.

Following their meeting, Gorbachev again accepted reunification but not that a reunified Germany should remain in NATO.

The NATO Secretary General and former West German Defence Minister Manfred Wörner, invited to Camp David, told George Bush that 'in the next few weeks or months, you personally will have to make decisions that can decide the future of Europe'.

A neutral Germany or a demilitarised Germany without US forces would create instability at the centre of Europe. They must avoid the classic German temptation: to 'float freely and bargain with both East and West'. It was Bush's 'historic task' to prevent that from happening. He was confident that the Soviets could not now prevent reunification.

In separate talks between Baker and Shevardnadze, agreement had been reached to ban chemical weapons and on conventional force limits of 195,000 on each side in central Europe, plus 30,000 for the US forces in Europe outside that zone.

On 24 February, Kohl arrived at Camp David. Bush saw the purpose of the meeting as being to 'keep Germany on the NATO reservation'. On the Polish border, Kohl said that the vast majority of Germans accepted the Oder–Neisse line. But at the end of the war, Germany had been obliged to cede one third of its territory to Poland and 12 million people had been displaced. The frontier could only finally be approved in a treaty ratified by an all-German Parliament.

'ONE FRANCE IN NATO IS ENOUGH'

Kohl was adamant that a united Germany would remain in NATO, with a continuing US presence. But there would need to be a transition period. NATO units should not be stationed on East German soil. Perhaps a united Germany could be in NATO like France (outside the integrated military structure). Bush reacted sharply that one France in NATO was enough. Baker said that US forces could only remain with full German NATO membership.

Bush said that Kohl would have to address the issue of US nuclear weapons in Germany, which were seen by Americans as essential to protect the US forces there. Kohl said that the Soviets needed financial assistance and that the final arrangements for Germany 'could end up being a matter of cash'. With the US government unwilling to contribute, Bush's response was: 'You have deep pockets.' Bush said that he wanted a good summit meeting with Gorbachev to help him at home.

Bush then proposed a 'bracing walk' around Camp David, which ended with the massive, jet-lagged German Chancellor struggling to make it up a sharp incline. On the following morning, they reaffirmed the intention not to position US forces on East German territory but agreed that the former East Germany could not be left outside the NATO security guarantee.

With the press, Kohl again was evasive about the Polish border, to the annoyance of Mitterrand as well as Thatcher. Mitterrand said that the alliance's security concerns could not be subordinated to German domestic politics, adding, 'Let's not believe that the USSR has vanished from the scene.' As George Bush observed, 'It was not a happy Mitterrand.'

Bush phoned Gorbachev, who said that they did not have an understanding with Kohl. If no one should be concerned about a united Germany, why was the US so determined to keep it in NATO? If the outcome was going to negatively affect the Soviet Union, they would have to think long and hard about it. But the East German elections had resulted in a clear majority for reunification, leaving the two Germanys to negotiate the modalities, including early monetary union.

The Polish border issue was defused, with Kohl now saying that both the German Parliaments approved the existing border, earning him a message of congratulations from Thatcher. Once Germany was reunified, the issue became moot anyway, as the act of reunification automatically ratified the existing frontiers, though Kohl still insisted on having this approved by the all-German Parliament.

On 23 March, Genscher annoyed the Americans by suggesting that, post-reunification, both NATO and the Warsaw Pact would quickly wither away and the GDR part of unified Germany could be left outside NATO. Kohl was exasperated enough to contradict him.

In May, Marshal Akhromeyev told his US counterpart that a unified Germany within NATO was something they could never accept. This was a grassroots issue. Every Soviet family had suffered in the Second World War. Shevardnadze, meanwhile, talking to Baker, seemed very worried about the prospects for Gorbachev's hold on power.

On 17 May, Kohl returned to Washington to tell Bush that he was about to sign a treaty between the two Germanys providing for economic and monetary union. He too was concerned about keeping Gorbachev in power in this crucial period. The Soviet economy was in a very poor state. The Soviets had asked through him for $12 billion in credits from the West. Bush said that the US could not extend any credits so long as the Soviets were threatening the Baltics, and even thereafter, with Bush acknowledging that US assistance to the Soviet Union was extremely modest.

On 18 May, in Moscow, Gorbachev poured out his frustrations to Baker. A united Germany in NATO would have a very serious effect on the strategic balance. Shevardnadze said that 'if united Germany becomes a member of NATO, it will blow up *perestroika*'. There was another plea for temporary financial support. Baker said that the US was not seeking to separate Eastern Europe from the Soviet Union.

It was clear that, unquestionably, Gorbachev was in danger. To add to his problems, Yeltsin was about to be elected chairman of the Supreme Soviet of Russia. When Mitterrand met him in Moscow, Gorbachev remained strongly opposed to a united Germany in NATO and to Lithuanian independence.

Baker, however, had been working very skilfully on a series of 'assurances' to the Soviets which might encourage a moderation of their reactions. These were that the US was committed to further agreement on conventional force levels in Europe and to pursue negotiations on short-range nuclear forces thereafter; Germany would reaffirm its intention never to produce or possess nuclear, biological or chemical weapons; NATO would conduct a strategic review of both conventional and nuclear weapons' requirements; extension of NATO forces to East German territory would be delayed during a transition period; there would be a transitional period for Soviet forces leaving East Germany; and Germany would make firm commitments about its borders and would aim to act in support of *perestroika*.

At the end of May 1990, Gorbachev arrived in Washington to full military honours. His conversation with Bush in the Oval Office was 'philosophical', with Gorbachev saying that the confrontation between them after the Second World War had wasted their time and energy; the old suspicions between them must be set aside. Bush recognised the immense sacrifices the Soviet Union had made in that war. The Soviet Union was an equal partner. He did not want it to be threatened by any power or there to be winners and losers. He assured Gorbachev that Germany in NATO would never be directed at the Soviet Union. Gorbachev said that his reforms were at a crucial stage. He was aiming for a market economy, but it would take time to get there.

In a larger meeting in the Cabinet Room, Gorbachev argued that a united Germany within NATO would isolate the Soviet Union. If Germany were united, it should either belong to no alliance or be allied both with NATO and with the Soviet Union.

A 'VIRTUALLY OPEN REBELLION AGAINST A SOVIET LEADER'

Bush pointed out that the Helsinki Final Act, agreed between the Western countries and the Soviets in 1975, had stated that all countries had the right to choose their alliances. Did Gorbachev agree?

To the dismay, indeed horror, of the other members of the Soviet delegation, Gorbachev, shrugging, said that he did.

There followed a heated discussion among his advisers, including Marshal Akhromeyev and the Soviet Defence Minister and future attempted coup leader Dmitry Yazov, in what Bush described as a 'virtually open rebellion against a Soviet leader'. It clearly was about trying to get Gorbachev to change his response. Even Shevardnadze was agitated at what Gorbachev had said. Gorbachev did not withdraw what he had said but added that they should work on an extended transition period.

Scowcroft 'could scarcely believe' what he was witnessing. It was obvious that Gorbachev's remark had created a firestorm in his delegation, arousing bitter opposition from most of its members.

Gorbachev also said that he hoped that the US military would remain in Europe for an extended period – and that he was prepared to say so publicly.

Gorbachev, that evening, told Bush that it was vital for him to have a new trade agreement with the US granting the Soviet Union Most Favoured Nation status (which would facilitate the purchase of large quantities of low-cost US grain). He was 'very agitated'. It would be a disaster if this were not agreed. It would make or break the summit for him.

The problem for Bush was that, while Gorbachev had been showing forbearance elsewhere in Eastern Europe, old-style Soviet tactics were being used against those demonstrating for independence in Lithuania, regarded as a vital strategic asset by the Soviet military.

Thinking about this overnight, Bush came up with an imaginative solution. The US would sign the trade agreements but not send them to Congress for ratification until the Soviets had met all the requirements for Most Favoured Nation status.

There was a further secret condition, which was that Bush would not ask Congress to vote on the trade deal until the Soviets had started negotiations with the Lithuanians and lifted the embargo they had imposed on Lithuania. This gave Gorbachev a public success, while keeping secret a condition that would have caused problems for him in Moscow.

On the helicopter flight to Camp David, Bush realised that their respective military aides both were carrying the codes that could have launched nuclear missiles at each other. Obliged to join in Bush's cherished game of horseshoes, Gorbachev was successful with his first throw. Gorbachev had been told that the Americans had used laser weapons against Panamanian troops. Having checked with Cheney and Powell, Bush told him that this was nonsense.

Gorbachev told Bush that he had not wanted to raise the question of needing money from the US in front of his own team. Bush explained American political realities: trade was one thing, financial aid another. If the Soviets could show further progress on cutting aid to Cuba, on allowing a reunified Germany to join NATO if it chose and on their own internal reforms, he would be better able to help.

Bush felt that he had got a long way towards establishing a genuine friendship with Gorbachev. The joint statement at the press conference included the formulation that future alliance membership would be for the Germans to decide.

In the Oval Office, Gorbachev saw Bush's schedule for a month ahead. He did not, he said, have such a thing in the Kremlin. Bush's chief of staff, John Sununu, was despatched to Moscow to help Gorbachev's staff to modernise his office, which, Sununu discovered, was badly needed. In one of the offices in the Kremlin, he found a table covered with more than two dozen yellow telephones.

Instead of a single phone with multiple lines, Gorbachev's staff were using a separate phone to call each government department.

On 8 June, Kohl was back in Washington. He reported that the Soviets needed between $20 and $25 billion to buy goods for consumption. They had approached Germany directly for a credit line and said that he could expect something in return.

But in a meeting subsequently with Baker in East Berlin, Shevardnadze rowed back on Gorbachev's remarks in Washington, demanding that Germany should remain divided for a further five years. Baker regarded this as being primarily for Soviet internal reasons. Shevardnadze said that a lot would depend on what came out of the planned NATO summit and the follow-up on Baker's 'nine points'.

'TRULY WEAPONS OF LAST RESORT'

To try to mitigate Soviet concerns about the prospect of a Germany reunified in NATO, Bush and Scowcroft drafted a new NATO declaration to be issued after the summit in July in London. The proposal was that NATO should shift its emphasis from being a military alliance to more of a political one and away from 'forward defence' incorporating the NATO doctrine that tactical nuclear weapons, if necessary, could be used to halt a Soviet military advance. Warsaw Pact countries were invited to send representatives to Brussels for liaison with NATO.

Thatcher, forcefully, and also Mitterrand objected to the initial draft, which they saw as being close to a pledge of 'no first use' of nuclear weapons by the alliance, which, Thatcher knew, also was opposed by the US chiefs of staff. It risked giving the impression that there no longer was a military threat, which was not the case.

Baker came up with a formula that preserved NATO flexibility while expressing the hope that nuclear weapons in due course would become 'truly weapons of last resort'. So both sides were satisfied in this debate, with Bush declaring that the alliance was 'moving away' from forward defence. He regarded this as 'a landmark shift' by the alliance, sending the text to Gorbachev as demonstrating a desire to transform its relationship with the Soviet Union.

At the end of June, Lithuania suspended its declaration of independence and Gorbachev lifted the Soviet embargo. In early July, he survived attacks on his domestic and foreign policies in an angry meeting of the Soviet Communist Party, winning a majority to continue on his course. Kohl and Genscher then met Gorbachev in Moscow and the Caucasus. They offered to take over all East Germany's debts to the Soviet Union, to provide a $3 billion credit at, Gorbachev said, 'just the right time' and to pay for the Soviet troops remaining in East Germany during the transition. Gorbachev told the press, 'Whether we like it or not, the time will come when a united Germany will be in NATO if that is its choice.'

Kohl reported to Bush that the NATO declaration had helped. Gorbachev had accepted a three- to four-year transition period in which there would be no allied troops on East German territory pending the withdrawal of Soviet forces. Thereafter, German forces not assigned to NATO could be there.

Kohl concluded that Gorbachev had burned all the bridges behind him.

The reunification treaty was signed by the representatives of the six powers in Moscow on 12 September 1990. The German armed forces were limited to 370,000 troops. All Soviet forces would withdraw from East German territory by the end of 1994. Until then, only German forces not assigned to NATO could be there. Once they were gone, German NATO forces could be stationed in eastern Germany, but no nuclear weapons. Kohl was emotionally grateful to Bush for the success of reunification. Success had been anything but preordained.

In October, the Pentagon wanted to leave 'the door ajar' for East European membership of NATO. But the State Department view, supported by Bush, was that NATO expansion was not on the agenda, as it was not in US interests to organise an anti-Soviet movement that might reverse the positive trends in the Soviet Union.

Bush reflected that, if the US had remained on the sidelines, the outcome of a negotiation between Germany and the Soviet Union was likely to have been very different.

When Bush told Thatcher that he was concerned to 'tie Germany to Europe', she replied that he might find that they had tied Europe to Germany! She doubted if Gorbachev would long survive German reunification. She professed to be unperturbed by the friction that had developed between her and the Bush administration over Germany, remaining convinced that, as she put it, the Americans soon would rediscover who their real friends were.

CHAPTER SIX

'THIS WILL NOT STAND'

O n the evening of 1 August 1990, Bush suddenly and quite un-expectedly was alerted to a brand-new crisis by Scowcroft and Richard Haass, the senior Middle East adviser on the NSC staff. 'It looks very bad,' they said. 'Iraq may be about to invade Kuwait.' They discussed whether the massing of Iraqi troops on the border with Kuwait was just posturing, as the intelligence agencies had tended to believe, and whether Bush should try to ring Saddam Hussein.

The seizure of Kuwait would leave Saddam in control of 20 per cent of the world's oil reserves. If he then attacked Saudi Arabia, which was unprepared to withstand an Iraqi offensive, that figure could go up to 45 per cent.

In 1981, Reagan had declared that the US would not allow Saudi Arabia to fall into the hands of any internal or external forces threatening to cut off oil supplies to the West. Bush told Thomas Pickering, the US Ambassador at the UN, to request an emergency meeting of the Security Council. Overnight, the Security Council approved fourteen to zero a resolution demanding the withdrawal of Iraqi troops.

The unanimity was a tribute to the dramatically improved rela-tionship with the Soviet Union, which had been a major sponsor and supplier of arms to Iraq, and to the better relationship with China. The unanimous condemnation of Iraq had been agreed while Baker was in talks with Shevardnadze in Siberia.

An inter-agency meeting convened by Scowcroft that night agreed to recommend the despatch of US F-15 fighter aircraft to Saudi Arabia, if the Saudis would accept them, and the freezing of Iraqi and Kuwaiti assets in the US. Bush ordered US warships based at Diego Garcia in the Indian Ocean to move towards the Persian Gulf.

At 8 a.m. the next day, before attending a meeting of the National Security Council, Bush told the press that he was demanding the immediate and unconditional withdrawal of Iraqi forces. Asked if he was contemplating intervention, he said twice that he was 'not contemplating such action', adding that he would not discuss it if he was.

The NSC meeting that morning was a low point in dealing with the crisis, in a discussion described by Scowcroft and Haass as 'rambling' and chaotic. Scowcroft was appalled that much of it seemed to be based on acceptance that Iraqi control over Kuwait was a fait accompli. The tone implied that the crisis was a vast distance away and doing anything serious about it would be just too difficult. Sharing in the confusion was George Bush, who told his diary: 'It's halfway around the world, US options are limited and all in all it is a highly complicated situation.'

Haass told Scowcroft that it was one of the worst meetings he had ever attended. Scowcroft agreed. 'Write me a memo about why we have to act,' he told Haass.

Scowcroft told Bush of his unhappiness about the NSC meeting, asking if, exceptionally, he could speak first at the next meeting about the absolute intolerability of the invasion to US interests.

They then boarded a small Gulfstream aircraft to Aspen,

Colorado, where Bush had a long-scheduled meeting with Margaret Thatcher and was due to make a speech. In the discussion on the plane, it became clear to Scowcroft that Bush was prepared to use force to evict Saddam Hussein from Kuwait, though he did not explicitly say so. Scowcroft undoubtedly had contributed to that determination himself.

Bush spoke to King Hussein of Jordan, who urged him to 'remain calm', as Saddam would pull out within days, and to President Hosni Mubarak of Egypt. Both wanted time to find an 'Arab solution'.

Meanwhile, in Washington, Defense Secretary Dick Cheney was asking, 'Shouldn't our objective be to get him out of Kuwait?' Sanctions would not work. The key was US military power.

When Colin Powell, chairman of the joint chiefs of staff, presented Cheney with a plan to defend Saudi Arabia, he was told to produce one also for the liberation of Kuwait.

Bush met Thatcher in the Aspen home of Henry Catto, the US Ambassador to Britain. As she made clear in her memoirs, she saw no lack of resolution on the part of George Bush. He said that he had told the Arab leaders that they couldn't accept the status quo. It had to be withdrawal and restoration of the Kuwaiti government. The US carrier group was on its way to the Gulf.

Thatcher said, 'If Iraq wins, no small state is safe.' Iraq had seen its chance to seize a major share of the world's oil. 'It's got to be stopped.' They needed to get a sanctions resolution through the UN. Getting Saudi support was critical: they could not do much without them.

Addressing the press jointly with Thatcher, when asked about possible military action, Bush gave a far better answer than the day before. 'We're not ruling any options in,' he said, 'but we're not ruling any options out.'

When, later that day, he got through to King Fahd of Saudi Arabia, Bush found him 'emotional' and furious with Saddam Hussein, whom he compared to Hitler. But when Bush offered to send the F-15s to Saudi Arabia to ensure air superiority, Fahd asked for more time before accepting.

This 'rang alarm bells' in Bush's mind. There was, he believed, an Arab propensity to work out deals. Were the Saudis going to settle for a promise that Saddam would not attack Saudi Arabia? There could not be a solo US effort in the Middle East. There must be Arab allies, in particular those who were threatened the most – the Saudis.

The memo drafted by Haass for Scowcroft to use at the NSC meeting said that he knew 'how costly and risky a conflict would prove to be. But so too would be accepting this new status quo. We would be setting a terrible precedent.'

Bush returned to Washington overnight to hear the CIA director, Bill Webster, tell the National Security Council that Saddam had no intention of withdrawing. Scowcroft spoke first to remind everyone of the stakes. With the fourth largest army in the world, Iraq now controlled the world's second and third largest oil producers.

Scowcroft said that in the previous NSC meeting, he had 'detected a note … that they might have to acquiesce in an accommodation'. The stakes for the US were too high for that. Baker's deputy, Larry Eagleburger, and Cheney supported him, setting a far more determined tone for the meeting.

But, Bush told his diary, 'the Arabs don't seem to have the resolve'. Bush was trying to 'stiffen the spine' of the Saudis. The status quo, he told his diary, was intolerable.

Mitterrand agreed that they could not accept it. Baker and Shevardnadze issued a joint statement condemning the Iraqi invasion.

On 4 August, Bush summoned his senior military advisers to Camp David to discuss plans to defend Saudi Arabia and to enforce an embargo against Iraq. The Saudis were unprepared for war and their forces were vastly inferior to those of Saddam Hussein.

Bush continued to worry about King Hussein and Mubarak, both of whom he found still 'in the hand-wringing stage', with neither of them really wanting action by the United States or by the Arabs themselves. A lot of Arab countries, he concluded, were scared to death of Saddam Hussein.

At 11 that morning, Scowcroft saw the Saudi Ambassador, Prince Bandar. Trained by the British as a fighter pilot, Bandar entertained grandly at his houses in McLean and Aspen and was popular with the Bush team. Having pointed out how exposed Saudi Arabia was to an Iraqi attack, Scowcroft offered US forces for the defence of the kingdom, only to find Bandar not at all keen on this proposal. 'He seemed ill at ease and did not react with enthusiasm to the idea.'

Bandar pointed out that in 1979, during the Iranian revolution, the Americans had sent F-15s to Saudi Arabia, only then to announce that they were unarmed. Later, they had despatched US Marines to Beirut, only to withdraw them after a suicide bomber attack. Manifestly, there also were concerns about the presence of American troops in the strictly Islamist kingdom.

Bandar was despatched to see Cheney, who said that the US was planning to deploy up to 200,000 troops. 'We're serious this time.' There was no time to lose to forestall Saddam launching an attack on Saudi Arabia.

Bush told the National Security Council that his worry was the 'lack of Saudi will'. Fahd agreed to receive a senior US team for consultations but still was being evasive. Bush told him that the defence of Saudi Arabia was vital to the US and the West and, 'on his word of honour', the Americans would stay until they were asked by the Saudis to leave.

On Sunday 5 August, Scowcroft told Bandar that the Saudis had a choice between being defended or being liberated. But Bandar, meanwhile, was discovered to have been telling the Turks to take no action while the Saudis worked things out.

To avoid any danger of a public rejection, Bush decided not to send Cheney and his team to Saudi Arabia without a prior assurance that the kingdom would accept US troops. It was at this point that King Fahd agreed to accept the offer of US troops on the ground to defend Saudi Arabia.

When Cheney saw Fahd, with Bandar as interpreter, the King's half-brother, Abdullah, argued that the Saudis should delay before accepting the US offer. Fahd brushed this aside: 'The Kuwaitis waited and now they are living in our hotels.' He confirmed to Cheney, 'OK, we'll do it,' with two conditions. The US must bring enough troops to finish the job and they must then leave when asked to do so.

On the South Lawn of the White House on 5 August, George Bush made his dramatic statement to the press: 'This will not stand, this aggression against Kuwait.' Colin Powell, watching on television, felt that this had a 'Thatcheresque' ring to it. Struck by the certainty of what Bush had said, he realised that planning must now indeed be for the liberation of Kuwait. Saddam told the US chargé d'affaires that Iraq would never leave Kuwait. 'The Kuwaiti royal family is history.'

The following afternoon, on 6 August, Bush still was worrying that Saddam might stage a pre-emptive invasion of Saudi Arabia. On her way back from Aspen, Thatcher joined in a long meeting at the White House. In her memoir, she wrote that, close as she had been to Reagan, she was never taken into the Americans' confidence more than she was in that discussion. 'The President that day was an altogether more confident George Bush,' displaying all the qualities of a Commander in Chief. She had always liked Bush. 'Now my respect for him soared.'

Bush gave her details of the planned US military deployment. During the meeting, Cheney called to confirm that King Fahd would accept US forces. The UN Security Council had passed another thirteen to zero resolution imposing economic sanctions against Iraq. Thatcher insisted that a blockade was needed to enforce them. Bush and Scowcroft agreed, though deciding to call it a 'quarantine'.

'HE IS SUCH A FOX THAT YOU FEEL THE IMPULSE TO CHECK YOUR WALLET WHEN YOU LEAVE HIS OFFICE'

The meeting also saw the beginning of an argument between Thatcher and Baker as to whether a further UN Security Council resolution was going to be necessary, authorising member states to use 'all necessary means' to dislodge Saddam. Her worry was that this might not be attainable. She thought they could rely on the existing UN resolutions, plus Article 51 of the UN charter on self-defence.

Thatcher was never as comfortable with Baker as she had been with the solid and reassuring figure of George Shultz. She continued to regard him as a 'fixer' and was not alone in that view. Maureen Dowd and Thomas Friedman of the *New York Times* reported that he had 'a compelling presence, but he is such a fox that you feel the impulse to check your wallet when you leave his office'. Thatcher suspected, correctly, that he would prefer to avoid a military conflict in the Gulf, if he could.

Baker was unrepentant and determined to challenge her when he thought she was wrong, as in his view she had been about Germany. She considered Baker to be 'wet' for wanting to go back to the UN. No one else who ever had dealings with James Baker could detect any dampness in him at all. It was an unnecessary argument, as Bush assured her that they would not go back to the Security Council unless they had the votes to get an eventual resolution adopted authorising the use of 'all necessary means'. Baker's calculation was that if he could get such a resolution through, this would help Bush to get sufficient Democrats on his side to win the subsequent vote in Congress.

For far from being just a fixer, Baker's legendary quality in Washington was in *getting things done*. His achievements as Secretary of State, in helping to manage German reunification and the collapse of the Soviet empire, went far beyond those of any holder of the office since Henry Kissinger and further still beyond those of any of his successors.

On returning to London, Thatcher telephoned King Fahd to clear with him the despatch of RAF aircraft to Saudi Arabia. 'I feel great pressure, but I also feel a certain calmness,' Bush told his diary. 'I know that I am doing the right thing.'

He had known that he could count on Thatcher's support. When, on her return to London, he rang her later to thank her for her leadership, 'It was your leadership,' she said. 'I was just a chum.'

More surprisingly, to Bush's delight, disregarding prior French objections to the involvement of NATO outside Europe, Mitterrand told him: 'We will be there.'

The US troops are under way, Bush told his diary, 'the biggest step of my presidency'.

On the morning of 8 August, once elements of the 82nd Airborne Division had arrived in Saudi Arabia, Bush addressed the nation. He knew, he told himself, that he was not as good as Reagan at doing this. But he made a forceful case for the path he was taking. Appeasement did not work and America was at the head of a huge international coalition.

Thatcher told him that she was sending British naval forces to join in the blockade. Bush telephoned the Gulf leaders, all of whom supported action against Iraq.

'NO TIME TO GO WOBBLY'

As Bush then set off for his usual stay at Walker's Point in Maine, he noted that the public were with him – for now. But the support was shaky, with nearly all Democrats against military action. It could turn against him and be the end of his presidency. But, he said, 'I like wrestling with the foreign policy agenda. I don't like the negotiations on the budget.'

Bush realised that the press would attack him for leaving Washington in the midst of the crisis, but, he observed, 'a President is never truly on vacation'. They had secure communications and 'Brent could stay awake all night there just as well as in Washington'. Facilities were improvised for the press there, though the move put some strain on the relationship with the White House press corps.

Mubarak had organised an emergency meeting of the Arab League, at which all the Gulf states, Egypt, Morocco and a couple of others had pledged to join the coalition against Saddam, giving it an indispensably Arab complexion. Egyptian and Moroccan troops started arriving in Saudi Arabia.

King Hussein arrived by helicopter at Walker's Point to plead for an accommodation with Saddam, rejected by Bush. The Saudi Foreign Minister then arrived, now pressing for rapid military action.

The Iraqis had sent five oil tankers to Yemen in defiance of the UN embargo. Bush, Cheney and Scowcroft all wanted to intercept them. The French and the Soviets wanted a delay until there was a UN Security Council resolution authorising military action, limited to helping to enforce the embargo. Bush reluctantly accepted Baker's argument in favour of a delay until such a resolution was passed.

As Britain was the United States' principal military partner, Bush then had to ring Margaret Thatcher to tell her of his decision. He admitted that he 'wasn't looking forward to the call'.

In the middle of the night London time, Thatcher heard out Bush's explanation, responding with, 'Well, all right, George. But this is no time to go wobbly!'

It was the reaction he had expected from her. As he hung up the call, Bush burst out laughing. He claimed to think it 'a marvellous expression'. So did Scowcroft and other members of Bush's team, who at various times throughout the crisis would jokingly quote it to one another. Bush himself made the remark public.

The UN resolution on enforcing sanctions was passed. The tankers by then had reached Yemen, but, having secured the enforcement resolution, the Americans no longer cared.

Bush, continuing to manage the crisis from Maine, was in touch with the Situation Room in the White House by 5 or 5.30 every morning, which did not stop him being pilloried in the press for golfing and fishing amidst it.

By this stage, Bush had become convinced that it would be

necessary to use force. So had Scowcroft and Cheney. Baker wanted more time for diplomacy and sanctions to work. He worried that they could get bogged down in another Vietnam, losing public support and destroying the Bush presidency. He kept warning that a war would be popular until the body bags started coming home.

Given the massive size of the Iraqi armed forces (1 million men and nearly 6,000 tanks), the TV pundits were predicting high US casualties and Baker cannot have been reassured by the US forces taking with them 20,000 body bags in case of need. In a meeting with the joint chiefs of staff at Camp David on 1 December, the Air Force commander, General McPeak, projected that 150 US aircraft could be lost in the air war. (In the event, the Americans lost twenty-eight and the British seven fixed-wing aircraft.)

Bush and Scowcroft reflected that, in previous crises, the US and the Soviet Union almost automatically were never on the same side. This time, they were working together, leading them to wonder if this could not be the beginning of a 'new world order' – in a first, non-public use of the phrase.

But as opinions remained divided in Moscow, with the Soviet Middle East envoy, Yevgeny Primakov, who had been the chief sponsor of Saddam, and the old guard on the other side, Bush met Gorbachev in Helsinki on 9 September. Bush shared with him the prospect of a 'new world order' against aggression emerging from the crisis. He did not want to use force, but if Saddam remained in Kuwait, the US could not accept the status quo.

Gorbachev said that a military solution was not acceptable to the Soviet Union. He proposed pressure on Saddam to withdraw, coupled with an international conference on the Middle East, conflicting with Bush's determination to keep Israel out of every aspect of the crisis.

Gorbachev said that Primakov wanted to find a way for Saddam to save face. Bush would not accept anything that left Saddam in place in Kuwait. Also, he pointed out, Saddam had an incipient nuclear programme.

But Gorbachev then agreed to a joint statement calling on Saddam to withdraw from Kuwait and release the hostages he had seized. If the current measures failed, they were prepared to consider additional ones under the UN charter.

Throughout this phase of the crisis, Bush was battling with Congress on two fronts. On Iraq, nearly all the Democrats remained opposed to military action, with the opposition led by the normally centrist Senator Sam Nunn. To counter their attacks on the potential costs of action, Baker and Brady were despatched on what subsequently was described as a 'tin cup' trip to the Arab and Western allies, including Japan, returning with pledges of $6 billion. Thanks to Baker's indefatigable 'tin cup' efforts after the war, with Kuwait, the Saudis, other Gulf states and Japan, the amount eventually raised was $53.7 billion against costs of $61.1 billion. Administration officials at one point worried that Baker's efforts might result in the US making a profit from the war.

The Soviets, meanwhile, were trying to broker a compromise with Saddam, and Bush was anything but reassured when their envoy, Primakov, called on him in Washington.

In September, Bush flew to Helsinki for a meeting with Gorbachev. As Iraq was or had been a client state of the Soviet Union, Bush made clear to Gorbachev that future cooperation would depend on the Soviets not impeding action against Saddam Hussein. In a similar conversation in London, when Primakov asked Margaret Thatcher what the Soviet Union could do to help, he was told that the best thing they could do was to get out of the way.

In his diary, Bush congratulated himself on his personal diplomacy, believing, correctly, that his incessant phone calls to a raft of world leaders had contributed to the array of countries now aligned against Iraq.

In October, Israeli troops fired on a violent demonstration at the Temple Mount in Jerusalem, killing twenty-one Palestinians and injuring many more. To avoid a more radical resolution, which the Americans would have felt obliged to veto, they took the unprecedented step of joining the British and French in sponsoring a resolution, which then was passed, condemning the Israeli action. Baker, though a supporter of Israel, was no fan of the Likud government, led by Yitzhak Shamir, who had started his political career as a Zionist terrorist and was opposed to any settlement with the Palestinians. This unprecedented criticism of Israel, as Baker observed to me, came at a political cost, being fiercely attacked by the principal Jewish organisations in the US.

'WOULD YOU PUT YOUR PRESIDENCY ON THE LINE FOR THIS?'

As Saddam still was showing no intention of withdrawing from Kuwait by the UN Security Council deadline of 15 January, there remained mixed feelings in the Bush team about the prospect of a war to liberate Kuwait. Left to his own devices, Colin Powell would have preferred simply to defend Saudi Arabia. He invariably was extremely cautious about military engagements, subsequently opposing US involvement in Bosnia.

He was not the only one. After a meeting on Iraq at Camp David, Dan Quayle asked Baker: 'What do you really think about it?' 'I don't know,' said Baker, 'it's a big gamble.' Quayle asked: 'Would you put your presidency on the line for this?' As Quayle recalled it, neither of them had an answer for that. But so far as the instinctively cautious Baker was concerned, the answer was almost certainly not.

On 11 September, Bush told his diary once again that it was said of him that he much preferred to work on international affairs. He was indeed engrossed in the Gulf crisis and getting into much more detail on it than on the domestic scene. But he saw the budget deficit as 'something essential to resolve'.

If no budget agreement was achieved, the US faced the prospect of a government shutdown in October. In his address to Congress on 11 September, Bush said that he wanted to be able to tell the American people that, together, they had solved the budget deficit problem. When, three weeks later, he and the Democratic congressional leadership reached agreement on a programme to reduce the deficit, this was rejected in the House of Representatives thanks to Newt Gingrich. The Democrats having then secured an increase in income tax, the revised agreement was signed into law on 5 November 1990. Bush's budget director, Richard Darman, hailed it as the largest deficit reduction programme ever enacted.

For Bush, it was critical to have cleared the decks before a showdown with Saddam Hussein. But he had accepted this, to him, extremely damaging agreement because of his fundamental conviction that the budget deficit had to be addressed come what may.

Half a million US troops by now had been despatched to the Middle East, in accordance with what was described as the Powell doctrine that in any serious conflict the US must apply overwhelming force. In reality, this was not Colin Powell's doctrine but that of Reagan's Defense Secretary, Cap Weinberger, whose other principles were that the US must have so powerful a military that no one sane would want to challenge them and that it must never be used unless absolutely necessary. Powell had served on Weinberger's staff.

On 30 September, Thatcher saw Bush in New York. In his briefing note, Scowcroft wrote, 'As is usual when the chips are down, the British are there when it counts.' Bush talked of possibly responding to a 'provocation' by Saddam. Thatcher did not want a conflict to be started in that way. The *casus belli* needed to be the occupation of Kuwait. Bush noted that she did not want to go back to the UN 'and nor do I'.

But Baker would not give up on this, though Bush again assured her they would not do so unless they were sure that the resolution would pass.

On 11 October, Bush held a meeting with the military commanders. They laid out the plans for the air war, which they were confident of winning in short order. But it was agreed that air attacks alone would probably not suffice to dislodge Saddam from Kuwait.

So they laid out their plans for a ground offensive. These were based on a frontal attack on the Iraqi forces, with the US forces heading straight up the coast road to Kuwait.

Scowcroft was unimpressed. 'It sounded unenthusiastic, delivered by people who didn't want to do the job.' Rather than attack through the midst of the Iraqi forces, he asked, why did they not plan an enveloping attack to the west and north around the forces in Kuwait, to cut them off? He was told that the US forces deployed did not have enough fuel trucks for this, so the tanks would run out of gas and the desert sands might not support tanks either. 'Appalled' by the presentation, he called Cheney, who agreed that they had to do better.

'THE BRITS ARE STRONG, AND THE FRENCH ARE FRENCH'

On 12 October, Bush told his diary, 'The thing that weighs on me is sending kids into battle and the lives being lost.' This was reinforced by his own experience of war and the number of pilots with him who had been killed. Once he had resolved in his mind that he might have to do that, he felt 'a certain calmness' about everything else.

He still wondered whether an Iraqi provocation might offer the chance to respond. The Iraqis were preventing the staff in the US embassy in Kuwait from leaving, effectively holding them hostage. 'As I look at our allies in the Gulf: the Brits are strong, and the French are French.' Mitterrand had been great, but his Foreign Ministry were off wanting to compromise.

Scowcroft was looking for a definition of US war aims, including degrading the Iraqi military to a point at which it could no longer threaten Iraq's neighbours but, presciently, not 'to the point that a vacuum was created, destroying the balance between Iraq and Iran, further destabilizing the region for years'.

Meeting Thatcher in New York, Bush found her still keen to plan military action based on the existing UN resolutions. Going back to the UN 'would risk amendments'. She did not favour starting military action on the basis of a provocation. They should do so at a time of their own choosing. Due to weather in the Gulf, that would have to be between November and March.

Baker insisted that unless they tried for a further resolution at the UN, this would weaken the international consensus. Bush told her that the US forces would not be ready until December. They did not want to launch the military campaign during Ramadan. That left January or February.

Bush raised the idea of seeking a UN resolution to authorise them to re-provision their embassies. If Saddam refused, that could be the *casus belli*. Thatcher warned against putting the embassy staffs at risk. Scowcroft also was against launching the air war prematurely, with a limited objective, which could leave Saddam still in control of Kuwait.

CHAPTER SEVEN

DESERT STORM

As war drew nearer, Bush understood very clearly that he was gambling his presidency. The great majority of Democrats in Congress remained opposed to military action. The press was full of gloomy forecasts of US casualties. Baker feared that support would evaporate in that event.

The key issue was whether the President should seek the support of Congress before committing the country to a war. Bush was confident that, as Commander in Chief, he had the constitutional right to do so without a prior vote in Congress. Most constitutional jurists agreed. But he knew that if he did so and things then went badly, he would be impeached.

On 18 November, at the outset of the CSCE conference there, Bush met Margaret Thatcher in Paris. Although mired in the Conservative Party leadership struggle, she promised that Britain would provide more ships and troops for the allied campaign. At a meeting later that day, Gorbachev promised to support a fresh UN Security Council resolution giving Saddam a firm date by which he must withdraw his forces from Kuwait. That evening, Thatcher had dinner with Helmut Kohl, who, despite their quarrels over German reunification, could not believe she would be ousted.

'IF I GET IMPEACHED, SO BE IT'

On the evening of 20 November, Thatcher narrowly failed to win enough votes from Conservative MPs to stave off a second round of voting, in which she was unlikely to prevail. Bush was 'saddened and surprised' when he heard the news. 'Her downfall was amazing – so fast and almost unforeseen.' While their relationship had not been as close as hers with Reagan, it had become progressively warmer over his time in office. He found it typical of her that in her farewell letter to him on 20 November, she told him that she had persuaded her Cabinet to double the British military commitment with an additional British armoured brigade, so Britain would be contributing a full armoured division and 30,000 men. Bush described this as a 'marvellous commitment'.

She had told Mitterrand to go ahead with the grand state dinner at Versailles, as she would be late. He insisted on holding it up until she arrived. When the dinner ended, as she was being besieged by the press, the Bushes 'swept her up' and whisked her away in their car, causing her to write in her memoirs, 'It was one of those little acts of kindness which remind us that even power politics is not just about power.'

In his diary, Bush reflected:

> I have a good relationship with Thatcher – it's grown … I don't feel the warmth for her as I do to say Helmut, or even Mitterrand … but I have great respect for her, and I like her, and I think she's grown to trust me more … We do see eye to eye on most of these issues, and thank God she's as strong as she is in the Gulf.

From Paris, Bush invited the congressional leaders, George Mitchell and Tom Foley for the Democrats, Bob Dole and Bob Michel for the Republicans, to join him on a visit to Saudi Arabia, where they were magnificently received by King Fahd. Next day, they flew on to Dhahran in eastern Saudi Arabia to spend Thanksgiving with the US forces there. Plunging into the crowds of soldiers and marines, struck by how young they all looked (the same age as him in his combat years), he redoubled his prayers for their lives to be spared.

In the midst of Baker's masterly diplomacy to secure a Security Council resolution that the Soviets would support and the Chinese not veto, Jimmy Carter intervened, urging members of the Security Council to vote against it. Nevertheless, on 29 November, UN Security Council Resolution 678 was passed by twelve votes to two, with Cuba and Yemen opposed and China abstaining, calling on Saddam to withdraw from Kuwait by 15 January and for 'all necessary means' to be used to enforce the resolution.

Bush had debated with himself what he should do if he agreed to a prior vote in Congress and lost it. His conclusion was: 'It is only the United States that can do what needs to be done.' Therefore, 'If I don't get the votes, I'm going to do it anyway, and if I get impeached, so be it.' But Baker's calculation always had been that a positive UN resolution would help to change the minds of waverers in Congress.

On 20 December, to the alarm of the Americans, Eduard Shevardnadze resigned as Gorbachev's Foreign Minister. He had been the leading voice of moderation in dealing with the Baltics. In his memoir, he described his resignation as an act of disagreement and protest and as a warning. He had been losing out to Primakov in advising Gorbachev about Iraq and to the 'traditionalists' in Moscow in general.

Still struggling with Congress, and with a host of pundits

continuing to predict heavy allied casualties, on 21 December, with new Prime Minister John Major visiting Washington, Bush was pleased to find that 'the British are as resolute as ever'. It was the first time he had met John Major and he 'immediately liked him'. They had been scheduled to fly to Camp David by helicopter, but it was snowing hard. So they climbed into a car, with Scowcroft and Charles Powell on the jump seats facing them, to discuss the US war plan. Bush had wondered how much to tell John Major this far in advance. Scowcroft had advised him to tell Major everything.

Major understood that he needed to win the confidence of the Americans, which he did. Though they had never met before, he felt immediately at ease with George Bush. 'There was no holding back.' They both accepted that a military solution was the only way forward and there was no advantage in further delay.

So they went over the plans for first the air then the ground offensive in the back of the car. Bush said that the offensive would be launched on the morning after the deadline expired. Bush would have found it understandable if Major had wanted to go back to his colleagues or the military. Instead, 'he declared on the spot that the British would be with us all the way. I shall never forget that.'

Major observed that Bush had a distinguished war record, 'but he was not martial by temperament'. He was a reluctant warrior. A pioneer of telephone diplomacy, he had kept his friendships around the world in good repair, including with the key Arab leaders. He had pieced together an extraordinarily broad coalition against Saddam, despite Russia muttering from the sidelines. It was 'a first-class piece of diplomacy from a first-class President'.

In Washington, Scowcroft had asked the deputies' committee to work on objectives beyond that in the UN resolution. The conclusion was that the best way to weaken the regime was to attack the

Republican Guard forces. There was no plan to go after Saddam Hussein. But it was hoped that he would not survive a defeat.

On Christmas Eve, Bush told his diary, 'They say I don't concentrate on domestic affairs, and I expect that charge is true; but how can you when you hold the life and death of a lot of young troops in your hand?'

The year ended with the Democrat-supporting *Time* magazine christening Bush 'Man of the Year' as a wise and articulate leader on foreign policy but 'At Home: No Vision – A Case of Doing Nothing', notwithstanding the politically courageous role he had played in negotiating with the Democratic leaders the budget agreement to cut future deficits and the passage in 1990 of the new Clean Air Act, the Americans with Disabilities Act and the amended version of the Civil Rights Act. Bush felt that the article showed the same lack of objectivity he had experienced from *Newsweek*.

On 8 January, on the eve of a crucial meeting between Baker and the Iraqi Foreign Minister, Tariq Aziz, in Geneva, Bush formally sought endorsement by Congress of the mandatory 'withdraw by 15 January' resolution.

Bush was encouraged by polls indicating that most Americans supported, if necessary, the use of force. He was worried that many forecasters had scared people into thinking it would be a long, drawn-out conflict. He did not believe it would be but could make no promises about that.

In the event, Bush won the vote approving military action if necessary in support of the UN Security Council resolutions by 250 to 183 in the House of Representatives, with influential Democrats like Les Aspin and Steve Solarz supporting. In the Senate, Bush won only by the uncomfortably narrow margin of fifty-two to forty-seven, thanks to a handful of Democrats, including Al Gore, voting in favour. Gore's vote was a factor in persuading Bill Clinton to choose him as his running mate, while Aspin became his first Defense Secretary.

The final effort to avoid a war was made by Baker with Tariq Aziz at their meeting in Geneva on 9 January 1991. Baker found that sitting next to Aziz was Barzan al-Tikriti, Saddam's half-brother and former head of the Iraqi secret police, known for presiding over the executions of opponents in Iraq and the assassination of opponents of the regime overseas. Clearly present to ensure that the understandably nervous Aziz did not make any concessions, in the words of Stephen Hadley, accompanying Baker as Assistant Secretary of Defense, he had 'the eyes of a killer'.

Baker said that he had a letter from George Bush which he wanted Aziz to deliver to Saddam Hussein. He slid the envelope across the table, with an Arabic translation. The letter said, 'Unless you withdraw from Kuwait completely and without condition, you will lose more than Kuwait.' Reading it with shaking hands, Aziz refused to pass it on, as, he said, it was insulting to his President. Baker said that the only question was whether the Iraqis withdrew peacefully or by force. If peacefully, those in power in Iraq would have a say in the country's future.

'THIS IS NOT A THREAT; IT IS A PROMISE'

There followed a warning which Cheney and Colin Powell had asked Baker to deliver. If Iraq used chemical or biological weapons against US forces, the American people would demand vengeance. 'This is not a threat; it is a promise.' In that event, the objective would no longer be just the liberation of Kuwait but the elimination of the Iraqi regime.

The meeting lasted several hours, getting nowhere, until Baker left and an aide retrieved the letter to Saddam.

It was only at this point that Baker accepted that war was inevitable.

Bush still had to make 'the weightiest decision that any President has to make, ever'. His continuing hope was that the action he was about to take could lead towards acceptance of a 'new world order', a degree of international cooperation that, he acknowledged, had been sought unsuccessfully for 100 years.

On 14 January, he spent a sleepless night before instructing Cheney to unleash the air assault on the Iraqi forces. He telephoned Major to confirm the planned start of operations and formally to confirm permission to operate from the US bases on the British Indian Ocean territory of Diego Garcia, which had already been agreed.

Under Bush's and Scowcroft's guidance, the military mission had been precisely defined as the liberation of Kuwait. Bush was not seeking to march on to Baghdad or depose Saddam or occupy Iraq. An occupation was precisely what was to be avoided. Bush hoped and expected that a crushing defeat would lead the Iraqis themselves to get rid of Saddam Hussein, but overthrowing him was not a US war aim.

The US-led air attacks had forthwith achieved unquestioned air superiority. But Bush warned the press, 'There will be losses ... War is never cheap or easy.'

Saddam's response was to launch Scud missile attacks against Israel. Bush went into overdrive on two separate occasions to dissuade the Israeli Prime Minister, Yitzhak Shamir, from retaliating, which would have caused problems with the Arab states in the coalition against Saddam. Shamir was told that the Americans were targeting the Scud missile launching sites and US Patriot anti-Scud missiles were despatched to Israel.

By 20 January, Bush was noting that 'we own the skies' and that US casualties so far had been light. He badly wanted to get rid of Saddam, but the best outcome would be if he were 'taken out by his own people'. As the need to give approval for a ground offensive approached, Bush felt calm about doing so. 'I know that we'll lose lives ... But we can't stop now.' The US military were 'very optimistic about getting this done with few casualties, although I dare not say that'.

On 29 January, as the President was preparing for his State of the Union address, Scowcroft was flabbergasted to see a joint statement by Baker and Shevardnadze's replacement, Alexander Bessmertnykh, that a ceasefire would be possible if Saddam Hussein made an 'unequivocal commitment' to withdraw from Kuwait. When Bush was shown this, his face went ashen under the makeup for his televised address and he was as angry as Scowcroft had ever seen him. US policy was not to accept promises from Saddam on which he was likely to renege. A ceasefire depended on his actual withdrawal from Kuwait.

With the air offensive going well, Bush's State of the Union address was greeted with unanimous stamping and cheering by legislators who, not long before, had voted by not that much for the actions now being taken.

Baker apologised for a bad mistake. The reality, however, was that, personally, Baker might have been tempted to accept a promise to withdraw rather than face the risks of a ground war – contrary to the views of Bush, Scowcroft and Cheney.

On 20 February, Bush told Saddam to withdraw from Kuwait

or face a ground offensive. The US continued to worry about the possible use by Saddam of chemical or biological weapons. It was at this point that Cheney asked Powell a hypothetical question: how many tactical nuclear weapons would be needed to destroy an Iraqi Republican Guard division if circumstances required? Colin Powell dodged having to reply, then came up with the impossibly high figure of seventeen, on the grounds that the division might be widely dispersed.

This exchange was an entirely theoretical one, as the US military would never have recommended nuclear weapons for such a purpose and the chances of George H. W. Bush authorising it were zero. He was unaware that the question had even been asked. He had already ruled out threatening a nuclear response as it was wrong to threaten something he had no intention of carrying out. Cheney, however, was pleased to have been told after the war by the head of Iraqi military intelligence that the warning of 'devastating' consequences if chemical weapons were used against US forces had been taken to mean that the US might use nuclear weapons.

'I FIRMLY BELIEVED THAT WE SHOULD NOT MARCH INTO BAGHDAD'

Two days later, Bush again was telling his diary that he hoped that defeat would lead the Iraqis themselves to get rid of Saddam Hussein, failing which, he realised, victory would not be regarded as complete. But, 'I firmly believed that we should not march into Baghdad.' That would be way beyond the UN mandate, would divide the coalition, plunge the region into greater instability and condemn young soldiers to fight 'an unwinnable urban guerrilla war'.

These thoughts were ventured by him twelve years before his son George W. Bush invaded Iraq with exactly the consequences his father had foreseen and he had been warned of by Brent Scowcroft on the eve of the war.

Following a briefing on the revised plans for the ground offensive, now based on a major western flanking movement through the desert to cut off the Iraqi forces, Bush observed that Colin Powell always had been prepared to do what had to be done, 'but now he seemed genuinely enthusiastic', believing that the ground war could be won with very limited casualties.

Gorbachev had kept coming up with plans for a ceasefire, inspired by Primakov. On 19 February, he made a final try, citing a last-minute offer from Saddam to withdraw from Kuwait, subject to all sorts of conditions. Bush phoned Gorbachev to tell him, as politely as he could, that this was a non-starter.

Cheney and Powell then briefed Bush on what lay ahead. On potentially grisly reports about American casualties, Scowcroft told Bush: 'We may have to spare you some things.' 'I know,' said Bush, 'But that is not one of them.'

Powell said that he and General Norman Schwarzkopf, commander of United States Central Command, 'would rather see the Iraqis walk out than be driven out'. In an attack,

> there will be costs. We will lose soldiers in substantial numbers at a time. It will be grisly. There will be pool reports of dead Americans … There is a high probability of a chemical attack … We will get more of their tanks and stockpiles by attacking, but the cost in lives and later problems is not worth it.

The Iraqis would crack under attack. 'But at what cost?' asked Powell.

The ground offensive was launched at 4 a.m. Baghdad time, 8 p.m. Washington time on 23 February. While Bush was attending church next morning, Cheney passed him a note: 'Norm [Schwarzkopf] says it's going very well,' at which Bush found himself 'choking up … It's going to be quicker than anyone ever thought.'

Bush Senior understood the contradictions in his own position: 'We need a surrender, we need Saddam out, and yet our objectives are to stop short of all of that.'

On the encircling flank of the allied offensive, General Rupert Smith, commanding the British armoured division, had expected to have to fight his way across the border. Instead they found a six-lane pathway lit with flares and a sign saying 'Welcome to Iraq', courtesy of the US First Engineering Division. General Walter Boomer, commanding the US Marines' attack on the coast road, found that the engineers had made short work of the supposedly fearsome Iraqi minefields, losing just one Marine as they broke through towards Kuwait.

Before long, the world was watching images of the US blasting Iraqi troops and tanks on the road from Kuwait City back to Basra in Iraq. Colin Powell felt that the conflict was turning into a turkey shoot.

Bush asked his commanders if it was time to stop. Powell consulted General Schwarzkopf and advised that it was.

The ground war had been won in just 100 hours. One hundred and forty-seven US and forty-seven British troops were killed in action; for the Iraqis, an inestimable number. Nine British servicemen were killed by 'friendly fire' in a US air attack. Bush addressed the nation with the highest ever approval rating for a US President.

But it was at this point that two serious mistakes were made. Colin Powell contributed to them by advocating an early ceasefire, in part because he believed that Saddam Hussein could not possibly survive so crushing a defeat.

General Barry McCaffrey who, commanding the left wing of the US pincer movement, had cut off three Republican Guard tank divisions, was appalled to be told to allow them to withdraw to Basra *with their tanks*. In Washington, Baker had contended that requiring them to surrender their tanks exceeded the UN resolutions. In his diary, Bush was still saying, 'We must disarm the Republican Guard.' In the view of the US military on the ground, it was self-evident that the tank crews should have been required to leave their tanks behind.

Scowcroft did not agree with Colin Powell's advice. He phoned Charles Powell to say, 'You won't believe this – they are proposing to stop fighting straight away before dealing with the Republican Guard on the grounds that it is not American to shoot fleeing enemies in the back. Your people might want to express a view.'

The British War Cabinet expressed consternation and instructed Douglas Hurd, who was in Washington, to query the case for stopping so soon. He reported back that it was too late; the President had made up his mind. John Major's foreign policy adviser, Sir Percy Cradock, also was surprised at the hastiness of the decision to stop. As Cradock observed, the US had the Iraqi tank forces trapped. 'That was the whole purpose of the [flanking] manoeuvre.'

The Bush team soon realised that fewer Republican Guard divisions had been destroyed than anticipated, in part because the unexpectedly rapid advance by the Marines straight up the coast road, plus the early ceasefire, had accelerated their withdrawal to Basra.

The other major error was made by General Schwarzkopf in the ceasefire agreement, when he agreed to permit the Iraqis to continue using their military helicopters, supposedly for evacuation purposes. The tanks and helicopters were used by Saddam to suppress the Shia uprising which then broke out around Basra and to bolster his regime.

Bush regretted in his diary that the victory had not been 'clean', with no Iraqi surrender and Saddam remaining in power. His diary shows a period of exhaustion and some despondency, as he must have felt that his greatest achievement was behind him. He felt 'a little old, a little tired' and that maybe 'somebody else ought to have a shot now'. But Barbara 'wants to hear nothing of that'.

*　*　*

In March 1991, Bush was thrilled to attend a ceremony in South Carolina to welcome US troops coming home from the war. 'When you left,' he told them, 'it was fashionable to question America's resolve … No one, no one in the whole world does so now.'

Speaking at the Arlington National Cemetery in honour of those killed in the war, Bush was close to tears as he said that America had prevailed 'because we dared to risk our most precious asset – our sons and daughters'.

When, after the conflict, I took the families of the nine British servicemen killed by friendly fire to the White House, George Bush made a huge personal effort to console them and convince them that their loss had not been in vain.

As, after the war, the Kurds sought to assert their autonomy, with Saddam attacking them, John Major, with support from Kohl and Mitterrand, announced a plan for a safe haven for the Kurds rebelling against Saddam. This was contrary to Bush's intention not to get involved in Iraq's internal quarrels. Colin Powell told me with grim amusement that, unilaterally, we had announced something that could only be enforced by the US. Conscious that it would look bad if they did not respond, Bush and Powell changed tack. There was starting to be pressure from the US media for them to do so. But Major had pushed them into taking action earlier than they otherwise would have done to protect the Kurds by enforcing a no-fly zone over northern Iraq.

CHAPTER EIGHT

'I'VE LOST THE HEART FOR GUT POLITICAL FIGHTING'

It was in the aftermath of the war, in what came close to a requiem for the remainder of his own presidency, that George Bush told his diary: 'It's not that I don't want to fight, but it's that I've lost heart for the gut political fighting, as a result of trying to lead this country and bring it together in the Gulf.'

A 'MEANINGFUL DOWNTURN'

With his approval ratings now off the charts, Bush was clear-sighted that his popularity would not endure. He noted that the euphoria would soon dissipate and the economy was 'down, down, down'.

Greenspan had announced that the economy had suffered a 'meaningful downturn' by October 1991. Despite the budget agreement, the Fed did not cut interest rates soon or fast enough to revive it. The US economy remained in recession throughout the year, with unemployment rising to 7.8 per cent, the highest rate in a decade.

Instead of seeking to concentrate on this problem and to call on the Fed both publicly and privately to cut interest rates, as any other President would have done, Bush was too much of a gentleman and too distracted even to try to do so. This was a mistake, as, despite its vaunted independence, the Fed does not enjoy being pilloried in accurate public criticism and Bush would have been entitled to point out that they were failing in their statutory duty, which was and is to 'promote effectively the goals of *maximum employment, stable prices and moderate long-term interest rates*', which Greenspan subsequently had to admit they had failed to do.

Bush could scarcely have failed to win a fight with the Fed about this, but he did not even try and the Treasury Secretary, Nick Brady, was not a politician either. What Bush continued to be distracted by, and what he felt far better equipped to deal with and intrinsically more important, were all the issues arising in and around the Soviet Union.

'TO THOSE OF US WHO WATCHED HIM CAREFULLY, THE OLD ZIP WAS GONE'

When, soon after the war, Bush made a speech, badly written for him and full of platitudes, to a business audience, he noted that it had attracted scarcely any applause – his own fault, as he had taken little interest in it before delivering it. He told his diary that 'I'm not that much of a political animal', though he had been when seeking the presidency. 'The common wisdom today is that I'll win [re-election] in a runaway, but I don't believe that. I think it's going to be about the economy.'

In May 1991, on a run in Camp David with a secret service agent, Bush suddenly ran out of breath. The medical staff found that he was suffering from atrial fibrillation, or an irregular heartbeat. Transferred to the Bethesda Naval Hospital, he talked to Quayle, who found him in good spirits and joking. His press secretary, Marlin Fitzwater, declared that he had not lost consciousness or suffered a heart attack. The doctors thought that he might have to undergo a procedure under anaesthetic, which would have entailed a brief handover of power to Quayle. This proved not to be necessary, as overnight medication restored a regular heartbeat.

The doctors then discovered that he was suffering from Graves' disease, a thyroid condition, the medication for which required careful calibration. Barbara Bush, bizarrely, suffered from the same condition.

At the state dinner in Washington for Queen Elizabeth at around this time, George W. Bush was shocked to see his father looking so tired and worn. It was the first time in his life that his father had looked old.

Nevertheless, Bush remained hyperactive, getting up so early for his morning jog that he was pictured admiring the spring blossoms by the tidal pool in Washington while it was still dark.

It is impossible to determine to what extent his medical condition contributed to his lacklustre performance in seeking re-election, but Marlin Fitzwater had no doubt that it did. 'To those of us who watched him carefully,' he said, 'the old zip was gone.'

Seeing him periodically over the next eighteen months, his fatigue seemed as much mental as physical and related to the fact that his heart no longer was in domestic politics. So he continued to immerse himself in foreign policy, amidst events that demanded his attention.

BREAK-UP OF THE SOVIET UNION

On 2 January 1991, Soviet troops had seized public buildings in Lithuania and Latvia. Bush spoke to Gorbachev, urging moderation. But on 13 January, troops fired on demonstrators in Vilnius, killing fifteen people. Bush condemned the shooting, which Gorbachev said had not been approved by him. But four people then were shot in Riga, Latvia. Yeltsin responded by signing on behalf of the Russian Federation a pact with the Baltics, defying central Soviet authority.

Bush warned Gorbachev that he would freeze economic ties if violence continued against Lithuania. Gorbachev's economic reforms, still a long way from embracing a market economy, had delivered little in terms of results. The Soviets, meanwhile, were backtracking on the conventional forces treaty by refusing to withdraw a lot of equipment, which they claimed belonged to 'naval infantry'.

By April, Gorbachev had re-engaged with the republics and passed a law liberalising emigration from the Soviet Union, thus enabling Bush to remove the restrictions on trade with the Soviet Union imposed by the Jackson–Vanik amendment, which prohibited doing so otherwise. By then, there also was movement by the Soviets on withdrawing their military equipment. On 12 June, Yeltsin was elected President of the Russian Federation.

Gorbachev was requesting economic aid and membership of the International Monetary Fund and World Bank, all due to be discussed at a G7 summit in London in July, which Gorbachev wanted to attend. Bush warned Primakov, who by now was Gorbachev's chief adviser, that it would be no use appearing with impossible demands, which Primakov promised Gorbachev would not do.

On 20 June, Boris Yeltsin had a positive meeting with Bush in the Oval Office. He claimed to be working well with Gorbachev. Both Yeltsin and Gorbachev discounted a report of a possible coup by Gorbachev's opponents.

In July 1991, the NATO Secretary General, Manfred Wörner, told the Russians that the NATO Council and he both were against the expansion of NATO.

In July, Gorbachev was invited to attend a separate session with the G7 leaders, having produced a document promising somewhat more market-related economic reforms. The Bush finance team remained unwilling to offer direct financial aid, which they contended would be wasted anyway in the absence of more effective economic reforms. What the G7 offered was limited to technical assistance and special associate status at the IMF and World Bank. Brian Mulroney of Canada wondered if they should not have been more generous, as did Richard Nixon, who contended that more should have been done to help Gorbachev.

When Bush met Gorbachev after the meeting, Baker reported on a breakthrough in the START arms control negotiations. Bush got a sense of how overwhelming Gorbachev's problems were but urged him to grant independence to the Baltics.

Invited to Moscow at the end of July, Bush found Gorbachev optimistic about concluding a new union treaty giving greater autonomy to the republics, provided Ukraine joined. He found Yeltsin supporting independence for the Baltics but adamant that Ukraine must stay in the union. Bush, who felt a deep sense of loyalty to Gorbachev, was irritated by episodes of Yeltsin blatantly upstaging him. A meeting with Gorbachev at his dacha outside Moscow was interrupted by news of six Lithuanian guards being killed in a border incident.

Bush and Gorbachev signed the new START treaty, providing for further reductions in each side's inter-continental ballistic missiles. But Scowcroft found the Defence Minister, Dmitry Yazov, complaining that everything was going NATO's way, while the Soviet military was deteriorating – no new equipment, avoidance of the draft, no housing for troops returning from Europe etc. Bush had no idea, as he left, that this would be his last summit with Gorbachev.

'CHICKEN KIEV'

From Moscow, Bush flew to Kiev, to make what, unforgettably, was described by the columnist William Safire as his 'Chicken Kiev' speech, written for him by the NSC Soviet expert and future Secretary of State under George W. Bush, Condoleezza Rice. As always with Bush, his intentions were good: to help Gorbachev with his union treaty, granting greater autonomy to the republics, and to encourage reform rather than an attempted Ukrainian breakaway that he feared could provoke a conflict. He told Baker and Scowcroft, 'Whatever I do, I don't want to make trouble for Gorbachev.' But this was an occasion when his concern to protect Gorbachev went too far.

Bush told the crowd that 'freedom is not the same as independence'. Bizarrely, he added that Americans would not support those who supported independence to establish a new tyranny or pursue a 'suicidal nationalism'. This, it was contended afterwards, was not intended to refer specifically to Ukraine.

The speech went down like a lead balloon with the Ukrainians and the US press.

A COUP IN MOSCOW

While Bush had been a leading supporter of German reunification, provided the united Germany remained within NATO, he realised that the outcome carried with it serious risks to Gorbachev, including from the military leadership, many of whom by now had had enough of his reforms. Thatcher had been justified in questioning whether Gorbachev would survive such an outcome. In June 1991, Bush had warned Gorbachev about reports of a possible coup against him. A critical stage in the dissolution of the Soviet Union was now taking place, with the demands for independence in Ukraine.

At midnight on 18 August, while on holiday at Walker's Point, Bush and Scowcroft heard the news that Gorbachev, supposedly, had resigned 'for health reasons'. Since they had seen him two weeks before in good health, this was obviously false. Next morning, Gorbachev, while on holiday in Crimea, was said to have been 'relieved of his authority' by a committee including the leading members of his government, Prime Minister Valentin Pavlov, Defence Minister Yazov, KGB chief Vladimir Kryuchkov and a handful of other hardliners who saw this as their last chance to block the potential break-up of the Soviet Union.

Bush consulted John Major, who had already denounced the coup, and Mitterrand, who said that it might well fail. Bush praised Gorbachev, telling the press that what had happened in Moscow was 'extra-constitutional' and that 'coups can fail. They can take over at first and then they run up against the will of the people.' He did not want to see 'the new era of cooperation ending'.

This soon was followed by sharper condemnation of the coup and support for the demand by Yeltsin for the restoration of the constitutional order and reinstatement of Gorbachev. With the press observing that the Bush team had been taken by surprise, Scowcroft's response was, 'So was Gorbachev.'

Gorbachev was completely cut off, with Bush unable to get through to him, saying to his diary, 'Mikhail, I hope you're well. I hope they've not mistreated you. You've led your country in a fantastically constructive way.' Bush thought of his sense of humour, his courage and of the old guard military, Yazov particularly, 'who was grumbling all the time at the meetings we had in the Soviet Union'.

Yeltsin by this time had mobilised outside the Russian Parliament a huge crowd demonstrating against the coup and climbed on a tank to address them. The Bush administration, heavily invested in Gorbachev, up to this point had remained extremely wary of Yeltsin. But Bush by now was admiring the 'enormous guts' Yeltsin was displaying, standing on his tank.

A letter to Bush from the nominal coup leader, Vice-President Gennady Yanayev, was passed on by the Soviet Ambassador. It said that the coup leaders had acted to preserve the 'single economic space' and the single foreign policy – in other words, the Soviet Union. Bush had no doubt that it also was because Gorbachev was seen as being 'too close to us'.

On 20 August, Bush managed to speak to Yeltsin, who said that Gorbachev was cut off in Crimea. Yeltsin's base at the Russian Parliament building was surrounded and he expected an attempt to storm it at any moment. He was appealing to the tens of thousands of people outside to protect the legal government. He had given the coup leaders ten demands, the first of which was the restoration of Gorbachev.

Bush said that he did not want to call Yanayev or have any contact with him, as that could legitimise the plotters. Yeltsin strongly agreed. Bush should demand to speak to Gorbachev, which he did, with no success. Yeltsin concluded by saying that he could hear tanks moving.

By the morning of the 21st, Yeltsin was sounding more confident. He had talked to Kryuchkov to stop the tanks. The air assault division had come over to his side. The huge crowd outside had stopped any storming of the building. The tanks were now being withdrawn. Nursultan Nazarbayev for Kazakhstan and Leonid Kravchuk for Ukraine had denounced the coup. The Russian Parliament had declared that it was sovereign on Russian territory. He said that Bush's declaration against the coup was 'an important statement by the American President in support of the Soviet people'.

'THERE IS A GOD'

Later that day, when Bush returned from a boat ride at Walker's Point, he was told by the secret service that there was a call awaiting him from a 'Chief of State'. This turned out to be Gorbachev. While his staff scrambled to find Bush, Gorbachev told the interpreter, 'There is a God.' He had been shut up in a fortress for four days. When Bush arrived, 'My dearest George, I am so happy to hear your voice again,' said Gorbachev.

Yeltsin rang Bush to thank him for his support. The plotters were being detained. Bush told Yeltsin that his stock was now 'sky-high'.

On 23 August, when Yeltsin escorted Gorbachev to the Russian Parliament, it was obvious who now was in charge. Gorbachev made a lame attempt to defend Communism. But the real power now lay with the Russian Federation. The Gorbachev era was over.

Marshal Akhromeyev, though he had not joined the plotters, took his own life, in despair at the collapse of the Soviet Union. On the 24th, Gorbachev telephoned Bush to say that he was resigning as General Secretary of the Communist Party. He was calling for a new party to be established. A few days later, the Supreme Soviet banned Communist Party activities.

The republics were seizing the chance to break free. The Baltics had declared their independence. On 24 August, Ukraine, representing a fifth of the population of the Soviet Union, declared its independence, subject to a referendum on 1 December. Having forewarned Gorbachev, on 2 September Bush recognised the independence of the Baltics.

In the aftermath of the attempted coup, Bush invited John Major and his family to join him at Walker's Point. He had developed a real affection for Major, with whom, he told me, he found it much easier to get on than with Margaret Thatcher. Bush's warmth throughout the visit made it clear to the attendant press that Bush was hoping for Major to win the impending British election. He sympathised with Major about Thatcher's attempts at back-seat driving, observing that 'some people just won't let go'.

In the course of their meeting, over a year before the US presidential election, Bush told John Major that he liked Bill Clinton and thought he would make a pretty good President, but Ross Perot was 'a truly awful human being' who would be a disaster.

Bush had been impressed by Clinton as the spokesman for the Democrats at a conference he had convened with the nation's governors in 1989 on education, at which agreement was reached on new national performance goals. Clinton had joined Barbara Bush in her box to hear the announcement of agreement in Bush's 1990 State of the Union address.

An NSC meeting convened to consider what the US should do about the impending break-up of the Soviet Union sensibly concluded that there wasn't much they could do but wait to see how things played out. Their main concern was about the possibility of a diffusion of control over nuclear weapons. It would be best if these ended up under the control of 'one entity', which, predictably, turned out to be the Russian Federation so far as command and control were concerned, though the inter-continental nuclear missiles in Kazakhstan physically were under the control of Nazarbayev, who set about negotiating with the Americans for help in dismantling them. Kravchuk, meanwhile, appeared in Washington to tell Bush that the Ukrainians would vote for independence.

Bush and Scowcroft saw the opportunity to get rid of the US land-based (though not air-based) tactical nuclear weapons in Germany and South Korea and to propose to the Russians that both sides should get rid of the multiple independently targeted warheads on their remaining inter-continental ballistic missiles. This was incorporated in the START II treaty signed in January 1993, just before Bush left office.

Bush also announced that he was taking the US strategic bomber forces off alert, cancelling a couple of missile programmes and getting rid of tactical nuclear weapons on naval ships. He told Gorbachev that these measures would enhance stability for the Soviet nuclear forces.

These were unilateral actions by the US, but Gorbachev and Yeltsin agreed to reciprocate by taking their heavy bombers off alert and reducing the army by a further 700,000 men. They agreed to a one-year moratorium on nuclear testing and to discussions on reducing the amount of fissionable material.

Meanwhile, seeing Gorbachev and Yeltsin in Moscow in September, Baker had got their agreement that both sides should stop support to the combatants in Afghanistan. Gorbachev agreed to end all support to Cuba, confirming this to the Americans before he even told the Cubans.

On 29 October 1991 Bush met Gorbachev at the Middle East conference, which Baker had devoted months to convening in Madrid. The press were forecasting this as Gorbachev's last meeting with Bush in any official capacity. Bush asked about the relationship with Yeltsin, who was promising much more radical market economy reforms but behaving as if any central authority no longer existed. He was now demanding a confederation of sovereign republics. Gorbachev expressed confidence that Ukraine would remain within the union, though Kravchuk had told Bush that it wouldn't.

On the eve of the Ukrainian referendum, Bush told Gorbachev that the US would have to respect the outcome. Gorbachev was upset that the Americans were thinking of recognising Ukrainian independence. Yeltsin told Bush that if Ukraine wouldn't join, there would only be a weak union. He was talking direct to the Ukrainians, who, in their referendum, then voted by over 90 per cent in favour of independence.

Kravchuk told Bush that Yeltsin had promised to recognise Ukraine. On 8 December, Yeltsin phoned Bush from a meeting he was holding with Kravchuk and the President of the neighbouring republic, Belarus, to tell him that they were not satisfied with the union treaty, the centre was not adding any value and they were creating a Commonwealth of Independent States. Nazarbayev of Kazakhstan intended to sign up for this as well.

The four republics accounted for 90 per cent of the national product of the union. Nuclear weapons would be under central control. They would honour all existing treaty commitments. Yeltsin had just sounded the death knell of the Soviet Union. Gorbachev had not yet been told about this.

Bush rather feebly replied, 'I see.' He realised that they were fulfilling all the US conditions for recognition, but he 'felt a little uncomfortable'. He regretted that Gorbachev was being elbowed aside but accepted that all this could only be sorted out by the participants themselves.

A furious Gorbachev protested that the Yeltsin-sponsored declaration was illegal, but he had no power to stop it. Yeltsin phoned Bush to say that ten republics were now signing up to the Commonwealth of Independent States.

Bush lamented the treatment of Gorbachev, 'who had done so much for the Soviet Union'. Yeltsin kept assuring Bush that Gorbachev was being treated 'with respect', which, clearly, was not really the case.

'A MAN TO WHOM HISTORY WILL
GIVE ENORMOUS CREDIT'

On 21 December, all the republics except the Baltics and Georgia, which wanted no remaining ties, signed up to the Commonwealth. On Christmas Day, 'my friend Mikhail Gorbachev' telephoned Bush, just before resigning as President of the Soviet Union, to say how highly he had valued their work together. Bush replied that what Gorbachev had done 'would live in history'. He sincerely wanted them to stay in touch. He told his tape recorder that he had just heard 'the voice of a man to whom history will give enormous credit'.

Scowcroft observed that an event he had never expected to see in his lifetime had just happened. It was a rare great moment in history. An era of unrelenting hostility had come to an end – thanks to Gorbachev, though, sadly, he had never been prepared or felt able to go all the way with his reforms. The US suddenly was in a unique position, which they must use wisely.

Bush felt that their relationship had facilitated and smoothed matters at a crucial time. 'I trusted him, and I think he felt that he could trust me.' He felt strongly about the role the US should play in 'the new world before us … The importance of American engagement has never been higher. If the United States does not lead, there will be no leadership.' If the US instead became inward-looking, there would be a price to be paid later.

'WE'RE STILL GETTING POUNDED
FOR NO DOMESTIC PROGRAM'

Bush had forecast months before that the euphoria of the Gulf War would soon wear off, while throughout 1991 the economy was struggling. A recovery was under way by 1992, but the media, Bush was convinced, did not want to acknowledge this. The acclaim he had won for his victory in Iraq could not obscure a political tide that for years had been running in favour of the Democrats. Reagan was so well liked that, despite Iran–Contra, his term as President had ended with still high approval ratings for him. But Bush had to outperform his fellow Republicans to win the presidency in 1988 and the Republicans had suffered further setbacks in the November 1990 midterm elections.

Of the Democratic contenders lining up to consider challenging him, Bush noted that Al Gore was reputed to be a worse speaker than him, adding: 'The poor guy's in real trouble if he's worse than me.'

Early signs of the more formidable challenge he would face in 1992 were to be found in the activities of the Democratic Leadership Council, set up to move the party back towards the centre following the presidential election defeats of Mondale and Dukakis. Leading lights in this enterprise included Gore, Jay Rockefeller and the Arkansas Governor Bill Clinton, who understood better than anyone what was needed to get elected next time around. Bill Clinton co-invented the 'New Democrats' long before Tony Blair's 'New Labour', with a similar centrist agenda.

Meanwhile, George Bush threw himself into a cause he really believed in – the realisation of a North American Free Trade Agreement, enthusiastically supported by his friend Brian Mulroney, Prime Minister of Canada. Bush won an important victory when, following intensive personal lobbying of a host of members of both houses of Congress, in March 1991 he secured an extension of his 'fast-track' negotiating authority, enabling him to negotiate and present for approval to Congress a treaty that could be voted down but could not be amended.

Bush was delighted that, once elected and despite opposition from the Democratic trade unions, Bill Clinton adopted the same cause, ensuring that Congress eventually approved the agreement.

*　　*　　*

The campaign that took George Bush to the presidency in 1988 had been run by Lee Atwater, Roger Ailes and John Sununu, aided and abetted by James Baker, none of whom lacked a cutting edge. Bush's choice of a campaign team in the 1992 election was an unmitigated disaster. Bob Mosbacher was a major fundraiser but no organiser. Fred Malek, vice-chairman of Northwest Airlines, made no impact either. The campaign effectively was run by the pollster Bob Teeter, who proved accurate at telling the President why he was trailing in the polls but of little use at telling him what to do about it.

In August 1991, Bush convened a meeting at Camp David to discuss the upcoming presidential election. The presentation by Teeter was a clear wake-up call. While over 70 per cent of the electorate approved of Bush's handling of foreign policy, only 20 per cent were happy with domestic policy. Unemployment had replaced the deficit as the main issue. Yet there was no serious discussion of a strategy to address the perceived deficit in domestic policy.

As Bush reflected at Walker's Point on the forty-seventh anniversary of being shot down at Chichi Jima, a memo from his political staff arrived saying that, although this would bring his personal life under scrutiny, Bill Clinton was likely to run for President, though probably more with hopes for 1996 than for 1992. Bush told his diary that he liked Bill Clinton but thought he could beat him.

'IF HE RULES AGAINST WHAT I THINK, SO BE IT'

In the course of his presidency, George Bush made two nominations to the Supreme Court. The first was that of David Souter, a distinguished jurist from New Hampshire recommended by the Republican Senator Warren Rudman. Bush found that Souter 'seemed to be right on the key points – "interpret" versus legislating from the Bench' and regarded him as a 'safer choice' than a more right-wing candidate. But he worried that Souter might turn out to be a liberal once appointed to the bench. Sununu, also from New Hampshire, reassured him about this but proved to be mistaken, as Souter became 'a huge disappointment' to Bush by siding consistently with the liberal judges on the court.

In June 1991, Thurgood Marshall, the only black member of the Supreme Court, retired. Bush wanted his replacement to be another African American. Clarence Thomas was a Yale law graduate from an impoverished family, whom Bush had known for some time as a Republican supporter. It was a controversial appointment, as he clearly was less qualified than Souter. As with Souter, Bush did not ask for any assurances from him: 'If he rules against what I think … so be it.'

In October 1991, in the nomination hearings for Clarence Thomas, he was accused of sexual misconduct, which he strongly denied, by a former subordinate, Anita Hill. Bush and his wife invited Thomas and his wife to the White House to console them. In the end, Thomas was confirmed by the Senate by the narrow margin of fifty-two votes to forty-eight.

TRYING FOR PEACE IN THE MIDDLE EAST

George Bush and James Baker had come into office with a determination to pursue a more balanced policy in the Middle East than the well-nigh unconditional support for Israel that until then had prevailed. Following the successful outcome of the Gulf War, both were determined to honour the undertakings they had given the Arab leaders to try to advance the cause of peace in the Middle East, taking account of the rights of the Palestinians.

Bush and Baker were staunch supporters of the Israel of Shimon Peres but not of the current Prime Minister, Yitzhak Shamir, and his Likud party, which they saw as bent on seeking to make a two-state solution impossible through ever more Israeli settlements on the West Bank. In his first meeting as President with Shamir, Bush pressed him on the new settlements, only to be told that he should not worry, 'settlements ought not to be such a problem'. Bush understood this to mean that Shamir would do something about them. What the Israelis claimed Shamir meant was that the US should not concern themselves with the settlements, which he had no intention of suspending. But Bush considered that Shamir had misled him and never trusted him thereafter.

In May 1989, addressing the American Israel Public Affairs Committee (AIPAC), Baker pledged support for Israel and said that a peace agreement would require concessions from both sides, then caused a storm by warning against pursuing the 'unrealistic vision of a Greater Israel. Forswear annexation. Stop settlement activity.'

Bush strongly supported him. Shamir, correctly, regarded Baker's remarks as aimed at him. In March 1990, Bush called not only for a freeze on settlement activity but for an end to building in East Jerusalem too.

'WHEN YOU ARE SERIOUS ABOUT PEACE, CALL US'

Shortly afterwards, the Israeli Deputy Foreign Minister, Benjamin Netanyahu, made a speech accusing the US of being too gullible in its dealings with the Palestinians. A furious Baker banned Netanyahu from access to the State Department. Eventually, he was allowed back into the building, but only to see lower-level officials, not Baker. When a member of the House of Representatives Foreign Affairs Committee chided the Bush administration for being too harsh towards Israel, Baker replied that the problem was not the President but that the Shamir government was not serious about peace. When Shamir then came up with new conditions for talks, Baker said that, in that event, there wouldn't be any dialogue or any peace. Baker said his telephone number was 1-202-456-1414. 'When you are serious about peace, call us.'

Eight months later, at the end of the Gulf War, Baker was ready to try again. The Soviet Union and the Arab states were pressing for an international conference. The Israelis, not wanting to be outnumbered, favoured direct negotiations with the Palestinians but refused to talk with representatives of Yasser Arafat's Palestine Liberation Organization (PLO), declining to believe that his renunciation of terrorism was genuine. Under Baker's plan, the US and the Soviet Union would jointly sponsor a conference with Israel and the Arab countries, to be followed by direct negotiations between Israel and the Palestinians.

In March 1991, a few days after the war had ended, Baker met King Fahd, who said that if a Palestinian homeland could be established, Saudi Arabia would be inclined to open relations with Israel. 'We know there is a state called Israel. No one should deny it.'

This was a step forward, as Saudi Arabia hitherto had never formally recognised Israel's existence. But a few weeks later, the Saudi Foreign Minister refused to consider Saudi Arabia attending a conference with Israel. Baker finessed this problem by proposing that the Saudis should attend as members of a delegation of the Gulf

Welcome aboard, Sir: Lieutenant George H. W. Bush being rescued from the Pacific by the USS *Finback* (2 September 1944).

GEORGE H. W. BUSH PRESIDENTIAL LIBRARY AND MUSEUM

Lieutenant George H. W. Bush getting married to Barbara Pierce (6 January 1945).

GEORGE H. W. BUSH PRESIDENTIAL LIBRARY AND MUSEUM

The Bushes on their bicycles in Beijing (circa 1974).

GEORGE H. W. BUSH PRESIDENTIAL LIBRARY AND MUSEUM

ABOVE George H. W. Bush with Barbara Bush and President Ford, being sworn in as head of the CIA (January 1976).
GEORGE H. W. BUSH PRESIDENTIAL LIBRARY AND MUSEUM

LEFT President-elect Ronald Reagan and George H. W. Bush celebrating election victory on Capitol Hill (18 November 1980).
PHOTO BY JAMES K. W. ATHERTON/ *WASHINGTON POST* VIA GETTY IMAGES

ABOVE Vice-President Bush conferring with Reagan in the Oval Office (20 July 1984).
GEORGE H. W. BUSH PRESIDENTIAL LIBRARY AND MUSEUM

LEFT President George H. W. Bush and General Brent Scowcroft.
GEORGE H. W. BUSH PRESIDENTIAL LIBRARY AND MUSEUM

President George H. W. Bush and Prime Minister Margaret Thatcher in Aspen (August 1990).
GEORGE H. W. BUSH PRESIDENTIAL LIBRARY AND MUSEUM

'They all looked so young to me': President Bush meeting soldiers in Saudi Arabia before Desert Storm (22 November 1990).
GEORGE H. W. BUSH PRESIDENTIAL LIBRARY AND MUSEUM

George H. W. Bush's State of the Union address during the Gulf War (29 January 1991).
GEORGE H. W. BUSH PRESIDENTIAL LIBRARY AND MUSEUM

George H. W. Bush with General Colin Powell and his senior advisers on the eve of the Gulf War (11 February 1991).
PHOTO BY DAVID HUME KENNERLY/GETTY IMAGES

George H. W. Bush and John Major before a joint press conference in Kennebunkport after the coup in Moscow (August 1991).

President George H. W. Bush with Secretary of State James Baker (1991).

President George H. W. Bush welcoming President-elect Bill Clinton to the White House (18 November 1992).
PHOTO BY DIANA WALKER/GETTY IMAGES

A more civilised time: President-elect Barack Obama and President George W. Bush at the White House with all living former Presidents (7 January 2009).
PHOTO BY DAVID HUME KENNERLY/GETTY IMAGES

George H. W. Bush receiving the Medal of Freedom from Barack Obama (15 February 2011).
PHOTO BY JOSHUA ROBERTS/BLOOMBERG VIA GETTY IMAGES

Former President Bush skydiving in his seventies (June 1999).
GEORGE H. W. BUSH PRESIDENTIAL LIBRARY AND MUSEUM

Cooperation Council. Baker had support from President Mubarak, as Egypt already had relations with Israel.

President Assad of Syria remained the most obdurate of the Arab leaders. Baker had a total of eleven interminable meetings with him. Baker said that if Syria would make peace, the US would guarantee its border with Israel and perhaps the Golan Heights could then be returned to Syria. Assad claimed that Syria agreed to attend the conference because of Baker's 'guarantee' that Israel would withdraw from the Golan Heights. Baker denied any such guarantee, but the Syrians eventually decided to attend.

Baker had kept in constant touch with Shamir throughout this process, his calculation being that if the key Arab states all agreed to be present, the Israelis would find it difficult to refuse. The Israelis would not accept a separate Palestinian delegation. They would accept Palestinians as part of the Jordanian delegation, which, for Baker, meant making up with King Hussein, who had sided with Saddam Hussein in the Gulf War. The Israelis insisted that none of the Palestinian representatives could be from the PLO; they must be non-PLO representatives from the West Bank and Gaza. An Israeli demand that they must renounce the PLO was rejected by Baker, but he promised that they would be acceptable to Israel. A by now more friendly Shamir said that he would accept Baker's word on that.

Baker then had to stave off demands from the Palestinians that there must be PLO representatives on the delegation and someone from East Jerusalem. Baker told them that they had always wanted an international peace conference; they were now about to get one.

It had required a Herculean effort by Baker to get to this point. He had been on the road for twenty-three days, with only one member of the press corps surviving to the end of the journey. His exhausted aides could not believe his endurance. Baker prided himself on never appearing less than immaculate and unfrazzled and remained so at every stage of this journey.

With the collapse of the Soviet Union, hundreds of thousands of Jewish immigrants were flooding into Israel. The Israelis requested $10 billion in loan guarantees. Baker was concerned that some of this would be used for more settlement activity and that approving it could blow up the peace conference. Israel's supporters in Washington launched a full-scale lobbying campaign to get the funds released forthwith. Proud of Baker's achievement in securing attendance of all the key players at the conference, Bush would not give way. He declared that he was up against a 'very strong and effective lobby', triggering cries of outrage from AIPAC and pro-Israeli Congressmen.

Baker still had to make a further flight to Damascus to get Assad finally on board, at a meeting in the course of which he lost his temper ('Go to hell. Get your land back yourself,' which the interpreter declined to translate but Assad understood). In Jerusalem, the Palestinians still were insisting that their delegation must include a representative from East Jerusalem and that Israel must halt all settlements. This caused an equivalent explosion, with 'steam coming out of Baker's ears'. He declared that he was through with negotiating: they had better take the opportunity offered to them.

The conference was convened in Madrid on 30 October 1991, with Bush and Gorbachev delivering opening remarks. Baker declared that, for the first time, Israel and its neighbours were meeting to begin the search for peace, while warning, from his own experience, how laborious a process it was going to prove to be. The Syrians made an entirely negative contribution. But the Palestinians indicated that they could accept some form of self-government in the West Bank and Gaza as a step on the way to full statehood.

The conference paved the way for the first direct talks between the Israelis and Palestinians. In a private note to him, George Bush paid tribute to Baker's 'perseverance and determination. You hung in against great odds and gave the "vision thing" a new dimension.' Shamir too paid tribute to his 'stubborn diplomacy'. Baker observed that he had always been accused of being risk-averse, an opinion he had confounded in this case.

It had been thanks to the political cover provided by Bush that Baker had been able to be far blunter with the Israeli government and the pro-Israel lobby in Washington than any of their predecessors (or successors). Both Bush and Baker told me that the clashes with the Israeli lobby were going to be costly for them electorally. Baker went back to trying to help Bush win re-election, in which case he saw his principal mission as being to pursue the peace process he had launched. Instead, the election put an end to the career of by far the most remarkable US Secretary of State since Henry Kissinger.

The Saudis regarded the US initiative as a major step forward. The Palestinians, frustrated at the formal exclusion of the PLO, nevertheless understood that this was an important advance from their point of view. Baker declared that it was now for the Arabs and Israelis to decide how to carry this forward, though the US would make proposals on key issues whenever they were asked to do so.

When I congratulated Baker on this huge effort and a more even-handed policy, he said that the principal Jewish lobbying organisations in the US were more intransigent than the Israelis. They did not want any displays of even-handedness.

CHAPTER NINE

'I MUST ACCEPT ALL THE BLAME FOR THIS'

As Bush's poll numbers continued to fade, the White House chief of staff, John Sununu, was being pilloried in the press for having used his official car and driver to take him to New York for a stamp auction. The highly intelligent, autocratic Sununu had made a lot of enemies. As George Bush was incapable of saying no to almost anyone, Sununu had relished the role of enforcer.

George W. Bush was asked by his father to consult members of the White House staff and others and recommend what should be done. He found that almost everyone wanted a change and he volunteered to be the person to tell Sununu, who was persuaded to resign in December 1991.

The Transportation Secretary, Sam Skinner, was chosen to succeed Sununu for no obvious reason except that he was much easier-going. The Bush White House after Sununu lacked any real discipline, with frequent leaks, usually to the Democrat-controlled *Washington Post*. The domestic policy staff remained as uninspired and ineffective as ever, in the starkest of contrasts to the exceptionally competent national security staff.

If Bush was going to make a change, it was at this point that he should have tried much harder to persuade Baker to return as the

White House chief of staff, rather than waiting until August to do so, by which time it was far too late for Baker to make much difference. Baker would have sought to put a badly needed new stamp on domestic policy. But Bush knew how strongly Baker wanted to remain as Secretary of State and the importance of what he was continuing to do in that role. Bush seemed to believe that he had more time than was in fact available for him to turn things around.

At year end, a poll showed Bush down to a 47 per cent approval rating, 'the lowest I have ever been'. They were 'getting pounded on the economy'. 'I must accept all the blame for this,' he added.

'THE THREAT OF A WORLD WAR IS NO MORE'

On Christmas Day 1991, Gorbachev called Bush to say that the Soviet Union, by now on its deathbed, was abandoning Communism. He was resigning and would be handing over control of the nuclear arsenal to Yeltsin. Bush should not worry: 'Everything is under strict control.' Bush felt that he was 'caught up in real history with a phone call like this'.

To the world press, Gorbachev said, 'An end has been put to the Cold War, the arms race and the insane militarization of our country, which crippled our economy ... The threat of a world war is no more.'

But, for Bush, there was no respite from the kind of politics he detested, with everyone blaming him for the recession and failing to do anything about it. Teeter's polling was showing levels of confidence as low as they had been under Jimmy Carter. Bush had been having far more success in influencing world events than in doing so in the US.

In January 1992, there followed an unfortunate episode, of which much was made by the press, when a feverish and jet-lagged George

Bush threw up over the Japanese Prime Minister at an official dinner in Tokyo.

Less easy to shrug off was the challenge by now being mounted to him in the Republican primaries by the right-wing 'America First' commentator Pat Buchanan, supported by the populist talk show host Rush Limbaugh. Exploiting Bush's breaking of his 'read my lips' pledge, Buchanan was making progress in New Hampshire. He denounced Bush as an internationalist vainly pursuing the dream of a 'new world order' rather than putting American interests first. A campaigning visit to New Hampshire by Bush was a disaster, as it was felt that his message, 'I care', was all he had to offer to those suffering from the weak economy.

Buchanan lost to Bush but won nearly 40 per cent of the votes in New Hampshire. Before the Georgia primary, Bush felt obliged to say that raising taxes in the 1990 budget had been his 'biggest mistake'. James Baker was appalled at this, as he felt it to be a display of weakness, with Bush compounding his problems.

'THEY MUST NOT RESORT TO CAMPAIGN TACTICS THAT ASSAULT ANOTHER'S CHARACTER. PLEASE MAKE SURE THAT ALL HANDS GET THE WORD'

Lee Atwater, the driving force in the Bush 1988 campaign, had died of cancer and Bush did not want to run as negative a campaign anyway. In January, the *New York Post* published an article about Bill Clinton's alleged extramarital affairs. Bush's reaction in his diary was that 'sex stories ought to be out of the public arena'. Gennifer Flowers then sold her story about an alleged twelve-year affair with Clinton. Bush found this 'ugly and nasty ... There is no gain for anyone in all of this.'

Nor did he want to make much of what others regarded as

Clinton dodging military service. All members of his campaign team were told that 'they must not resort to campaign tactics that assault another's character. Please make sure all hands get the word.'

One person who had no such qualms at the time was Hillary Clinton, who, seeking to deflect attention from the Clintons' problems, asked in *Vanity Fair* why the press failed to investigate rumours about George Bush's extramarital life. 'They're going to circle the wagons on Jennifer [Fitzgerald] and all these people.' A furious Barbara Bush described this as 'lower than low'.

ROSS PEROT

By the spring of 1992, the Texan computer tycoon Ross Perot was ready to enter the race as an independent, presenting himself as an anti-establishment straight-talking outsider. Bush regarded his campaign as a massive ego trip, which it was. But he started gathering a lot of support and there was an animosity between the two, partly related to Bush having declined Perot's offer to work for him decades before.

To help manage his campaign, Perot hired a former Reagan political operative, Ed Rollins. His then wife, Sherrie, was working in the White House as an assistant for public liaison. When she told him about Ed Rollins's assignment with Perot, Bush said that he was making a terrible mistake. 'I know Ross Perot, and he's crazy … And the American people are not going to elect a person of Bill Clinton's character. This is all going to work out and we're going to win.'

While George Bush remained convinced that the character issue would see him through, his campaign team continued to be prohibited from attacking Clinton's character.

In the spring, Perot for a while was leading both Bush and

Clinton in the polls despite being, in Bush's opinion, 'outrageously ill-suited to be President of the United States' (an opinion Bush also held about Donald Trump). Perot was getting traction by campaigning hard against Bush's proposed North American Free Trade Agreement. The abolition of tariffs against imports from Mexico, Perot argued, would lead to the 'giant sucking sound' of US jobs being siphoned off south of the border, which to some extent was what did happen as, following the agreement, US car and other manufacturers relocated a good deal of production to lower-cost plants in Mexico.

By now Bush was regretting the departure of Sununu. 'Yes, there was a lot of china broken,' but he had helped to get the Disabilities and Clean Air Acts and the amended Civil Rights Act passed (Bush had vetoed an earlier version of the Civil Rights Act because it had imposed employment quotas). Bush was finding Sam Skinner failing to exercise control and not up to the job.

In the run-up to the Earth Summit in Rio de Janeiro in June 1992, there were divided views in the Bush administration about entering into any international commitments about climate change that could affect the US economy, with Darman adamantly against doing so, leaving the US negotiator, William Reilly, with a difficult hand to play.

But Bush signed the summit's Convention on Climate Change, which led on to the Kyoto Protocol, adopting, as Obama subsequently observed, a far more enlightened position on climate change than most members of his party. His doing so went almost unobserved at the time and was scarcely commented on by the US media, perhaps because it did not fit the narrative of Bush only being good at conventional foreign policy.

As Clinton and his running mate, Al Gore, staked out their claim to be the new generation now qualified to be running the country, Bush reflected in his diary that he was 'not getting the strong staff support we get in the foreign policy field'. They kept telling him that the polls 'show I'm disconnected and … I don't get it' but failed to offer much advice on what to do about it. He discussed the possibility of introducing a value-added sales tax, enabling him to promise to cut direct taxes, but some of his economic advisers objected and, anyway, there was no longer time to make headway with this before the election.

* * *

During the Democratic Party convention, Bush set off for a fishing trip with Baker in Wyoming. As Bush well knew, Baker definitely did not want to give up his post as Secretary of State, in which he excelled and had earned a worldwide reputation. But, once again, he accepted the appeal of his closest friend to rally round and go back to being chief of staff at the White House.

This was a job he didn't want to do. For, understandably, he had hoped for better than that. Formally, the argument went, Baker could not hope to be George Bush's running mate, as they both came from Texas. But Baker's standing and reputation were big enough to transcend that impediment. Having rendered such outstanding services to his country and the President, Baker would have been less than human if he had not hoped that, if Quayle were replaced on the ticket, it could be by him.

For Quayle, who had been such a contentious choice from the outset, had not improved in office. Few, if any, saw him as a credible replacement as President if Bush fell ill. The Clinton/Gore ticket now was leading Bush/Quayle by 57 to 32 per cent. As the Bush team debated what could be done to reduce the polling gap, replacing Quayle on the ticket was high on the list.

George Bush had his own doubts about Quayle, wondering whether he was 'quite ready' to be President. George W. Bush favoured replacing him with Cheney, who had performed well as Defense Secretary in the Gulf War. President Ford also urged Bush to make a change. But Bush told his diary that, rather than making him look strong, sacrificing Quayle would make him look weak. It also would be an admission that he had made a mistake in the first place. Nor did he believe that it would make a critical difference to the campaign: Americans voted for the President, not his deputy.

On 25 July 1992, the argument was cut short as the *Washington Post* reported that Bush had told Quayle that he would remain on the ticket. At the time it was believed that Quayle had sought a meeting with Bush, protesting that he had always been loyal, and had been assured that he would not be replaced.

In reality, as Bush recorded, 'there weren't any such discussions'. The *Post*'s report had been planted by Quayle's staff. But Bush had concluded that, if Quayle were dumped, he would be attacked for disloyalty and abandoning Quayle to save himself.

The Clinton/Gore team breathed a sigh of relief, for, as they told me, they had feared that such a move would look decisive on the part of a President whom they were depicting as asleep at the switch, and would narrow the gap in the polls, though they too did not believe that it would have changed the eventual result.

At this time, Bush experienced a further fit of weakness and dizziness, with a recurrence of irregular heartbeat due, as it turned out, to the increased medication his doctors were giving him to manage the effects on his thyroid of Graves' disease. An adjustment to his medication sufficed to resolve the problem, which was not disclosed at the time, as his doctors considered it transitory and of no lasting consequence. It did, however, leave him feeling very tired.

At the Republican convention, Reagan did his best to help. 'The presidency is serious business.' The country needed a man of serious purpose and unmatched experience, 'a steady hand on the tiller'.

Pat Buchanan endorsed Bush, attacking the Clintons about gay rights and abortion and for being on the wrong side of the 'cultural war ... for the soul of America'. Bush's private comment was that Buchanan's speech had made it a 'polarizing event', whereas he, Bush, 'wanted to stay out of the attack business'.

In his speech, to those who accused him of spending too much time on foreign policy, Bush said that their children used to fear the threat of nuclear war. He had seized the chance to rid their dreams of that nightmare. The Reaganite political operatives who had been brushed aside by them by this time had taken to calling Bush and his team 'country club Republicans', a critique all the more annoying as there was an element of truth in it.

'GEORGE BUSH KNOWS MORE ABOUT KUWAIT THAN CALIFORNIA'

Bush continued to be exasperated by the press suggesting that he did not care about domestic policy. But the truth was that he did not care as intensely about it as he did about managing foreign crises. Stu Spencer, a key political operative for Ronald Reagan, warned me that Bush was going to lose California by a mile, adding, 'George Bush knows more about Kuwait than California – and maybe cares more about it too.'

Still trailing by a long way in the polls, Bush was not enjoying the campaign, telling his diary in August, 'I just wish it were over.' The press and television continued almost exclusively to cover the ailing economy, leading Bush's assistant, Mary Matalin, to claim: 'The media has its own agenda – the same liberal one Bill Clinton's running on.'

Bush noted in his diary that the Soviet infantry brigade had left Cuba. 'What changes in the world and yet who gives a damn.' Ironically, the economy by now was showing signs of recovery, though too late to help Bush. GDP numbers published after the election confirmed that the economy had been growing strongly from mid-year.

James Baker was not optimistic about the prospects. 'People out there', he kept telling me, 'are hurting' from the flagging economy. Visiting him in the White House was a strange experience, as there were hardly any papers on his desk. If such a change was to have been made, it should have happened sooner. He did not feel that, at so late a stage, with only nine weeks of the campaign to run, there was a great deal of difference that he was going to be able to make.

This feeling must have been reinforced when Baker's special assistant, Robert Zoellick, was asked to draft a speech setting out Bush's vision for his second term. Zoellick asked why Bush wanted re-election. 'Because I would do a better job than the other guy' was the reply, leaving Zoellick with nothing much to work with. A proposed Bush speech on the economy was handed off to be delivered instead by the Treasury Secretary, Nick Brady.

When I took Margaret Thatcher to see Bush in the Oval Office in this period, her opening words were: 'George, why on earth don't you change your position on abortion?' which, at any rate nominally (though not in reality), he opposed. Bush replied that Teeter told him that it was only the seventeenth most important issue. Thatcher replied that, for many young women, it was *the* most important issue 'and in case you haven't noticed, you are level among men and ten points behind among women'. Government should not be interfering in such matters anyway.

Baker, who was present, observed to me afterwards: 'She was absolutely right.'

Bush had overcome long odds against Dukakis, but Clinton, as a moderate Democrat, was a far harder target. Bush kept telling me, against all the evidence, that the decisive period of the campaign would not be engaged until after Labor Day (early September). He kept telling himself, 'I'm a better person, better qualified, better character to be President', despite his shortcomings – 'and there are plenty of those'. He was tired of Clinton 'lying and ducking' about dodging military service.

Fundamentally, until very close to the end of the campaign, as a self-proclaimed believer in 'honor, duty, country', he refused to accept that the American people would elect someone with Clinton's character shortcomings, though in the end he realised that what had seemed so important to him mattered less to the new generation.

In early September, Ross Perot, who for a while had dropped out of the election race, made a conspiratorial approach to Baker, which led nowhere. Bush declined to speak to Perot himself or make him any offer. On 1 October, Perot announced that he was re-entering the race.

In the first presidential TV debate on 11 October, Bush made a feeble criticism of Clinton for attending an anti-Vietnam War demonstration while at Oxford. In the second debate, on 15 October, a young woman in the audience asked the three candidates, 'How has the national debt personally affected each of your lives? And if it hasn't, how can you honestly find a cure for the economic problems of the common people if you have no experience in what's ailing them?'

Glancing at his watch, Bush said, 'Obviously, it has a lot to do with interest rates.' Reminded that he was being asked how it had affected him personally, Bush said, 'I'm not sure I get it.' The questioner said that she knew people who had been laid off from their jobs, who couldn't pay their mortgages. Bush said that as President, of course he cared about that.

Clinton's reply was that as Governor of a small state, he had seen what happened when people lost their jobs. 'There's a good chance I'll know them by their names.' He had met 'people like you' who had lost their jobs, livelihoods and health insurance.

Realising that this had been a fiasco, Barbara Bush wanted to 'go negative'. Bush acknowledged that the debates 'were not good', but with *Penthouse* publicising details of Clinton's longstanding affair with Gennifer Flowers, he still hoped that the character issue would see him through.

As the Clinton team told me, their fear had been that in the debates, Bush, with his distinguished war record, would turn on Clinton, refer to his draft dodging and ask, 'What makes you think you are qualified to be Commander in Chief?' This was a question Clinton was dreading, but Bush was too much of a gentleman to ask it.

'MY DOG MILLIE KNOWS MORE ABOUT FOREIGN POLICY THAN THOSE TWO BOZOS'

As the vote approached, the polling for Bush showed some improvement. But the Iran–Contra prosecutor Lawrence Walsh chose this moment to charge Cap Weinberger, who had been against the whole venture, with obstruction of justice, publicising Weinberger's notes of a meeting in January 1996 saying 'VP approved'. It was an extraordinary and highly political move by the independent counsel to make such a determination on the eve of the presidential election.

Teeter and Baker offered three different attacks they could make on Clinton, including one about Gennifer Flowers. Bush said no, contenting himself instead with saying that 'my dog Millie knows more about foreign policy than those two bozos' – meaning Clinton and Gore.

In his last campaign speech, back in Houston, Bush said that 'I've never been too hot with words', with some pundits saying he couldn't finish a sentence. 'But I care very deeply about our nation.' In his diary, he described the campaign as 'the ugliest period in my life'.

LOSING THE PRESIDENCY

Thanks to Perot, who got 19 per cent, Bill Clinton was able to win the election with just 43 per cent of the votes, with Bush getting 37 per cent. Bush himself had told his diary that he would vote for Clinton 'in a minute' before the paranoid Perot. If Perot had not been in the race, it is doubtful if that would have made much difference. He contributed to the anti-establishment sentiment, but the exit polls indicated that he had drawn as much support from Democrat as from Republican voters.

Bush congratulated Clinton graciously and announced that he planned 'to get very active in the grandchild business'. At first, he had the feeling of a burden being lifted. But that was overtaken by the sentiment that 'I let everybody down'. He still could not understand 'how in God's name did this country elect a draft dodger?' It was small consolation that, as he noted in his diary, 'The overseas cables are wonderful, quote, "You'll have your place in history."'

It hardly was surprising that it had proved impossible to win a fourth consecutive term in the White House for the Republicans amidst a recession. Bush understood that there had been 'a generational disconnect'. But there had been a lot wrong with his campaign and the sentiment of having let his supporters down would not go away.

'YOU RAN THE WORST CAMPAIGN I EVER SAW, BUT YOU'RE GOING OUT A BELOVED FIGURE'

On 18 November, he showed Bill Clinton around the White House. Clinton was 'friendly and respectful' and seeking his advice. Bush spent two hours talking to him about the foreign policy issues he would face. In conclusion, Bush said, 'When I leave here, you're going to have no trouble from me ... I will do nothing to complicate your work.' He was more doubtful about Hillary: 'Very militant and pro-liberal-cause and that's going to get her into some difficulties.'

At a farewell lunch, the redoubtable former Democratic Speaker Tip O'Neill told him, 'You ran the worst campaign I ever saw, but you're going out a beloved figure; everybody will tell you that.'

In his valedictory weeks as President, another international trouble spot caught Bush's attention. Civil war in Somalia had created a humanitarian crisis. There was 'a feeling that we won't help black nations ... and that we don't care about Muslims' that he wanted to counter. He also wanted to help save 'thousands of innocents'.

Announcing that he was sending 28,000 troops to help restore order in Somalia, in what turned out to be not a well-conceived venture, Bush said, 'I understand the United States alone cannot right the world's wrongs,' but added that some crises could not be solved without American involvement. In January 1993, before leaving office, he visited the US troops in Somalia.

When his friend and ally John Major, who had won re-election, was invited to Camp David in the uneasy interregnum before he left office, Bush appeared close to tears in a speech suggesting that, in losing the election, he had 'let everyone down'. Major replied that no one had ever done less to let people down. People around the world owed a huge debt of gratitude to him.

To lighten the mood in the White House, the comedian Dana Carvey, known for his imitations of Bush giving a speech, waving his arms around like a windmill, was invited to perform there.

Bush then was thrilled to go to Moscow to sign the START II treaty, which, in return for US nuclear arms reductions, eliminated an especially threatening class of Soviet missiles, the massive land-based SS-18s. Bush had reason to regard this as 'a great thing to bow out on'.

As President, he then pardoned Weinberger, plus four officials who, unlike Weinberger, actually had been involved in the Iran–Contra affair. Ronald Reagan, described as his 'friend and mentor', was invited back to the White House to receive the presidential Medal of Freedom. As Saddam Hussein was violating the terms of the end-of-war agreements, Bush authorised air strikes against new missile sites in southern Iraq.

In April 1993, having left the Oval Office, Bush visited Kuwait with Baker to receive the thanks of the country he had liberated. A huge car bomb was discovered and several people were arrested for plotting to kill the former President, in an operation directed by the Iraqi intelligence service. Clinton was furious, the more so as, if the attack had succeeded, he could have been obliged to embark on a fresh war with Iraq. As it had failed, the retaliation was limited to a Tomahawk missile attack on the Iraqi intelligence headquarters.

Bush seemed curiously diffident about the fuss that was being made about the failed attempt on his life. As Clinton's adviser George Stephanopoulos observed, 'Maybe his bred-in-the-bone patrician modesty made him a little embarrassed by all the trouble everyone was going to for him.'

In September 1993, Bush was invited back to the White House by Clinton for the signature of the agreement between Yitzhak Rabin and Yasser Arafat, recognising both Israel's right to exist and the Palestinians' right to self-rule.

Clinton and Bush used the opportunity to set out the case for NAFTA. Bush was delighted that Clinton had adopted a cause Bush had initiated and felt strongly about. After listening to Clinton making the case for the agreement, Bush said that he now understood why Clinton was President and he wasn't.

Clinton thought this a 'wittily generous' thing for Bush to say. Bush was thrilled when, in 1993, Clinton got NAFTA approved by Congress, thanks to the support mainly of Republican members, with the Democratic trade unions and many of Clinton's own supporters still opposed.

After decades in the government service, Bush, who had been reputed to be very rich all his life but was no more than comfortably well off, at last was able to make a fortune from speaking around the world, for which he was so well paid that he described these ventures as 'white collar crime'.

Meanwhile, he formed more of a friendship with his successor. At the opening of the Clinton Library in Little Rock in November 2004, Bush declared, 'It has to be said that Bill Clinton was one of the most gifted American political leaders in modern times. Believe me, I learned that the hard way. He made it look too easy and oh, how I hated him for that!'

In December that year, when a devastating tsunami struck southeast Asia, George W. asked his father and Bill Clinton to travel there to show US concern and help to raise money for relief. Bush Senior had been horrified by the Monica Lewinsky affair and Clinton lying under oath. The far less easy-going and more judgemental

Barbara Bush could not abide the Clintons and was extremely reluctant to return to the White House so long as they were there.
When she was obliged to do so at a reunion of former Presidents,
she was amazed to hear Clinton, post-Lewinsky, reciting John Adams's prayer that 'none but honest men' should serve under that
roof. But Bush could not help liking the 'outgoing and gregarious'
Bill Clinton, the more so after they made the trip together. Even
when Clinton talked eloquently on subjects he knew little about
and was late most of the time, Bush concluded, 'You cannot get
mad at the guy!'

George W. sought the help of this duo again after Hurricane
Katrina. When they accepted an award together in Philadelphia,
Bush observed, 'It was like traveling with a rock star.' Clinton kept
declaring, 'I love George Bush,' recalling that his predecessor had
scrupulously refrained from ever causing any problems for him as
President.

Bush kept in touch with Gorbachev, Brian Mulroney and John
Major and other world leaders he had known but refused to join
any club of former heads of government. He horrified his wife by
insisting on celebrating his eightieth birthday by making a parachute jump. From 2012, he compensated himself for being confined
to a wheelchair by wearing brightly coloured socks. He made his
last assisted parachute jump at ninety.

Barack Obama, who credited George H. W. Bush with having
conjured away the threat of nuclear war, observed that the person
he had come to know 'was exactly the gentleman I had perceived
him to be'.

In November 2010, presenting him with the Presidential Medal
of Freedom, Obama declared, 'As good a measure of a President as
I know is somebody who ultimately puts the country first, and it

strikes me that throughout his life he did that, both before he was President and while he was President, and ever since.'

Amidst the laudatory articles written about him worldwide when he died, what would have pleased him most was a headline in the London *Daily Mail*: 'He was proof that a good man can change the world.'

CHAPTER TEN

THE GEORGE H. W. BUSH LEGACY: THE INDISPENSABLE NATION?

George H. W. Bush assembled the most impressive US foreign policy team since Acheson and Truman. With Scowcroft ironing out the differences, there was a striking camaraderie between his team and the President they all admired. When he failed to secure re-election, to my great regret at the time, they departed with him, convinced that he would go down in history not just as a good but as a great President, at a time when the world had so badly needed the leadership he provided.

For this was a period in which, for all the talents around him, one man did make a difference. The distinguishing feature they all saw in him was the determination to act never in his own political interests, but as a statesman.

The fact that he was not much of a politician, rather a great public servant, contributed to his political demise. In response to the repression in Tiananmen Square, they believed that any other President would have given way to the clamour for punitive sanctions against China. He knew, from his own experience in Beijing, that this would not help the dissidents and that, in the interests of both countries, the US had better try instead to preserve its ability to communicate with the Chinese leadership.

In response to the invasion of Kuwait, James Baker, Colin Powell and others would have favoured the far less risky course of restricting US intervention to helping with the defence of Saudi Arabia. It was the President who decided that 'this will not stand', knowing full well the danger of serious US casualties, of no approval by Congress and that he was risking his presidency in that cause.

In the reunification of Germany, much was owed to Baker's skilful diplomacy, but it was Bush's early decision to back Helmut Kohl to the hilt that also made a crucial difference. He made a strange error in not meeting Gorbachev until a year after his election, but thereafter Baker's diplomacy was overlaid by the skill and sensitivity with which Bush developed that relationship. James Baker told me that he did not see how, in either case, his diplomacy could have succeeded without his great friend as President.

Nor could Baker have ventured to pursue a more even-handed policy towards Israel and Palestine, at some political cost to both of them, without the protection of his President. It was the conference Baker convened with such difficulty that led on to the first ever agreement between Israel and the Palestinians in the Oslo accords.

It was Bush's decision, against the grain in his own party, to approve the climate convention, for which he got no credit at the time but which drew a tribute from Barack Obama, that led on to the subsequent climate change agreements.

George H. W. Bush sought to leave a legacy not just in foreign policy but in domestic politics as well. A convinced Republican, he detested extremism of any kind. He regarded the ultra-right-wing John Birch Society, confrontational politicians like Newt Gingrich and culture warriors like Pat Buchanan as a danger to his own party and to American democracy. He was devoid of any malice towards his political opponents. He had many friends on the moderate Democrat side of the aisle. He was insistent on the need for civility in politics and had no respect for those who ignored it.

Even in his presidential campaign run by the no-holds-barred Lee Atwater, he denounced the 'Massachusetts liberal' ideas Dukakis represented with no personal attacks, which he flatly vetoed in the election he lost (by not that much) against Bill Clinton. He saw the brushfire development of negative campaigning as a threat to American democracy. He regarded the increasingly vast number of special interest lobbyists infesting Washington in much the same way.

He liked Clinton personally and approved his determination to govern from the centre. He got on well with Barack Obama and admired his rhetoric about seeking to unify the country and overcome racial divisions. For George H. W. Bush and George W. abhorred the deliberate divisiveness of the Trump presidency and did not see how this could possibly be in the nation's interests. Lifelong Republicans, neither voted for Donald Trump for President; George H. W. Bush voted for Hillary Clinton.

They also, both of them, believed in free or at any rate freer trade. When that fell out of fashion, they remained convinced that protectionism would never work well for so great a trading nation as the United States.

George H. W. Bush was unique among American Presidents in the proportion of his time he devoted to overseas affairs, largely in response to such pressing developments but also at the expense of domestic politics. Unsurprisingly, therefore, he devoted a great deal of thought to America's role in the world. Such was the warmth of his relationship with Gorbachev that he hoped for a time that this might herald a 'new world order' under which the great powers might start to work with rather than against each other, though he realised that this was liable to prove an impossible dream.

His experience of seeking to manage the break-up of the Soviet Union, the reunification of Germany and the liberation of Kuwait left him convinced that without American leadership there would risk being no leadership in dealing with world crises. Most other Arab states opposed the invasion of Kuwait, as did most of the rest of the world. But without the US, nothing would have been done about it. Without US leadership of the coalition against him, Saddam Hussein would have remained in possession of Kuwait and a threat to the Saudi oilfields.

That the United States, therefore, was indeed the 'indispensable nation', capable of doing what no other nation could or would try to accomplish in world affairs, was his deepest core belief in foreign policy. The members of his foreign and defence policy team, from their own experience, subscribed to that doctrine too. He and they were convinced, however sharp the divisions in domestic policy, of the need for bipartisan support for America's policies overseas.

To what extent did his successors, in words and in action, uphold his legacy in that respect? He was the antithesis of an aggressive inter-ventionist. How then did he manage his relationship with the presi-dency of his son? How did such very different people spring from the same family, with such different consequences? To what extent did his successors accept his mantra of the necessity for US leadership in the world and the doctrine of America as the 'indispensable nation'? It was directly contested by Barack Obama ('We should not be the world's policeman') and Donald 'America First' Trump, whose presidency, both in style and in substance, was the antithesis of everything George H. W. Bush believed in and stood for. What price has been paid by the US turning inward? And where does that debate stand today?

CHAPTER ELEVEN

BILL CLINTON

On arriving at the Oval Office on the day of his inauguration as President, Bill Clinton found on the desk a handwritten letter left for him by his predecessor, George H. W. Bush, stating:

> When I walked into this office just now I felt the same sense of wonder and respect that I felt four years ago. I know that you will feel that, too.
>
> I wish you great happiness here ... There will be very tough times, made even more difficult by criticism you may not think is fair ... just don't let the critics discourage you or push you off course.
>
> You will be our President when you read this note. I wish you well. I wish your family well.
>
> Your success now is our country's success. I am rooting hard for you.
>
> Good luck – George

The letter caused Hillary Clinton to burst into tears. When, fifteen years later, it was published – not by Bush – Bill Clinton declared, 'I will be for ever grateful for the friendship we formed.' He recalled the kindness President Bush had shown him when, as a young Governor, he, Hillary and Chelsea Clinton had been invited to Kennebunkport and the support Clinton felt he had received from him throughout his presidency.

A host of commentators hailed it as an outstanding example of grace in politics, bearing witness to a far better time.

*　　*　　*

The last thing the Secretary of State, Larry Eagleburger, told me before the presidential election was that if George Bush won, they intended to set about dealing with Serb aggression in the former Yugoslavia. For no sooner had the Gulf War been won than fighting broke out between the Serbs and Croats.

But Bill Clinton had been elected President not to resolve foreign crises but to fix the US economy, his predecessor having become so enmeshed in foreign affairs that he scarcely seemed to have a domestic policy.

'IT'S THE ECONOMY, STUPID'

From the outset, Clinton made it crystal clear where his priorities lay and this was reflected in the strength of his economic team, led by Lloyd Bentsen as Treasury Secretary, with a continuing influence on his former colleagues in Congress. He and Bob Rubin from Goldman Sachs as chairman of the National Economic Council were extremely close to Alan Greenspan, who was awarded pride of place at Clinton's first State of the Union address. By contrast, the lawyerly and meticulous Warren Christopher as Secretary of State needed no encouragement to keep his head down, as that was in his nature anyway.

The first phase of Bill Clinton's presidency was devoted to Hillary's ambitious plans for healthcare but, above all, how to further improve the already recovering economy. With the Democrats in control of both houses of Congress, Bentsen and Rubin combined with Greenspan to persuade Clinton to enact major tax increases.

The 1993 Tax Reform Act raising personal, corporate and other taxes was passed at a high political cost, with the Democrats losing their majority to Newt Gingrich and the Republicans in the House of Representatives. But by 1998, the federal government had produced its first budget surplus in almost thirty years.

Overseas, in October 1993, the US troops in Somalia launched a raid in Mogadishu to capture allies of the Somali warlord General Aidid. Two Black Hawk helicopters were shot down, with the dead bodies of US servicemen being dragged through the streets. This ended what little public support there had been for what was supposed to be a humanitarian mission there, causing Clinton to order the withdrawal of US troops from Somalia.

In the wake of that episode, when the genocidal murder of hundreds of thousands of members of the Tutsi tribe took place in Rwanda in 1994, there was no appetite whatever for the US to get involved, to the subsequent regret of the national security advisor, Tony Lake. Threatened US intervention against the military government in Haiti brought the elected President Aristide back to power, though, sadly, that did not do the Haitians much good.

But there were some foreign problems that would not go away. Saddam Hussein still needed to be contained and Europe was riven by a crisis that was getting worse.

'THE WHOLE OF THE BALKANS ARE NOT WORTH THE BONES OF A SINGLE POMERANIAN GRENADIER'

The Bush administration, in the process of bringing hundreds of thousands of US troops back from the Gulf, had no intention of turning them around and sending them to the Balkans. It was far from clear that any US interests were at stake, with James Baker, while still Secretary of State, concluding that, 'we do not have a dog in this fight'. (Baker denied having said this but subsequently admitted that he had!) Scowcroft and Eagleburger, both of whom had served in the Balkans, knew all about their ancient quarrels and at this stage also were very wary of getting involved.

They were happy to leave the problem to the Europeans. The Luxembourg Foreign Minister, on behalf of the EU, had declared that this was 'the hour of Europe'.

Britain sent 1,800 soldiers under UN auspices to distribute humanitarian supplies, as did the French. Mission creep soon turned this into an attempted peacekeeping mission in the absence of a peace to keep.

In the presidential election campaign, Clinton had begun to advocate lifting the arms embargo to help the Muslims, with possible air strikes against the Serbs ('lift and strike'). But in reality, at this stage, he had no real intention of getting involved.

For Bill Clinton told me that Hillary had given him a copy of *Balkan Ghosts* by Robert Kaplan, and I found the brand-new President trying to quote to me Bismarck's dictum that the whole of the Balkans were not worth the bones of a single Pomeranian grenadier. A no-fly zone was declared, backed by the Americans, but that was the limit of their involvement.

By the spring of 1995, the situation of the UN forces in Bosnia had become critical. A new commander in Sarajevo, General Rupert Smith, believed that no solution was possible without doing more to deter the Serbs. I was asked to warn Colin Powell's successor, General John Shalikashvili, that the British and other UN forces there might have to be withdrawn and that we might have to ask for US help in extricating them.

In July there followed the attack by General Mladić on the enclave of Srebrenica, brushing aside the Dutch peacekeeping contingent, who were powerless to stop the Serbs rounding up and massacring the 8,000 men and boys.

The British military contingent, surrounded by the Serbs in Goražde, clearly was next in line. Richard Holbrooke for the State Department and the national security advisor, Tony Lake, were advising that a serious ultimatum should be delivered to General Mladić by the US, Britain and France. President Clinton, by this time, had reached this conclusion himself.

When the Serbs shelled Sarajevo again, on 29 August General Smith withdrew the exposed British military contingent from Goražde and NATO launched air attacks on all Bosnian Serb military targets. Helped by military advances by the Croats, it resulted in an end to the fighting being agreed through forceful diplomacy by Richard Holbrooke in the Dayton peace accords.

It had taken longer than it should have done for this to happen, but Bill Clinton in the end had provided the decisive US leadership without which the crisis could not have been resolved, and an especially brutal war on European territory ended without a single allied casualty.

'THE BRITISH WERE FURIOUS'

The same evolution of Clinton towards acting in a more statesmanlike fashion was evident in Northern Ireland. In January 1994, the Sinn Féin leader, Gerry Adams, applied for a visa to visit the United States. Against the advice of the State Department, the FBI, the

CIA and the US embassy in London, but in response to being lobbied by Teddy Kennedy, Pat Moynihan and other Irish American political leaders, Clinton decided that a visa should be granted, with no undertaking from Adams to cease supporting violence. The British, as Clinton observed, 'were furious', with John Major for several days refusing to take his calls. Major had discovered that, unlike George H. W. Bush, Clinton had an 'affinity' for appeasing domestic opinion.

But this offered the opportunity to demand that, to justify their decision, the Americans should now put real pressure on Adams to deliver an IRA ceasefire. When, seven months later, the IRA declared a ceasefire, Clinton felt that he had been vindicated. In March 1995, Adams was invited to attend the St Patrick's Day celebration at the White House, as were the unionist leaders, with the White House then pressurising Adams for movement on the decommissioning of their arsenal of weapons, with Clinton's special envoy, Senator George Mitchell, playing a very constructive role.

Clinton's attention engaged, he became a passionate student of the politics of Northern Ireland, regarding the peace process as a cause of his own. This led to him developing a newfound admiration for the political courage and determination displayed by John Major in the pursuit of peace in Northern Ireland. When he visited Britain and addressed Parliament in November 1995, he paid a sincere tribute to Major's efforts, before making with Hillary a highly emotional visit to Northern Ireland. Switching on the Christmas lights at the city hall in Belfast, the reception they got made a lasting impression on both of them, as did their equally enthusiastic reception in Dublin.

The resumption of violence by the IRA with the London Docklands bombing in February 1996 thereby became as much of a setback for the US as for others and was followed by determined efforts by Clinton and his administration to help to get the ceasefire reinstated, which eventually it was in July 1997.

When Blair took over as Prime Minister, Clinton supported to the hilt his efforts with the Irish Taoiseach, Bertie Ahern, which culminated in the signature in April 1998 of the Good Friday Agreement, providing for power-sharing between representatives of the Protestant and Catholic communities in the province. This remained a personal cause for him and for Hillary, with Clinton ready to talk to the party leaders in Belfast whenever he was asked to do so, maintaining steady pressure on Sinn Féin to conclude the agreement.

The transcripts of their calls at this time show the extraordinarily close relationship with Blair, with Clinton offering to help whenever he could, wondering where Adams really stood with the IRA and complaining about the Northern Ireland leaders' constant need for time-consuming psychotherapy.

In August 1998, a dissident faction of the IRA exploded a car bomb in Omagh, killing twenty-nine people. The Clintons responded by visiting Omagh with Blair and George Mitchell to meet the victims of the bombing, with Martin McGuinness of Sinn Féin declaring that he would now oversee arms decommissioning by the IRA.

Bill Clinton personally and his administration had made a significant contribution to the achievement of an end to thirty years of violence and a more hopeful future for the people of Northern Ireland.

'A DUTY TO PROTECT'

In June 1997, the Clintons flew to London to congratulate Tony Blair on his victory in the British general election. Blair had modelled his centrist New Labour on Clinton's equally centrist New Democrats. Both were believers in the 'third way' and Hillary 'could not see any policy differences between them'.

But in relation to the conflict in Kosovo, Blair was developing the ideas about humanitarian intervention he espoused in a speech to the Chicago Council of Foreign Relations in April 1999, in which he talked of 'a duty to protect'. This horrified Henry Kissinger and the US military as an open-ended invitation to get involved in other people's wars.

There was no appetite whatever in the US to become involved in the fighting in Kosovo. As Blair acknowledged, his campaign for the West to intervene there put 'the most colossal strain' on his relationship with Clinton.

The Americans felt that, as with Bosnia, the Europeans had failed to deal with a problem in their own backyard, with Blair wanting to commit ground forces, the great majority of which would have to be American. With Clinton, reluctantly, getting closer to agreeing to US intervention, this proved not to be necessary, as the prospect caused the Russians to advise the Yugoslav Prime Minister Slobodan Milošević to withdraw the Serb forces from Kosovo. But, as with Bosnia, this smaller drama had again exposed the 'indispensability' of the United States in helping to end conflicts in Europe's own backyard.

ISRAEL AND PALESTINE: THE HARDEST PEACE

On 13 September 1993, I was invited to witness the meeting and handshake between the Israeli Premier, Yitzhak Rabin, and the head of the Palestine Liberation Organization, Yasser Arafat, on the lawn of the White House, Israel having agreed to withdraw its forces from Gaza and from much of the West Bank of the Jordan.

This outcome could never have been realised without James Baker's achievement in 1991 in getting all the key players in the Israel–Palestine dispute around the same conference table in Madrid. For that had been followed by direct talks between the Israelis and the PLO, facilitated by the Norwegian Foreign Ministry. Rabin and Arafat were in Washington to ratify the Oslo accords, which gave the Palestinians an important degree of interim self-government. The PLO recognised the state of Israel. Israel recognised the PLO as the representative of the Palestinian people.

The Oslo accords were supposed to lead on to a permanent peace settlement. Dennis Ross, who had been the principal US Middle East negotiator under George H. W. Bush, was asked by Bill Clinton to play the same role for him. In November 1995, Rabin paid with his life for the accords, as he was assassinated by a Jewish extremist. Arafat became President of the Palestinian National Authority with partial self-government on the West Bank, but the more radical Palestinian organisation, Hamas, rejected the accords and Israel's right to exist.

As Bill Clinton approached the end of his term as President, in 1999 in the Israeli elections the Labor Party leader, Ehud Barak, defeated Benjamin Netanyahu, who wanted no further agreements with the Palestinians. Barak resumed negotiations with the PLO. Clinton convened a summit with Barak and Arafat at Camp David in July 2000. Barak offered to form a Palestinian state based initially on 73 per cent of the West Bank and 100 per cent of Gaza, later increasing potentially to 86 per cent of the West Bank. Israel would withdraw from sixty-three settlements, though keeping the larger ones. The Palestinians demanded sovereignty over East Jerusalem and its holy sites, the Al-Aqsa Mosque and the Dome of the Rock located on the Temple Mount site, holy in both Islam and Judaism.

Israel offered the Palestinians 'custodianship' though not sovereignty on the Temple Mount. The Palestinians objected that their territory in East Jerusalem would amount to just six small and two larger sections, while the Jewish settlements there would remain. The Palestinians sought to insist on the right of return to Israel for the by now 4 million descendants of the Palestinians displaced in the first Arab–Israeli war. Israel would not accept a right of return for more than 100,000 returnees but envisaged an internationally financed $30 billion fund to compensate others. A fundamental Israeli requirement was that Arafat should declare the conflict over and make no further demands.

As Clinton was leaving office in January 2001, the two sides issued a statement that they had never been closer to an agreement. But in this window of opportunity, they had failed to achieve one. Barak's proposals were far in advance of Israeli opinion. In new elections, Barak was defeated by the far harder-line Ariel Sharon. Likud Prime Ministers of Israel thereafter encouraged new Jewish settlements at a rate designed to render a two-state solution virtually impossible, while the rise of Hamas, regarded as a terrorist organisation by the Israelis and most Western countries, was another insuperable obstacle.

Clinton and Ross and the rest of the US team had kept pointing out to Arafat and his colleagues that this was the best offer they were ever likely to receive from Israel. But Arafat was not prepared to give up the right of return and nor was he prepared to declare the conflict over, clearly fearful that he might suffer the same fate as Rabin.

So Clinton's attempt to achieve the hardest peace ended in failure and a resumption of violence, as every other effort had done. But he won George H. W. Bush's esteem for having used his final months in office to build on James Baker's achievement to try to help secure a better future for the Middle East.

CONTAINING SADDAM HUSSEIN

When Clinton took over as President, the US and Britain were continuing to enforce a no-fly zone over northern Iraq and that inspectors should be allowed to visit suspect installations. Air strikes could be called in if inspections were blocked. It was in this period that the beginnings of a rudimentary Iraqi military nuclear programme were dismantled.

In response to Saddam's attempt to assassinate George Bush, the Iraqi intelligence headquarters was destroyed in a Tomahawk missile strike. In 1995, a no-fly zone was imposed also over southern Iraq. The Shia rebellion was crushed and the regime remained firmly in power, but the intention was to contain it 'through sanctions and occasional resort to force'.

Containment, however, proved progressively harder to maintain. Major breaches stemmed, ironically, from the UN-sanctioned 'oil for food' programme, which was successfully manipulated by the Iraqis to enable them to buy vehicles and other material for potential military use and not just food. The French and Russians wanted to get rid of sanctions and did not enforce them. Saddam found the inspections increasingly irksome, becoming steadily more obstructive.

In 1998, Congress passed the Iraq Liberation Act stating that it should be US policy to remove Saddam from power. Clinton signed the act into law without, however, intending to give effect to it. He had no intention of starting a fresh war in Iraq, though financial support was given to the main exile organisation, the Iraqi National Congress, led by Ahmed Chalabi. In December that year, as Saddam was refusing the UN inspectors access to suspect installations, Clinton responded with 400 air and Tomahawk missile strikes, criticised by his opponents as a distraction from the Monica Lewinsky affair.

FIRST NATO ENLARGEMENT

No East European countries sought to join the NATO alliance during the presidency of George H. W. Bush and nor were they encouraged to do so. Under the Clinton presidency, in 1993 the US launched the Partnership for Peace as a way of building further bridges across the European divide. But subsequently, in 1994, Clinton delivered his 'not whether but when' speech about the Czech Republic joining NATO at a meeting in Prague. In response, Yeltsin warned of the danger of a 'Cold Peace'. But the East Europeans wanted NATO membership and the Polish and other immigrant communities in the Midwest were pressing for this, gathering congressional support.

In a campaign speech in the 1996 US election, Clinton formally espoused NATO enlargement, having assured Yeltsin that this would not come into effect until after the Russian elections in that year. Yeltsin was not by background or temperament a member of the tight-knit group of *siloviki* (securocrats) in Russia. At one point he told Lech Wałęsa that he did not really mind about Poland joining NATO, though he subsequently rowed back on that. In view of the generally cooperative and relaxed atmosphere in his numerous meetings with Yeltsin, Clinton felt that his reaction to NATO enlargement should prove to be manageable.

The US and Russia were cooperating on the withdrawal of nuclear weapons from Kazakhstan, Belarus and Ukraine. Clinton was showing political support for Yeltsin and urging the international financial institutions to help with Russia's economic difficulties. In March 1999, Poland, the Czech Republic and Hungary eventually were admitted to NATO. In the same month, Yeltsin remonstrated strongly with Clinton about the US air strikes on Serbia, but when Yeltsin resigned as President later that year, they parted with the usual expressions of friendship.

Following al-Qaeda attacks on the US embassies in east Africa and on the USS *Cole*, Clinton was accused of not having tried hard enough to capture or kill bin Laden. The 9/11 Commission concluded that he had never been presented with a convincing opportunity to do so.

Clinton had not set out to be a foreign policy President – anything but. His performance in the overseas policy domain was never likely to be as stellar as that of George H. W. Bush and nor did he face the same challenges. But his impeachment for lying about Monica Lewinsky failed because the US was at peace and doing well economically. Clinton, having held firmly to the centre ground, left office regarded by his compatriots as not a great but certainly not a bad President, and the same could be said of his foreign policy, including in relation to that of his successors.

George H. W. Bush strongly approved of Clinton's interventions in the former Yugoslavia and his vain effort to achieve a settlement in the Middle East. He had fulfilled the promise that the US would remain actively involved in world affairs.

CHAPTER TWELVE

A DIFFERENT KIND
OF BUSH

As George W. Bush plunged into politics, Bush Senior warned him, 'Your father will be an issue. I hope not an albatross.' He would need to establish very quickly that he was his own man, that they agreed on many issues, but there were others on which they didn't.

Bush Senior was always ready to talk to George W. and to Jeb Bush, but never to interfere in their political lives. In 1994, George W. ran for Governor of Texas against the Democrat incumbent, Ann Richards, who, his mother told him, was far too popular for him to have any chance of winning.

James Baker was among the many friends of the Bush family who saw the more studious and serious Jeb Bush as far more likely to succeed in politics than his wilder brother George W. This led to a belief that the family too saw Jeb as 'the One', an opinion not shared by Jeb, who said, 'If I were "the One", no one told me about it. I didn't get the memo.'

George W. knew that he was seen as a less serious person, more like his mother than his father, more irreverent and unattached, more interested in adventure and in girls than in settling down like his seven years younger brother, Jeb.

George H. W. Bush described the alleged family preference in politics for Jeb as 'bullshit'. But he did think that Jeb had a better chance in Florida than George W. did against Ann Richards. 'Nobody thought he could win.'

But by this time, there was a very different George W. Bush. Friends of his father had arranged for him to do his military service as a fighter pilot in the Texas National Guard. Having graduated from Harvard Business School, he had married Laura, whom his parents adored, found religion and given up drinking and he was by now very close to his father.

Having worked, like his father, in the oil leases exploration business, he had become part owner and manager of the Texas Rangers baseball team and helped to put together a consortium of investors to fund a new stadium. Asked about his previous misadventures, his reply was: 'When I was young and irresponsible, I was young and irresponsible.'

Anyone who knows Texas and the Texans will feel bound to agree with John Steinbeck that 'Texas is a state of mind' and George W. exemplified that state of mind. Andover, Yale and Harvard had left few traces on him, though he did become the first President to hold an MBA. Growing up in Midland, Texas, and making his way in the oil business and as manager of the Texas Rangers made a far deeper impact.

It was precisely for this reason that his future political adviser Karl Rove became convinced that in the next election George W. could defeat the popular and apparently unbeatable Democrat Governor of Texas, Ann Richards. From their first meeting, Rove found George W. in manner, attitude, dress and personality to be as Texan as anyone could possibly be, which was the response he then got on the campaign trail. In his Texas National Guard fighter

pilot's jacket, cowboy boots and blue jeans, the hallmark he bore
was that of the Texas heartland.

Ann Richards took to referring to her challenger, George W., as
'Shrub'. But although very feisty and personally popular, she was
not a great administrator. George W. avoided attacking her personally but seemed to know more about problems in the schools and
the criminal justice system than she did.

Unlike his father, he loved campaigning and proved to be very
good at it, including courting the Hispanic population. His obses-
sion with education led Ann Richards to observe that if you asked
her opponent what time it was, he would say, 'We must teach our
children to read.' When, against all the odds, George W. won in
Texas, telephoning his father from the midst of a huge celebration,
he found him, instead of congratulating George W. on his victory,
upset about Jeb's distress at losing in Florida, which, George W.
observed, was typical of his father. Jeb Bush went on to win subsequent elections and serve as the two-term Governor of Florida
from 1999 to 2007.

George W.'s indelible association with the ill-fated invasion of
Iraq, undertaken on false premises, led most of the outside world
to wonder how on earth he had become President of the United
States. But in domestic policy, which he had expected to be his
main focus as President, he did have a vision and abilities that far
exceeded those of his father.

For George W. had proved to be a successful, moderate and pragmatic Governor of Texas. As the Texas legislature was controlled by
the Democratic Party, he worked with the Democrat Lieutenant
Governor and Speaker on school reform and the reform of tort
law to rein in excessive lawsuits. School boards were given greater
authority, charter schools were established, minimum standards in

core subjects were set and teacher salaries were increased. Welfare recipients were required to do some work or to train for work, causing relief rolls to fall by half. During his tenure, Texas also became the leading producer of wind-powered electricity in the US.

The Texas Rangers, meanwhile, aided by their huge new ballpark, had become the most profitable franchise in major league baseball. The club now was sold at a big profit to a Dallas businessman, earning $15 million for George W. Bush, who described it as 'more money than I had ever dreamed of'.

'I KNOW WHAT THE FUTURE IS GOING TO LOOK LIKE HERE'

In his re-election campaign, George W. showed that he had indeed become, as he put it, 'a political animal'. His speeches were funny, self-deprecating and short, followed by plunging into the crowds. Taking to heart Ronald Reagan's dictum that the Hispanic population 'are our voters, they just don't know it yet', George W. courted the Hispanic vote with an op-ed in the *New York Times* urging Americans to be less critical of Mexico and Mexican immigrants. 'My state shares a 1,248-mile border with Mexico.' Texas was a richer place because of the Hispanic relationship. He told the *Houston Chronicle*, 'I know what the future is going to look like here.' They needed to help ensure that Hispanic children were well educated and Hispanic businessmen encouraged.

Billing himself as a 'compassionate conservative', with the striking support of the *Democratic* Lieutenant Governor, he won re-election in a landslide with two thirds of the votes, including half the Hispanic and a quarter of the black votes.

In June 1999, George W. announced his intention to run for President. His father observed with approval that he had (conservative) principles but was no ideologue. 'He doesn't need a voice from the past.'

Before George W. had even declared his intention to run, since he knew nothing about foreign policy, his father arranged a meeting with his Saudi friend Prince Bandar. George Shultz arranged one with policy experts from the Hoover Institution, just as he had many years before for Ronald Reagan. George W. then invited Shultz, Dick Cheney, Condoleezza Rice and the neo-conservative Paul Wolfowitz to a follow-up meeting in Austin.

The George W. foreign policy team were nicknamed by Rice 'the Vulcans', which was the emblem of her home town, Birmingham, Alabama. The name stuck because some of them believed themselves to be made of tougher stuff than their predecessors. Rice was recommended by Brent Scowcroft as a potential future national security advisor, becoming a frequent guest at the Bush family holiday home at Walker's Point in Maine.

As a presidential candidate, George W. believed in the importance of 'defining himself', which he felt his father had failed to do. His anti-extremist father always had regarded himself as a moderate conservative but did not have nearly as much of a domestic policy agenda to back this up. George W. did so by emphasising rehabilitation programmes for prisoners, tax cuts for lower-income groups and greater education funding. On the – to the Republicans – vexed subject of gay issues, he opposed same-sex marriages, as did a vast majority of Americans at the time, but declared that he did not believe in discriminating against anyone.

Continuing to win over many Hispanics to his cause, he told Americans that 'family values do not stop at the Rio Grande' and was to make a serious effort at immigration reform. By nature more deeply conservative than his father, this and his real, publicly advertised, religious faith enabled him to adopt relatively advanced positions on some subjects without losing the Republican base.

Nevertheless, George W. lost badly in the New Hampshire primary to the popular, independent-minded Republican Senator John McCain, a war hero who had been tortured while in captivity in Vietnam and a favourite of the media at the time. There followed a rough-house contest in South Carolina, with Bush massively outspending McCain while local Republican-supporting groups, though not the Bush campaign itself, spread all sorts of calumnies about his opponent. In a campaign of which Lee Atwater would have been proud, Bush prevailed, then swept the southern states, forcing an embittered McCain to withdraw.

'THEY MISUNDERESTIMATED ME'

In the primary debates, George W. had been asked who was his favourite philosopher. His answer was: 'Christ, because he changed my heart.' To his astonishment, his father rang to say, 'Don't worry, son. I don't think the Jesus answer will hurt you very much.' George W. did not believe that such an answer, which was true, could possibly hurt him at all.

George W. also believed that his father had allowed Bill Clinton to 'set the agenda', which he was determined not to do.

A feature the two Bushes did have in common were their periodic assaults on the English language. Off-the-cuff remarks by Bush Senior, as in his private conversation, would be full of sentences without a verb, or else they would be unfinished. His meaning usually was clear, but his mind seemed to be operating faster than he could talk.

This was taken to new levels by George W., who did know how to laugh at himself. He claimed to be proud when, later, a book was published entitled *George W. Bushisms: The Accidental Wit and Wisdom of Our 43rd President*, which he compared to Mao's Little Red Book. It included such celebrated Bushisms as 'They misunderestimated me' and 'Rarely is the question asked: Is our children learning.' He also was alleged to have opined that the French did not have a word for entrepreneur.

In the presidential race against Al Gore, the Bush campaign remained firmly based in Austin, Texas. Gore was a centrist Democrat and, except on environmental issues, there was not very much distance between him and Bush. But he was stiff and wooden and could appear robotic. His speeches often were long and sleep-inducing. Those of Bush, though full of fractured syntax, at least were humorous and short.

Before announcing Dick Cheney as his running mate, George W. did consult his father, who warmly endorsed his choice. Karl Rove upset Bush Senior by saying that it was important that he and Barbara Bush should not feature too much at the Republican Party convention. But, accepting that the focus must be on George W. and Cheney, the former President decided against making a speech there at all.

With the country at peace and with a strong economy, Clinton had remained popular and the election appeared to be the Democrats' to lose. As a moderate Democrat, Gore was hard to attack on most policy issues. But he was determined to distance himself from Clinton, making an extraordinary error in keeping Clinton out of his campaign.

He also had a habit of making embellished claims about his CV which allowed his opponents to make fun of him. He exaggerated his role in helping to develop the internet and believed that he and his attractive wife, Tipper, were role models for *Love Story*. He had not been under fire in Vietnam, nor had he helped to establish the Strategic Oil Reserve. To underline the difference with Clinton, Tipper was subjected to the longest stage kiss ever at the Democratic Party convention (sadly, they later separated).

The debates, as on previous occasions, were won and lost less on substance than on style, with Gore appearing pompous and wooden and Bush more at ease with himself. In the last week of the campaign, Bush suffered a setback when Fox News revealed a conviction for drink driving in 1976, which he had not disclosed.

'WHETHER YOU VOTED FOR ME OR NOT, I WILL DO MY BEST TO EARN YOUR RESPECT'

Gore won half a million more votes than Bush, but the outcome in the electoral college depended on Florida, where the result was effectively a tie, with Bush credited with winning a handful more votes than Gore. With James Baker called in to represent the Bush cause, the Supreme Court controversially ruled by the five more conservative judges to four liberals against any further recounts, handing the flimsiest of victories to Bush. Bush declared that he had not been elected to serve one party but one nation. 'Whether you voted for me or not ... I will do my best to earn your respect.'

Following his inauguration, the first person George W. invited into the Oval Office was his father. There was an emotional embrace. But he did not consult him about the appointment as Secretary of Defense, on Cheney's advice, of his father's old rival, Donald Rumsfeld, as he 'knew what the answer was' or would have been; George H. W. had never made any secret of his distaste for Rumsfeld ('an arrogant fellow').

In her memoir, *No Higher Honor*, Condoleezza Rice describes the dysfunctional nature of the Bush foreign policy team in the run-up to the Iraq War and its aftermath, with Colin Powell and Rumsfeld totally distrustful of one another, in Powell's case with good reason, and Cheney and his staff aligned against Powell. In Rice's view, 'the problem was that the Vice-President's staff, which seemed very much of one ultra-hawkish mind, was determined to act as a power center of its own'.

George H. W. Bush agreed with her. He found, he said later, Cheney very much changed from the person he had known as his Defense Secretary. He regarded Cheney as being responsible for an excessively hawkish image, that he was not behaving as a Vice-President should and should never have been allowed to take such a large and interfering staff with him into the administration.

Told much later of his father's reservations about Cheney, George W. said that he had not expressed them to him. 'He would never say to me, "Hey, you need to rein in Cheney."' That was not his way. Nevertheless, in his second term, George W. did rein in Cheney.

Cheney said that what had changed him was 9/11. He had been asked to play an active role and the nation thereafter was at war.

Powell's deputy, Rich Armitage, also a Vietnam veteran, never bothered to disguise his contempt for warlike civilians in the Pentagon with no military experience and no idea what war was like. It was not surprising that, caught between the clashing ideas and egos of Rumsfeld and Powell, though closer to the President than either of them, Rice must have felt at times like a rabbit caught in the headlights.

Another fateful decision was to ask George Tenet, head of the CIA under Clinton, to remain in the post. Tenet was not an intelligence professional but had been head of the agency for the past three years and deputy head before that. A very political figure, in the run-up to the war with Iraq, he proved far too eager to tell the politicians above him what they wanted to hear, ending up by assuring George W. that the intelligence about biological and chemical weapons in Iraq was 'a slam dunk'. The equally flawed advice given by his British counterpart to Tony Blair was based to a significant degree on the relationship with Tenet.

'NEVER UNDERESTIMATE WHAT YOU CAN LEARN FROM A FAILED PRESIDENCY'

George W. was quick to demonstrate that he did not lack self-confidence and that he was different to what had gone before. He was determined to protect his conservative base better than his father had done. As a former Governor, he saw himself as far more of a chief executive than his father had been. A key declaration by him was: 'Never underestimate what you can learn from a failed presidency.'

In his extremely short (fourteen-minute) One Nation-style inaugural address, he called for greater civility in politics and a greater effort to help those being left behind. As a key theme of his presidency, he majored on public education, launching a group of educational programmes under the title No Child Left Behind, which was a cause he really believed in and in which he was supported by Senator Ted Kennedy and other Democrats.

The antithesis of his father, who, with the important exceptions of the Disabilities, Clean Air and Civil Rights Acts, had only a broad-brush approach to domestic policy, George W. had a detailed interest in it. In foreign policy, the very obvious problem was that he didn't know what he didn't know, in particular about the Middle East.

As George W. himself observed, he did not deal in nuances. In July 2001, his apparently unconditional support for Israel against the Palestinian uprising had infuriated Crown Prince Abdullah of Saudi Arabia. Meeting his son at Walker's Point, George H. W. Bush telephoned the Crown Prince to try to reassure him. News of this leaked to the press, to the embarrassment of Bush Senior. When George W. then called on Arafat to end the violence, with no appeal for restraint or negotiations with the Palestinians to the Israelis, who were using tanks to counter it, Bandar had to deliver a message from the Crown Prince threatening abandonment of the relationship with the United States. In his reply, George W. Bush expressed support for Palestinian self-determination and, for the first time explicitly by an American President, an eventual Palestinian state, placating the Saudis.

George W. came into office expecting to be primarily a domestic policy President and to try to make a difference in that respect, as he had done in Texas. Tony Blair, invited to meet the new President at Camp David, found that his priorities at this time were domestic – about education, welfare, tax reform and cutting down on big government as he saw it. He shared his thoughts about Putin ('one cold dude') and Israel's Prime Minister, Yitzhak Shamir ('one mean sonofabitch'). Though Blair found Bush deeply conservative, a conclusion he reached was that George W. was politically shrewder and more in touch with US opinion than the European or Democratic-leaning press seemed to realise.

'THE UNITED STATES IS UNDER ATTACK'

On 11 September 2001, the world changed for Bush, Blair and the rest of us. It was while visiting a school in Florida to participate with children in a reading class that George W. Bush was told by his chief of staff, Andy Card, about the planes crashing into the Twin Towers in New York and that America was under attack.

Once back in Washington, he declared that the US would make no distinction between the terrorists who had committed these acts and the countries that harboured them.

The focus of his presidency had changed fundamentally, he wrote later. 'I had expected it to be domestic policy.' Now he was a wartime President. In the NSC meeting, Paul Wolfowitz, Deputy Secretary of Defense, suggested that Iraq must have been involved. Rumsfeld asked, 'Is there a need to address Iraq as well as al-Qaeda?' Bush asked Richard Clarke of the CIA to look into this, though Clarke said there was no evidence of any Iraqi involvement.

At midnight, Condoleezza Rice turned on her television to find the band of the Coldstream Guards outside Buckingham Palace, in a gesture of solidarity, playing 'The Star-Spangled Banner', at which she burst into tears.

*   *   *

When asked later about the influence of the 'neo-conservatives' on his policies, George W. claimed not to know who they were. Mainly Jewish in origin, with close ties to and unconditional supporters of Israel, they had formidable intellectual firepower, prior governmental experience and no lack of confidence in their beliefs.

Leading lights among them pressing for action against Iraq were Richard Perle, an adviser to the Pentagon, and Paul Wolfowitz, who was the most fervent advocate of the advantages of overthrowing Saddam. A war to do so, he claimed, would pay for itself from the revenues from the Iraqi oilfields. There was an alternative government in waiting – to be led by the dubious Ahmed Chalabi, wanted for securities fraud in Jordan but leader of the main Iraqi exile movement, the Iraqi National Council.

Wolfowitz's ambition was to establish Iraq as the first function-ing Arab democracy, which, he believed, would create a permanent ally of the US in the Middle East. Cheney's hyperactive chief of staff, 'Scooter' Libby, had been a pupil of Wolfowitz, and another true believer, Douglas Feith, became his deputy in the Pentagon.

Wolfowitz's vision chimed in an important respect with that of Bush that 'people love freedom' and the world was going to have to be remade. As Henry Kissinger observed, the trouble with the neo-conservatives was that they were not conservatives at all. In his earlier government roles, I had found Paul Wolfowitz very likeable and impressive. But when I said so to Reagan's Defense Secretary, Cap Weinberger, his response was, 'Yes, but he must never be al-lowed anywhere near the Middle East!'

The full agenda of some core members of this group was set out by Richard Perle and Bush's speechwriter David Frum in their book *An End to Evil*, published after the invasion of Iraq, calling for regime change also in Syria and Iran.

An apparent mystery about the neo-conservatives was why their close friends and colleagues in Israel did not inject greater realism into their thinking about Iraq. The Israelis wanted to get rid of Saddam but knew that it would trigger a sectarian war in Iraq and open the way for Iran to seek to dominate the country through their Shia allies. They also knew that the Americans would be regarded as an occupying force. But this was no longer the Israel of Rabin, Barak or Peres. With a Likud government in control in Tel Aviv, what Netanyahu wanted was an American invasion of Iraq, so no element of caution was expressed to their closest American friends.

Their fellow neo-conservative Ken Adelman predicted that the military invasion of Iraq would be a 'cakewalk'. As for what tran-spired thereafter, he confessed that he had believed his friends and

Rumsfeld to be exceptionally competent. In fact, in his view, they had turned out to be 'both individually flawed and dysfunctional together'.

The neo-conservatives were not the decisive factor in arguing for the invasion of Iraq, though they pressed hard and worked incessantly to skew the intelligence in favour of it. Cheney and Rumsfeld were more influential and so, above all, was George W., who liked to describe himself as, and indeed was, 'the Decider'. But they made it far harder to contain the ensuing insurgency, in pursuit of their doctrine of 'de-Ba'athification', by dismantling the Iraqi Army and civil service.

'WHATEVER IT TAKES'

Visiting the smoking ruins of the World Trade Center, Bush never forgot the cries from the crowd of 'Whatever it takes' and 'Do not let us down'.

With the nation at war, the CIA was authorised to kill, capture or detain al-Qaeda members anywhere. Bush told reporters that he wanted Osama bin Laden 'dead or alive', a remark his wife urged him to tone down. Bush was unrepentant. 'They understood me in Midland,' was his response.

On 13 September, Cofer Black of the CIA briefed Bush and the National Security Council on a well-thought-out plan to intervene, with US special forces and air strikes, alongside the anti-Taliban Northern Alliance, against the Taliban in Afghanistan. The Taliban leaders, including Mullah Omar, were asked through the Pakistan intelligence agency and directly by the CIA to stop providing safe harbour to al-Qaeda and Osama bin Laden, which they categorically refused to do.

US-led military operations against them in Afghanistan were launched on 7 October, starting with an air bombardment. Kabul was captured on 13 November and the Taliban stronghold of Kandahar in December, with bin Laden narrowly escaping across the border into Pakistan.

The intervention in Afghanistan, given the attack mounted from there on the US, was a war of necessity. What was to happen in Iraq was a war of choice.

Wolfowitz continued his campaign for an attack on Iraq. He warned about the difficulties of war in Afghanistan, whereas Iraq was a brittle, vulnerable regime. The concern was that Saddam still was attempting to develop or obtain weapons of mass destruction and since he had expelled the UN inspectors from Iraq, it was impossible to know how far he had got. Wolfowitz argued that the US would have to go after Saddam if the war on terrorism was to be taken seriously.

Rumsfeld also raised Iraq. States were easier targets than al-Qaeda, shifting between their camps in Afghanistan. Bush had said that he did not want to fire multi-million-dollar missiles at patches of sand in Afghanistan.

'I DON'T HAVE THE EVIDENCE AT THIS POINT'

Bush, at this stage, was against pursuing Iraq. He did not want to get distracted from dealing with Afghanistan and al-Qaeda. Bush told the NSC that he believed that Iraq was involved but was not going to strike them then. 'I don't have the evidence at this point.' They could work on military plans for Iraq, but over time.

On the difficulties of holding together the international coalition against al-Qaeda, 'two years from now', Bush said, 'only the

Brits may be with us'. On 20 September, he agreed with Blair that Iraq was not the immediate problem. Some members of his team thought differently, but he was the one making the decisions.

Clinton had approved the Iraq Liberation Act, calling for regime change and supported by both sides in Congress. In the British Parliament, Tony Blair supported the 'objective' of regime change. 'If we can find a way to remove Saddam, we will.'

On 28 December, Bush was briefed by the US military on the options for Iraq. The existing plan envisaged sending 400,000 troops. The military were instructed to work on a revised plan, with Rumsfeld insisting that victory could be achieved with far smaller forces, but paying no attention to the aftermath. The formal plan for invasion was not finally submitted until August 2002.

CHAPTER THIRTEEN

'THROUGH THE LENS OF 9/11, MY VIEW CHANGED'

No one seriously doubted at this time that Saddam had an arsenal of chemical weapons. He had dropped several thousand chemical bombs on the Iranians and the Kurds and thousands more were unaccounted for. He also had pursued a rudimentary nuclear programme. This had been interrupted by International Atomic Energy Agency inspectors after the Gulf War, but they had then been expelled.

It was against this background that Bush observed that 'through the lens of the post-9/11 world, my view changed ... Saddam must be disarmed.' They should remain hopeful that international pressure would succeed in achieving this. 'But we cannot allow weapons of mass destruction to fall into the hands of terrorists. I will not allow that to happen.'

In November 2001, he gave Iraq a stark warning to re-admit the UN weapons inspectors. In a telephone call to Blair in December, Bush raised the issue of regime change in Iraq, arguing that the threat of Saddam using weapons of mass destruction could no longer be tolerated.

Blair's focus was on disarming Saddam. But if getting rid of Saddam was the only way to achieve this, he told Bush that 'we were going to be up for that', though there was no support in his party for such an undertaking at the time.

In his State of the Union address on 29 January 2002, Bush declared that states like North Korea, Iraq and Iran, developing weapons of mass destruction and supporting terror, constituted an 'axis of evil'. His national security advisor, Condi Rice, regretted later that this term, concocted by the neo-conservative speechwriter David Frum, made the administration seem 'given to hot rhetoric and a preference for military force', though she did not object at the time.

George H. W. Bush also regretted this kind of 'harsh rhetoric', though he too did not tell George W. so at the time. The phrase did not make much sense, as there was no 'axis' either between Iraq and Iran, who had just been at war with each other, or with North Korea.

The Patriot Act was passed to give the administration sweeping powers to do whatever was necessary to pre-empt terrorist activities. Terrorists were to be tried by military commissions, not in a court of law. The authorisation for 'enhanced interrogation techniques', including waterboarding, in the no-holds-barred war on terror, though supported by Cheney and Rumsfeld, came not from them but from Bush. Bush and Cheney were unrepentant about these measures, which they regarded as having helped to keep America safe from any further terrorist attacks on their watch.

*   *   *

During a meeting with Tony Blair in April 2002, Bush was asked if he had made up his mind to attack Iraq. He replied that he had made up his mind that Saddam had to go, a statement he also made to the ITN correspondent Trevor McDonald. In a speech at West

Point, he declared that the war on terror could not be won on the defensive. 'We are in a struggle between good and evil.'

In July 2002, Richard Haass in the State Department was taken aback to be told by Rice that the President had made up his mind to attack Iraq if Saddam did not disarm. Until then, he had regarded her as someone who would be more cautious about going to war. But she was simply reflecting the President's view. On 23 July, the British were told by the head of MI6 that the Bush administration was preparing for military action and 'the intelligence and the facts were being fixed around the policy'.

'WE DON'T WANT THE SMOKING GUN TO BE A MUSHROOM CLOUD'

Condoleezza Rice became a higher achiever in the United States than any African American woman until the far less accomplished Kamala Harris became Vice-President. Academically brilliant, provost of Stanford University and associated with the right-wing Hoover Institution there, extremely likeable and popular with everyone, as national security advisor under George W., she did not have the stature to mediate between the frequently clashing egos and opinions of Cheney, Rumsfeld and Powell, though she was closer to and more trusted by Bush than any of them. Unmarried, she was virtually adopted by the Bushes as if she were family.

But that became part of the problem, for the lack of any distance between her and the President resulted at times in a lack of objectivity. She failed to support Colin Powell as strongly as she should have done, as she was to find out in her own difficulties with Cheney and Rumsfeld when she became Secretary of State. Her relationship with the President was one of dependency. When Bush started leaning towards an invasion, there was no question of her leaning back. She did not display sufficient scepticism about some of the intelligence, though nor did others at the time. To the contrary, it was Rice who first declared, 'We don't want the smoking gun to be a mushroom cloud.'

In August, Colin Powell went through all his concerns during two hours alone with Bush and Rice. If the US did decide to attack Saddam Hussein, he warned, winning the war would be the easy bit. But they would then end up 'owning' Iraq. They would become the government, struggling in a quagmire of intractable problems. Iraq, he pointed out, had never had a functioning democracy. Bush was more optimistic, believing that 'freedom is something people long for'. But he listened to Powell's arguments about the need to mobilise international support.

'IF HE THOUGHT I WAS HANDLING IRAQ WRONG, HE DAMN SURE WOULD HAVE TOLD ME HIMSELF'

George W. revered his father, though he was confident that he had better political skills. He flatly rejected the 'psychobabble' about wanting to compete with him, which was indeed far-fetched, except in one respect. For, ever present in his mind was a determination to be a two-term President. He also referred frequently to the fact that Saddam had tried to kill his father.

Speculation about the relationship between the two reached a new level of intensity over the Iraq War. Maureen Dowd of the *New York Times* was a premier exponent of the son versus father rivalry story. She and others had a field day when, on 15 August 2002, Brent Scowcroft published an article in the *Wall Street Journal* entitled 'Don't Attack Saddam'. Dowd annoyed both Bushes by entitling her article 'Junior Gets a Spanking'.

George W. was furious that Scowcroft had published his advice in the press, because of the inevitable speculation that this was his father's way of sending him a message about Iraq, which he discounted. 'If he thought I was handling Iraq wrong, he damn sure would have told me himself.'

Scowcroft had told Bush Senior what he was going to write and no effort was made to stop him. But there was no question, Bush Senior claimed, of using him to send a message to his son. 'We don't work that way.'

In reality, Bush Senior must have believed that Scowcroft's arguments deserved to be heard, given that they were exactly the same as those he had used against pursuing regime change at the end of the Gulf War. The furore this caused reinforced his determination not to allow any public divergence on this issue to appear between him and his son.

In a meeting with Blair at Camp David on 7 September, George W. agreed to seek a new UN Security Council resolution to require compliance from Iraq, including the return of UN weapons inspectors, or face the consequences. Bush added that if diplomacy failed, there would be only one option left, leading Blair to confirm that 'I will be with you', as he already had told Bush in July.

Dissatisfied with the more ambiguous intelligence from the normal channels – the CIA and the Defense Intelligence Agency – Cheney's staff, led by 'Scooter' Libby, would supplement these with more lurid allegations of their own, and Doug Feith had set up a separate Iraq intelligence group in the Pentagon to do the same. Cheney continued to lead the charge for an attack on Iraq, including making public statements about the supposedly imminent risk of Saddam developing nuclear weapons. The CIA Intelligence Estimate distributed to Congress on 1 October claimed bizarrely that Iraq could make a nuclear weapon in several months or a year (an estimate that later was revised to 'by the end of the decade'), had developed advanced biological weapons, had resumed production of chemical weapons and was developing ballistic missiles.

This was followed by Bush deciding to apply his doctrine of military pre-emption. He had reached a decision. 'We would confront the threat from Iraq.'

The report that Saddam had developed a dozen or more mobile biological weapons laboratories came from an Iraqi exile in Germany codenamed 'Curveball'. Despite warnings from the German secret service that this came from a single untested and possibly unreliable source, in his 2003 State of the Union speech Bush said that Iraq had several mobile biological weapons laboratories. This claim also featured in Colin Powell's presentation to the UN Security Council and in the Blair government's case for war with Iraq. The conclusion of the post-war inquiries in the US and the UK was that 'Curveball' had simply made it up, as he subsequently admitted.

Tenet, after the war, tried to disown his own report, which turned out to be wrong in most respects and had been contested at levels below him in the agency, including by the Iraq desk officer. Knowing the direction in which the President was heading, he allowed intelligence that should have been challenged or at least properly evaluated to escape any rigorous examination.

In October, Bush quoted the CIA report, adding that ties between Iraq and al-Qaeda 'went back a decade'. In fact, the US intelligence assessment finalised in January 2003 showed no evidence of cooperation between Iraq and al-Qaeda at the time of the 9/11 attacks. But from May 2002, as al-Qaeda leaders came under pressure in Afghanistan, a sizeable affiliated group led by Abu Musab al-Zarqawi did establish a presence in northern Iraq, with indications of them attempting to make primitive biological and chemical weapons. There was no evidence of any control by Saddam, but their presence appeared to be tolerated by Iraqi intelligence.

After the allied invasion, al-Zarqawi became a major problem for the occupying forces, making successful efforts to help to trigger a revolt by the Sunni minority and to worsen sectarian conflict between the Shia and Sunni populations until, eventually, he was killed in a US drone strike in 2006.

To increase the pressure on Saddam Hussein, on 10 and 11 October, Bush secured large majorities in Congress to give the President authority to attack Iraq.

The UN Security Council Resolution 1441 giving Saddam Hussein a 'final opportunity to comply' with earlier resolutions was passed unanimously on 8 November 2002.

'IT'S A SLAM-DUNK'

On 12 December, Bush asked Tenet about the public case for attacking Iraq, only to be told by Tenet, 'It's a slam-dunk.' At Christmas, George W. did ask his father what he thought about Iraq. Bush Senior approved the negotiating strategy, agreeing that if Saddam would not comply with the demand to give up weapons of mass destruction, the US would have to use force.

A myth since has developed that Bush agreed with Scowcroft and must have tried to dissuade George W. from invading Iraq. But according to the direct testimony of both George W. and his father, this was simply not the case. George Bush Senior was receiving the same intelligence briefings as his son, convincing him that Saddam Hussein was indeed intent on developing weapons of mass destruction. This was why he too now accepted the need for regime change, as he had not done in the war to liberate Kuwait.

What he did appreciate, far better than George W., were the

potential unintended consequences of marching all the way to Baghdad. He had been clear in the earlier conflict that occupying Iraq was precisely what was to be avoided, but he now was determined never to appear to be second guessing his son.

When, in 2004, Peter and Rochelle Schweizer, authors of a book about the Bushes, wrote that 'George H. W. Bush was opposed to his son's plan to attack Iraq', Bush Senior responded with an indignant denial. A spokesperson said, 'The truth is that, from the very first day, President Bush, No. 41, unequivocally supported the President on the war in Iraq. He had absolutely no reservations of any kind.' The second sentence was not actually true. He *did* support the invasion but wondered if his son fully realised the potential consequences.

On 27 January 2003, the chief UN inspector, Hans Blix, reported that Iraq appeared not to have come to a genuine acceptance of the disarmament that was demanded of it. Stocks of chemical and biological weapons remained unaccounted for. However, Mohamed ElBaradei, head of the International Atomic Energy Agency (IAEA), reported no evidence that Iraq had reconstituted its nuclear programme.

Blair told Bush that to get his party to support a war, he needed to get a further UN Security Council resolution.

On 5 February, Colin Powell was required to present the administration's case against Iraq to the UN Security Council, with Tenet sitting behind him. It was a speech he spent the rest of his life regretting. Like George H. W. Bush, he believed that Saddam probably was continuing to conceal his chemical weapons and he referred to the fact that the al-Qaeda group led by al-Zarqawi was operating in northern Iraq. He quoted a number of intercepts suggesting that the Iraqis were successfully hiding weapons from the inspectors. Powell's personal authority and the knowledge that he was extremely cautious about going to war gave special weight to his presentation.

On 10 February, the French, Russian and German leaders, Jacques Chirac, Vladimir Putin and Gerhard Schröder, issued a joint statement that 'nothing justifies war', rendering it impossible to secure yet another UN Security Council resolution. On the 14th, Blix reported that they had carried out 400 inspections at 300 sites without finding proscribed weapons, which did not necessarily mean that they did not exist. They needed more time to continue with their inspections. But by now even Colin Powell was doubtful that disarmament through inspection was possible.

On 25 February, the US Army chief of staff, General Shinseki, testified to the Senate Armed Services Committee that 'something of the order of several hundred thousand soldiers' would be required to stabilise post-war Iraq, provoking furious rebuttals from Rumsfeld and Wolfowitz.

'I HOPE THAT'S NOT THE LAST TIME WE EVER SEE THEM'

On 27 February, Bush met the Auschwitz survivor and Nobel Prize winner Elie Wiesel, who told him that Iraq was a terrorist state. 'In the name of morality, how can we not intervene?' By this time, the US military build-up had generated a momentum of its own, having reached a stage at which there was no leeway to argue for the UN inspectors to be given more time, as Blair, otherwise, would have wished to do. No US President, having despatched over 200,000 troops to the Gulf, was likely to keep them simply waiting there, or to bring them back, barring a complete climbdown by the Iraqi regime.

On 9 March, Bush was so worried about the possibility of Blair losing a vote in Parliament on going to war that he asked Blair if he would prefer to drop out of the coalition or just to participate in peacekeeping after the invasion, only to be told by Blair, 'I am with you to the end.' After a final pre-war meeting with Bush and the Spanish Prime Minister in the Azores, as Blair and his team got on their plane, Condi Rice was so uncertain about their political survival that she exclaimed, 'I hope that's not the last time we ever see them.'

In a final ultimatum, Bush gave Saddam Hussein seventy-two hours to leave Iraq. In the House of Commons, one third of Labour MPs voted against Blair, but the Conservatives voted with him, resulting in a huge majority in his favour.

On 20 March 2003, George W. Bush wrote to his father to say that he had issued the order to invade Iraq. His father, still believing that Saddam had weapons of mass destruction, replied immediately, 'You are doing the right thing.'

The military victory was not quite the 'cakewalk' Ken Adelman had forecast, but, with astonishing speed, by 9 April, US forces had reached Baghdad, where the statue of Saddam was pulled down. On 1 May, on the deck of the aircraft carrier *Abraham Lincoln*, Bush declared that major combat operations had ended. A large banner in the background unwisely proclaimed, 'Mission Accomplished'.

In May 2003, an experienced diplomat, Paul 'Jerry' Bremer, was appointed head of the Coalition Provisional Authority.

In October 2003, the head of the Iraq Survey Group, David Kay, reported that 'we have not yet found stocks' of weapons of mass destruction. In December 2003, Bush told Bob Woodward that he did not suffer any doubts about the decision to invade Iraq. He could not recall any extended discussion with his father about it. His father's role was one of reassurance.

On 28 January 2004, David Kay, who by then had resigned as head of the Iraq Survey Group, declared that the work was 85 per cent done and he did not expect ever to find weapons of mass destruction stockpiled in Iraq. He called for an independent inquiry into why the intelligence had been so wrong. Less well publicised were his conclusions that Iraq had been developing long-range missiles and that the regime had the means and intention to resume banned activities once international pressure subsided. In February, Bush declared, 'I expected there to be stockpiles of weapons ... We thought he had weapons.'

*　　*　　*

It had been agreed that the post-war administration of Iraq should be under the authority of the Defense Department. The planning was supervised by Wolfowitz's neo-conservative deputy, Doug Feith, Under-Secretary in the Pentagon, whose department had initiated a flood of allegations about the supposed Saddam Hussein/al-Qaeda relationship and Iraqi weapons of mass destruction which proved to be wrong. Feith sought to oversee the creation of an Iraqi exile brigade to join in the invasion of Iraq, which ended up with just seventy members.

Feith was responsible for the de-Ba'athification policy being pursued irrespective of the consequences for the post-war governance of Iraq. For most ordinary members of the army, police and civil service were not members of the Ba'ath Party out of conviction, but because they had to be. General Tommy Franks, commander of the coalition forces, was not a fan of Feith. He complained about having to spend his time dealing almost every day with 'the fucking stupidest guy on the face of the earth', as he considered Feith to be totally devoid of any vestige of common sense.

The President's vision, which a somewhat sceptical Dick Cheney thought was 'bold', was not just to get rid of Saddam but to replace his regime with a democracy.

Bush and his key advisers had been convinced that the coalition forces would be greeted as liberators. The British chief of the defence staff, Admiral Boyce, thought they would be – very briefly. Thereafter, as they tried to run the country, they would be regarded as an occupying force.

As Blair acknowledged, there was a failure to anticipate the likelihood of a full-scale sectarian war as the Shia, backed by Iran, pursued vengeance against the better-educated and hitherto predominant Sunni minority, many of whom joined the insurgency. The Iranians quickly established their dominance over the Shia militias and most of the Shia political class.

'THOUSANDS OF ARMED MEN HAD JUST BEEN TOLD THEY WERE NOT WANTED'

In his memoir, Bush concluded that he was badly advised by Rumsfeld to draw down rapidly the 200,000-strong US invasion force. Along with Colin Powell, Rice realised that the US did not have sufficient forces in place. She 'watched the chaos unfold'. The postwar administration of Iraq having been entrusted to the Pentagon, Rumsfeld and his deputies resisted any consultation with or interference from the State Department or others and Rice failed or was unable to exercise any oversight either.

On 16 May 2003, Jerry Bremer, the US pro-consul in Iraq, head of the Coalition Provisional Authority, in consultation with Feith in the Pentagon, issued Coalition Provisional Authority Decree No. 1 on 'de-Ba'athification', followed by a decree disbanding the Iraqi Army in pursuit of the Wolfowitz concept of getting rid entirely of Saddam Hussein's Ba'ath Party in Iraq.

General Jay Garner, in charge of reconstruction, and the CIA head of station in Iraq warned that these orders would drive tens of thousands of Iraqis, with their weapons, into rebellion, but they were overruled. It also meant that there was no longer any functioning civil service.

Condoleezza Rice had no notice of the terms of these decrees until she 'read about them in the newspaper' and nor did the British, who were appalled. Bush recognised subsequently that they had been a dreadful mistake. 'Many Sunnis took [Bremer's orders] as a sign that they would have no place in Iraq's future ... Thousands of armed men had just been told that they were not wanted. Instead of signing up for the new military, many of them joined the insurgency.' Rice belatedly resolved to 'get a better handle on what was going on in Baghdad'.

Thanks to his mentors in the Pentagon, the de-Ba'athification process was to be overseen by Ahmed Chalabi but, as well as the persistent allegations of corruption, he turned out to have little support within Iraq. He boasted subsequently that the false intelligence he and his organisation had supplied to the US had led to the American invasion. Though zealously supported by Wolfowitz and Feith, he soon fell out with the Americans, as he was found to have transferred his allegiance, plus some sensitive information, to the Iranians.

By August 2003, the British forces were down to 9,000 troops. Yet the British were supposed to help control an area the size of

France and they had lost control of Basra to the Iranian-backed militias. The Americans, by now, were engaged in bloody battles against a full-scale Sunni insurgency in cities like Fallujah.

In May that year, Rumsfeld had acknowledged that weapons of mass destruction might never be found. Blair remained convinced that getting rid of Saddam was justified. He would have remained a danger had he remained in power, including to the Iraqi people.

'NO ONE WAS MORE SHOCKED OR ANGRY THAN I WAS'

Blair had felt all along that getting rid of Saddam was a worthwhile cause.

Bush was more introspective. He noted that every major Western intelligence agency believed that Saddam still had weapons of mass destruction: 'No one was lying. We were wrong.' Yet,

> while the world was undoubtedly safer with Saddam gone, the reality was that I had sent American troops into combat based in large part on intelligence that proved false ... No one was more shocked or angry than I was when we didn't find the weapons. I had a sickening feeling every time I thought about it. I still do.

Saddam Hussein told his US interrogator that it was essential for him to have the Iranians and his own people believing that he still had such weapons. The definitive post-war study by the US Iraq Survey Group concluded that Saddam did not have weapons of mass destruction, but also that his intention was to resume such programmes as soon as he could do so.

When it came to George W.'s hoped-for re-election night in November 2004, George H. W. Bush was a bundle of nerves, as the exit polls were suggesting that his son had lost to the Democrat candidate, John Kerry. George W., whose nerves were stronger, went to bed, before discovering in the morning that he had won, this time with a small majority in the popular vote, unlike in his previous win against Al Gore.

'CHOOSING VICTORY'

By 2006, George W. was paying for the situation in Iraq. The Republicans took a beating in the midterm elections. Before the results came in, George W. had decided that Rumsfeld would have to go and this time he did consult his father about who to appoint to replace him. James Baker, by now seventy-six, politely declined the offer. Instead, George W. thought of Robert Gates, head of the CIA under his father and very close personally to him, an idea enthusiastically endorsed by Bush Senior.

Duly appointed, Bob Gates brought a new rationality to decisions about the armed forces, restoring relations with the military and doing the best he could with the war in Iraq. Barack Obama was sufficiently impressed by Gates to take the extremely unusual step of asking him to stay on as Defense Secretary when Obama became President.

By this time, much of Congress and the US press had had enough of the war in Iraq. But the US now had some outstandingly able military leaders there – Generals David Petraeus, Stan Mc-Chrystal and Ray Odierno. Their focus was firmly on training the Iraqi security forces to do a much better job in combating terrorism themselves, while the Sunni tribes in Anwar province were turning against the insurgency and especially the predominantly non-Iraqi al-Qaeda, the so-called 'Sunni awakening'.

With Bush coming under near universal pressure to wind down

the US presence there, he came to the opposite conclusion. General Jack Keane and the neo-conservative writer Frederick Kagan published an article entitled 'Choosing Victory', in which they argued for sending 30,000 additional US troops to concentrate on securing Baghdad.

Contrary to most expectations, the Bush 'surge' in Iraq succeeded in helping to stabilise the situation there sufficiently to enable the bulk of the American forces to withdraw in good order and on good terms with the Iraqi military, thereby laying the foundations for the US to work effectively with them later to crush the Islamic State 'caliphate' in Iraq.

Needless to say, no Jefferson-style democracy came close to emerging in Iraq. Politics there continued to be skewed by sectarian interests and the determination of Iran to maintain its dominance through the militias it financed and controlled in Iraq. The strategic outcome of the war was greatly to increase the aggressively exercised power and influence of Iran, now controlling Hamas in Gaza, Hezbollah in Lebanon and the Houthis in Yemen, and allied with Assad in Syria.

Today, however, elections are held in Iraq that do result in changes of leadership there, while resistance has been increasing to Iranian dominance. There is little doubt that, as Blair and Bush both contended, Iraq and the world are better off without Saddam Hussein. But that was not the rationale given for the war.

'NOT ONE INCH EASTWARD'

Russian leaders ever since have pointed out that, as part of his 'assurances' to the Soviets, James Baker at one point told Shevardnadze that NATO troops would not move into East Germany and nor would NATO's jurisdiction be extended 'one inch' further east.

He was overruled on the latter point by Bush and Scowcroft on the grounds that the mutual security guarantee under Article 5 of the NATO treaty could only apply if it extended to the whole of Germany. Shevardnadze was informed of this and, over time, in the atmosphere of ending the Cold War and the Soviets being invited to establish a liaison office to NATO, it was accepted that West German troops could move into East Germany.

Article 5, which is the cornerstone of the NATO treaty, provides that an armed attack against a NATO member shall be considered an attack against them all and NATO members will assist the party or parties attacked by taking forthwith such action as they deem necessary, including the use of armed force, to restore and maintain the security of the North Atlantic area.

While this falls short of an absolute mutual defence guarantee, it has generally been accepted that, more likely than not, an attack on one would be treated as an attack on all NATO members, with the United States likely to join in resisting such an attack, with bipartisan support in Congress. The East European countries formerly occupied by the Soviet Union, having rushed to shelter under the NATO umbrella, have put their faith in it ever since.

Clinton had set in train the process of NATO enlargement, with Yeltsin objecting formally but not very vehemently to the admission of Poland, the Czech Republic and Hungary to the alliance. The expansion of NATO was given an entirely new dimension under his successor.

In 2001, George W. Bush had a first meeting with Vladimir Putin in Slovenia. Bush told him that the US intended to withdraw from the anti-ballistic missile (ABM) treaty to develop anti-missile defences but wanted to do so 'in a manner that would not cause a breach with Russia'. Putin said that he could not agree to that.

With the revolt in Chechnya encouraged by them, Putin had his own reasons to detest radical Islamists. He denounced the protection Pakistan was giving to them as a major danger for the future.

He impressed Bush by telling him that the cross he was wearing had been given to him by his mother. When his dacha had been destroyed by fire, workmen had found the cross in the ashes and returned it to him.

At the subsequent press conference, Bush was asked whether he trusted Putin, replying that he did. To Rice's alarm, he added, 'I looked the man in the eye ... I was able to get a sense of his soul.'

Following the 9/11 attack on the United States, Rice forewarned Putin that the US was putting its forces on alert and that this was not aimed against Russia. Putin said that he had told the Russian forces to stand down. What more could they do to help? In a phone call with Bush, he agreed to use Russian influence with the central Asian states to give the US the transit and base facilities they needed to deal with the Taliban. He saw what had happened in the US as equivalent to the war he was fighting against the rebels in Chechnya.

The Russians already were helping the anti-Taliban Northern Alliance. When Bush urged them to accelerate arms supplies, the Russian Defence Minister, Sergei Ivanov, told Rice that they were having difficulty finding enough donkeys to transport the weapons across the mountainous terrain in Afghanistan!

Meeting Bush on the eve of the fall of Kabul, Putin was impressed by the speed with which the US ousted the Taliban from power, apparently concluding that George W. was a fellow tough guy. He was invited to a friendly meeting with Bush at his ranch in Texas at which they talked about further cooperation. In Rice's view, the two men 'enjoyed a certain degree of personal chemistry'.

A return meeting in St Petersburg also was positive, with signature of a further strategic nuclear arms reduction treaty, despite the differences over missile defence. When they fell out over the US invasion of Iraq, still a Russian client state, Bush despatched Rice to see Putin about trying to get relations back on track.

But as the Americans established large bases in Uzbekistan and Kyrgyzstan, Putin regretted his earlier cooperation and had started protesting about 'encirclement' by the US.

In November 2003, Eduard Shevardnadze was ousted as President by mass demonstrations in Georgia known as the Rose Revolution. The ensuing election was won by the pro-Western Mikheil Saakashvili. But the Russian-speaking territories within Georgia of South Ossetia and Abkhazia remained under Russian occupation.

The three Baltic countries, Estonia, Latvia and Lithuania, were admitted to NATO in 2004. There was a debate within the Western defence community over their admission, as they all had been annexed by the Soviet Union and would be difficult to defend effectively against a serious Russian attack. But having declared their independence in 1990, all three countries had been subjected to pressure and intimidation from Russia, with threats of intervention on the side of the sizeable Russian minorities there.

For good reasons, therefore, they saw hopes of greater safety in joining the alliance as well as the European Union. Putin at one stage said that he was not very worried about Estonia in NATO. Lithuania was more sensitive, because of continuing Russian control over the militarised enclave of Kaliningrad. On his way to the commemoration in Moscow of the sixtieth anniversary of the end of the Second World War, Bush told the Baltic states that their accession to NATO meant that they could never be threatened with impunity again but that they must respect the rights of the

Russian-speaking minorities living among them. Romania, Bulgaria, Slovakia and Slovenia joined NATO in the same year.

In May 2004, Rice, as national security advisor, met Putin at his dacha outside Moscow. Putin produced from a side room Viktor Yanukovych, making clear that he was going to be the Russian candidate for the presidency of Ukraine. In November, Yanukovych appeared to have won the election in Ukraine, but mass demonstrations against extensive vote rigging and his close ties to Russia (the Orange Revolution) caused a re-run of the election which the strongly pro-Western Viktor Yushchenko won convincingly, despite having nearly died from dioxin poisoning, generally attributed to agents of the Russian security services.

Putin's reaction was to express to Rice his bitter 'disappointments' with US policy and to denounce the 'revolution from the streets' which had resulted in the pro-Western regimes in Georgia and Ukraine.

By 2007, relations with the Russians had soured completely. They were making a huge fuss about the US preparing to install missile defence systems in Poland and the Czech Republic. The Americans contended that these were aimed primarily against possible future missile launches by Iran. In reality they were responding also to pressure from the Poles and Czechs, who did not feel safe without them. The Russian concern evidently was that long-range interceptors could be used against their strategic nuclear missiles.

Putin announced Russian withdrawal from the treaty placing limits on conventional forces in Europe. Rice understood that as the alliance moved steadily east, Moscow's tolerance was being tested.

To try to improve relations, George W. invited Putin to stay at the Bush family home at Walker's Point, with George H. W. Bush also looking in at the meeting, as the Russians regarded him as having been respectful of their sensitivities at the end of the Cold War. The atmosphere was positive – there still was some personal chemistry – but Bush was not prepared to give way on missile defences in Eastern Europe.

Georgia and Ukraine were next to be considered for Membership Action Plans (MAPs), which did not confer NATO membership but prepared countries for it. In a very emotional meeting, Yushchenko had pleaded with Rice to support NATO membership, which he saw as the only way of ensuring that Ukraine would remain independent. In a very threatening conversation, Putin was reported to have told him that, if he wanted, the Russian Army could seize the capitals of the Baltic states, Ukraine, Poland and the Czech Republic in forty-eight hours!

It was at this point, Rice observed, that 'Moscow's patience finally broke'. Although she knew this perfectly well, she also knew that George W. Bush was an ardent supporter of further NATO enlargement. At the National Security Council meeting to consider the issue, therefore, Rice presented the pros and cons, with no recommendation. With no strong advice against, the President decided to support admitting Georgia and Ukraine to MAPs.

At the NATO summit in April 2008, the German Foreign Minister pointed out that the Russian-speaking areas of Abkhazia and South Ossetia had tried to secede from Georgia, with Russian support. The risks of a conflict there were high. There was no case to admit Georgia to NATO.

Angela Merkel, having witnessed Putin's increasing paranoia about NATO expansion in a meeting with him, warned that Russia could see the admission of Georgia and Ukraine to NATO as an existential threat. She was supported by the French.

Rice, eager to fulfil the President's wishes, declared unwisely to the other Foreign Ministers that 'Russia needs to know that the Cold War is over and Russia lost'. Merkel was furious that her warnings were being ignored but, bizarrely, agreed to the summit statement about Georgia and Ukraine that 'we agreed today that these countries will become members of NATO', so long as there was no actual plan to admit them.

So NATO had managed to tie itself in knots on this crucial issue. In a meeting with the NATO ministers, Putin declared that the eastern half of Ukraine was Russian, both ethnically and historically.

After the NATO meeting, Bush went on to visit Putin in Sochi, to see the preparations for the 2014 Winter Olympics. Rice was struck by the still ramshackle appearance of Sochi. It was about to be transformed. The end of Communism was enabling Putin to help to achieve an increase in living standards in many parts of Russia.

There followed the crisis in Georgia, with the Russians actively supporting the secessionists in the two enclaves. Visiting Georgia, Rice warned Saakashvili not to respond to provocations. Bush also had cautioned him not to be provoked into 'doing something stupid'. Rice was explicit that he must not engage Russian forces. If he did, no one would come to his aid.

Yet in August 2008, in response to the shelling of Georgian villages in South Ossetia, Saakashvili launched an offensive against the secessionists, provoking a ferocious Russian military response, with their tanks soon closing in on the Georgian capital, Tbilisi. The French President, Nicolas Sarkozy, negotiated a ceasefire. Russia declared the two enclaves independent. Several NATO members pointed out that this demonstrated that US demands for a NATO Membership Action Plan for Georgia had been an extremely bad idea.

The US signed the agreements for missile defence systems with Poland and the Czech Republic, triggering threatening Russian reactions. In 2009, to the dismay of the Polish President, Lech Wałęsa, implementation of these plans was cancelled by Obama, but defensive systems against short-range missiles were offered instead.

Rice had not distinguished herself in this episode. If Georgia had been admitted to NATO, that would have been likely to undermine the mutual defence provisions in Article 5 of the NATO treaty, as there would have been no appetite on the part of NATO members to intervene in a conflict between Georgia and Russia. It was a classic example of the failure of George W. Bush fully to understand the implications of his policies and the failure of his Secretary of State to point these out to him.

But Rice was correct in concluding that the irreconcilable difference with Russia was Moscow's conviction that it still had a right of oversight on the territories of the former Soviet Union and of the Warsaw Pact. The short-range missile defences currently deployed in Eastern Europe could not threaten Russian strategic nuclear deterrence. The demand that all missile defences must be removed had been followed by one that no NATO forces should be stationed in the former Warsaw Pact territories – the Russian, and specifically Putin's, ambition evidently being to reinstate a form of tutelage over them.

*   *   *

Rice had not proved to be a very successful national security advisor, in exceptionally difficult circumstances. Appointed Secretary of State in George W.'s second term, she felt far more comfortable in that role, playing an important part in a serious effort to make progress towards a Palestinian state on the West Bank and in helping to ensure a different focus in the Bush second term.

Bush agreed with Rice that his second term should have a very different tone, with the emphasis on diplomacy rather than the use of force. As Secretary of State, Rice soon found herself barely on speaking terms with Rumsfeld and was hugely relieved when he was replaced by Gates. Her other persistent problem was with Cheney, which should have caused her to regret not having shown more support for Colin Powell, facing similar problems in Bush's first term.

But George W. and Cheney themselves became more distant from each other in the course of his second term, with Bush less disposed to follow Cheney's advice, and Cheney subsequently was embittered that Bush refused to pardon Cheney's chief of staff, 'Scooter' Libby, convicted in the investigation of the leak of the identity of a CIA agent, Valerie Plame, whose husband had discredited reports about Saddam Hussein acquiring uranium.

George W. remained 'the Decider', as was demonstrated when Cheney wanted to bomb a nuclear site in Iran. George W. did not agree. Nor did he agree when, at the end of his administration, he came under pressure to bomb a suspect nuclear reactor in Syria. Overruling Cheney, he vetoed doing so. The Israelis bombed the reactor instead.

The George W. Bush presidency rightly is remembered above all for the Iraq War. But he was a far more complex and better-intentioned figure than the caricatures of him. He tried every bit as hard as Bill Clinton had done to advance a cause he really believed in – the achievement of a two-state solution to the Arab–Israeli dispute. It was on his watch that the arch-hawk Ariel Sharon himself adopted a very different approach, first withdrawing from Gaza, then agreeing that there must be a solution for the Palestinians on the West Bank as well.

Having seen the evidence that Yasser Arafat, despite his denials, was continuing to encourage terrorism, Bush called publicly for a change in the Palestinian leadership, with Mahmoud Abbas emerging as Arafat's deputy, then his successor on Arafat's death. The Americans initially had to pursue negotiations separately with the Israelis and the Palestinians, until the Israelis then got used to dealing with Abbas direct, albeit still wanting US involvement. The effort continued up to Bush's last days in office with Sharon's successor Ehud Olmert, who was prepared to relinquish all but 6 per cent of the West Bank.

These efforts failed, firstly because of the emergence in control of Gaza of Hamas, Iranian-controlled and designated by the US and its allies as a terrorist organisation. To stop fighting between Hamas and Abbas's Fatah party, King Abdullah forced them together in a single Palestinian entity with which negotiation was impossible, Hamas being committed to the destruction of Israel.

Abbas continued to talk to Olmert, but he could not commit to Olmert's offer on the West Bank which Hamas was certain to oppose and which did not offer a right of return for the millions of descendants of the Palestinians displaced when Israel was created, which no Israeli government could accept.

Olmert, ousted on corruption charges, was replaced by Benjamin Netanyahu, who was totally opposed to any two-state solution, continuing to do his utmost to make it impossible through the proliferation of Jewish settlements on the West Bank. The US initiatives had failed, but Bush had made a more determined effort to make headway in resolving the problem than Barack Obama felt himself able to do.

George W. Bush is remembered in Africa for having launched in 2003 and funded the US President's Emergency Plan for AIDS Relief, under which, by 2020, $90 billion had been provided for AIDS prevention and treatment there. The programme is credited with having saved 20 million lives.

In an emotional ceremony during his last days in office, in the presence of his father, George W. Bush commissioned a new aircraft carrier named the USS *George H. W. Bush*.

CHAPTER FOURTEEN

'WE SHOULD NOT BE THE WORLD'S POLICEMAN'

Barack Obama won the presidential election in November 2008 against Senator John McCain, a recognised national security expert but with a much weaker grasp of domestic policy issues. As the junior Senator from Illinois, Obama had no foreign policy credentials, but it was a plus for him that he had opposed the Iraq War. It was clear that his intention was to prioritise domestic policy, for good reasons at the time. For the United States was mired in the depths of the 2008 financial crisis.

Before his election, showing a keener understanding of what was required than, initially, George W. Bush and especially John McCain, Obama had supported Treasury Secretary Hank Paulson's $440 billion Troubled Asset Relief Program to refinance the major financial institutions, only to find as President that an additional $780 billion was required to stabilise and help to revive the US economy.

When, immediately after his election, he was told by the CIA analyst Bruce Riedel that the prospect of nuclear weapons falling into the wrong hands was 'scary', Obama said that he had just been told by the US Treasury that virtually every bank in America could fail by the end of the month. 'Now that's *really* scary!'

What Obama will be remembered longest for, the overriding priority of his first year in office, is the passage in March 2010 of the Affordable Care Act. Obama, who was a realist and a pragmatist, rejected demands from the 'progressive' wing of his party to try to enact state-funded 'Medicare for all'. He kept asking them if they could count to sixty, which was the number required to get legislation through the Senate. Instead, the act extended Medicaid coverage and was based on individual insurance mandates. It came into effect in 2014. By 2016, the uninsured portion of the population had roughly halved, with more than 20 million additional people covered.

The act prohibited insurance companies from refusing coverage to those with pre-existing conditions but mandated that individuals must buy insurance or pay a penalty. This was intended to force participation by many millions more young and healthy Americans to achieve lower average premiums – a requirement that rendered it unpopular with many in the younger half of the population.

The fiendishly complicated bill was able to be steered through the Senate only because the Democrats could just muster the sixty votes needed to override a Republican filibuster.

Obamacare did not help in the 2010 midterm elections, when the Republicans won control of the House of Representatives and seven seats in the Senate, though the main reason was the still-lagging economy. It was not until 2015 that a majority of Americans supported the act. Thereafter, as people got used to the new system, it became increasingly accepted. The Republicans continued to attack what they regarded as 'socialised medicine' but became wary of actually trying to repeal it. Donald Trump vowed to do so and replace it with 'something better' but proved unable to propose a credible alternative.

It was said of Obama by one of his closest associates that he was 50 per cent idealist, genuinely wanting to try to make the world a better place, and 50 per cent street smart Chicago politician. The combination helped him to be a successful two-term President, pursuing his and his party's goals with a Clinton-like focus on not alienating too many of the swing voters on whom his re-election would depend, enabling him narrowly to defeat the moderate Republican candidate, Mitt Romney, in 2012.

'AMERICA SHOULD NOT BE THE WORLD'S POLICEMAN'

In foreign policy, a turning inwards of the United States became evident in his presidency, unsurprisingly, given that when he took over as President in January 2009, the US had 146,000 US troops in Iraq and 38,000 in Afghanistan. He attacked head on the notion of America as the 'indispensable nation' when it came to dealing with world crises. Addressing the students at the military academy at West Point, he declared that the US had underwritten world security for the past six decades. 'We have not always been thanked for these efforts … The nation that I'm most interested in building is our own.'

Obama was declaring his own version of 'America First', tempered by a declared belief in multilateralism, but reinforced by a conviction that nation building elsewhere was beyond its power.

Having defeated her for the Democratic Party nomination in the presidential election, to the surprise of Hillary Clinton, he asked her to serve as his Secretary of State, which she did very creditably for the next four years. Robert Gates, Defense Secretary under George W. Bush, was even more surprised to be asked to stay on in that role, an imaginative appointment by Obama, showing his understanding of the need for experience on matters of which he had none. The very capable Leon Panetta, formerly Clinton's chief of staff, was a vast improvement on George Tenet as head of the CIA.

On national security, there was more continuity than most had expected with the prior administration. Obama continued the rendition of suspects from overseas and the detention of persons considered likely to pose a threat to national security. The decision to close the detention centre in Guantánamo Bay was rescinded, as no one in the US or elsewhere would take the suspects held there (and when they eventually were released, many of them resurfaced as regional commanders for the Taliban). Far from curtailing, Obama expanded the targeted killing of suspects through drone attacks. Cheney noted with amusement how little seemed to have changed.

In the presidential election campaign, Obama had denounced the conflict in Iraq as a 'bad' war, launched on false pretences, while Afghanistan was a conflict that had been forced on the US. He had indicated that he wanted to draw down the US forces in Iraq but was prepared to send a couple of additional brigades to Afghanistan, though the Hamid Karzai government's corruption and paranoia about his US allies had been making him an increasing disappointment.

The Taliban were solidly installed in the virtually ungoverned tribal areas within Pakistan, on the border with Afghanistan, and controlled from the Quetta Shura (Council) in Pakistan. The Pakistan Inter-Services Intelligence (ISI) agency had one set of operatives liaising with the Americans and another supplying and supporting the Taliban. Their overriding concern was to ensure there must never be an Indian-dominated government in Afghanistan.

The number of coalition troops deployed could not make much difference except locally and in the main population centres, given the topography of Afghanistan. The Taliban funded themselves locally by levying 'protection' taxes and from the opium trade. The Haqqani terrorist network, linked to the Taliban and al-Qaeda, had complete immunity in Pakistan.

An initial meeting between Karzai and Biden as Vice-President ended in recriminations about civilian casualties and corruption. Obama agreed to send an additional 17,000 troops to help provide greater security during the Afghan elections, plus 4,000 to train the Afghan forces. Half went to an area of Helmand province which had just 1 per cent of the population.

Nothing would change Pakistani behaviour. In the initial discussions within the Obama administration, Biden made an impassioned plea for the US to stop fighting the Taliban and get out, while still trying to prevent terrorist actions from Afghanistan. Otherwise Afghanistan, in his view, would simply gobble up as many additional troops as were sent there.

In September 2009, General McChrystal, commanding the US forces in Afghanistan, requested an additional 40,000 troops as, otherwise, the campaign would 'likely end in failure'. This would bring the number of US troops there close to 100,000. Biden urged Obama to refuse: 'We're into Vietnam.' But Obama felt that, as President, he could not afford to lose or be seen to be losing a war.

There followed a deluge of leaks about McChrystal's recommendation, with the head of the joint chiefs of staff, Admiral Mike Mullen, and General Petraeus supporting it. Obama was infuriated by what he regarded as the military 'gaming' him through the press.

But his question to the National Security Council, 'Does anyone think we should leave Afghanistan?' showed only Biden to be in favour. Gates as Defense Secretary, Hillary Clinton as Secretary of State and the US military formed an unbreakable alliance on the other side.

Victory was modified to mean preventing the Taliban from taking over consequential parts of the country, the essential goal being to deny the Taliban the opportunity to overthrow the Afghan state. The main effort was to be on training and supporting the Afghan forces. According to Obama's account, Biden and the NSC staff by now acknowledged that operations against al-Qaeda 'could not work if the Taliban overran the country'.

It took more agonised discussions than it should have done eventually to decide in November that the increase in troop levels should be 30,000, not 40,000. But Obama could not be criticised for failing to heed the military advice about Afghanistan. Within a year of taking office, he had increased the US presence there to 100,000 troops. However, the second increase was accompanied by a declaration that it would be followed by a withdrawal of troops, beginning in July 2011. There could be no objection to planning to do so, but declaring this publicly at the time was criticised as the worst possible kind of message to be sending the Taliban, whose entire strategy was based on outlasting the Americans.

In October 2009, nine months into his presidency, Obama was surprised to be awarded the Nobel Peace Prize, it being unclear what he had yet done to deserve it, other than not being George W. Bush.

*   *   *

Meanwhile, thanks to the Bush surge and to the US commanders there, Obama was able to head towards delivering on his pledge to withdraw 'responsibly' from Iraq, which Petraeus attributed to the US showing clear resolve, a sense by insurgent Sunnis that they were not going to prevail, Sunni weariness of insurgent activity, disenchantment with foreign leadership of al-Qaeda in Iraq, improvement in the performance of the Iraqi security forces and an Iraqi political process with some legitimacy.

The US, which had been on the brink of failure in Iraq, was no longer so. Bush had agreed with the Iraqi government a phased withdrawal of all US forces by 2011. With relations with the Iraqi government now in good shape, Obama signed a future cooperation agreement with the Iraqi Prime Minister, Nouri al-Maliki, promising to retain strong security as well as economic ties.

General Stan McChrystal, who had defeated al-Qaeda in and around Baghdad, had found very frustrating the arguments in Washington about the 'surge' in Afghanistan. As Obama wryly observed, 'McChrystal's eyes narrowed when, on more than one occasion, Biden started explaining to him what was necessary to conduct successful counter-terrorism operations.' Gates also was irritated at attempts at micro-management of military affairs by NSC staff with no perceptible national security expertise.

While on furlough in Paris in June 2010, McChrystal and his staff were foolish enough to make unflattering remarks about Obama's advisers, Biden and others to, of all people, journalists from the *Rolling Stone* magazine, reflecting the frustration of commanders in the field.

McChrystal was relieved of his post and Petraeus took over direct command in Afghanistan as well as Iraq. Understanding that what could be attainable in Afghanistan was not victory but a stalemate, his strategy was to aim to reduce US forces there over time to the thousands, and to train and build up the Afghan security forces, while supporting them with air strikes and logistics. By the time Obama left office in 2017, US forces in Afghanistan were down to 8,400 men.

*　　*　　*

The Russians had invaded Georgia just three months before Obama won the presidential election. Obama had criticised George W. Bush for not doing more to penalise Russia for the invasion. But on taking office Obama supported Hillary Clinton's attempt to 'reset' relations with Russia. When Obama visited Moscow in July 2009, he had to suffer an hour-long lecture from Putin about the invasion of Iraq and other US misdeeds, especially the admission of former Warsaw Pact countries into NATO.

In his memoir, Obama described Putin as reminding him of an old-style Chicago ward boss, for whom bribery and corruption were legitimate means of control. 'In such a world, a lack of scruples, a contempt for any high-minded aspirations beyond accumulating power were not flaws, they were advantages.'

But Obama did his best to form a personal relationship with the – at the time – more user-friendly Dmitry Medvedev, interim President of Russia from 2008 to 2012, though still firmly under Putin's control. Obama argued that the US effort against radical Islam in Afghanistan was in Russia's interests too. Medvedev was supportive about the US supply base in Kyrgyzstan, for which Russia supplied all the fuel. Medvedev cooperated in the nuclear negotiations with Iran.

In return, in September 2009, Obama cancelled the Bush plans for long-range missile defences in Poland and the Czech Republic, ostensibly because of a supposedly reduced threat from Iran, but in reality because of the Russian reactions, with Putin welcoming the decision to do so. The Poles instead were offered a shorter-range anti-missile system, the first three phases of which could not threaten the Russian strategic nuclear forces. In March 2010, the US and Russia agreed on a further 'New START' reduction in their nuclear arsenals to around 1,550 deployed strategic nuclear warheads on each side.

In June 2010, Obama and Medvedev celebrated the apparently successful 'reset' over a cheeseburger in Arlington. When I asked the White House at this time which foreign leader the naturally rather aloof Obama felt he had a particular rapport with, the answer was not Merkel, Cameron or Sarkozy but Medvedev.

In 2012, Obama was overheard telling Medvedev that he would have more flexibility over missile defences after his re-election. In 2013, the US duly cancelled phase four of the planned new anti-missile systems, which could have enabled them to intercept inter-continental ballistic missiles. The short-range defensive system was not due to be operational from Poland until the end of 2022, but in response to the crisis in Ukraine, the Biden administration deployed Patriot short-range anti-missile defences to Poland in March 2022.

No lasting improvement in relations followed from the abandonment of the longer-range anti-missile systems, as Putin was infuriated by pro-democracy demonstrations in Moscow in the run-up to the 2012 Russian elections and accused the US of supporting his opponents. Having won the elections, he took back the presidency in the following year, from which point, despite Obama's concessions on missile defence, more adversarial relations were resumed. In February 2014, there followed the first Russian invasion of Ukraine.

'PROGRESSIVES COULD NOT AFFORD TO IGNORE ECONOMICS'

Obama realised that he had to tread warily about action to combat climate change, given the strength of the oil and gas industries and the views of the big Democratic-led unions. But he was able to use the powers under George H. W. Bush's Clean Air Act to tighten the fuel efficiency standards for all vehicles produced in the US, which George W. Bush had resisted doing, and he paid generous tribute to George H. W. for overriding Republican objections to what became the Kyoto climate change programme, which Obama sought to salvage by agreeing at the Copenhagen conference that the Chinese and Indians could set their own emissions targets. As US industry was reducing emissions anyway through greater efficiencies, plus incentives for 'green' energy, the US was ready to pledge to reduce carbon emissions by 17 per cent below 2005 levels by 2020 and to agree to contribute to a $10 billion a year fund to help developing countries to cope with the problem.

But China had surpassed the United States in carbon dioxide emissions in 2005 and with, as Obama put it, Americans seething at the outsourcing of their jobs, the Kyoto Protocol, which the US still had not ratified, had imposed no binding obligations to curb their emissions on China or India at all. Both countries since have continued firmly to prioritise economic growth, with both continuing to build coal-fired power stations at a rate of knots.

'WITHOUT PUTTING A SINGLE US SOLDIER ON THE GROUND, WE ACHIEVED OUR OBJECTIVES'

In February 2011, anti-Gaddafi demonstrations broke out in Libya. The regime responded with lethal force, killing over 1,000 demonstrators and issuing blood-curdling threats to kill tens of thousands more. The inhabitants of Benghazi, the centre of the uprising, were told that they would be slaughtered like cockroaches. President Nicolas Sarkozy of France led a campaign to stop the slaughter, supported by the UK. The UN Security Council passed a resolution authorising military intervention in Libya.

The French and British sought US support to enforce a no-fly zone. Robert Gates and the US military were extremely reluctant to get involved. Gaddafi had abandoned his military nuclear programme and was opposed to al-Qaeda. But when Sarkozy and Cameron consulted together about intervening militarily without the US, they were advised that it would be too risky to do so without the Americans first taking down the Libyan air defences.

Obama agreed with Gates that there could be no question of committing US ground forces, but Hillary insisted that the US must support its allies. Gates pointed out that a no-fly zone would not stop Gaddafi's tanks. In meetings at the White House on 15 March, Obama decided that if the US intervened, it must be on the basis of 'all necessary measures' to prevent a massacre, not just a no-fly zone.

On 19 March, the US, with support from Britain and France, began a campaign of air strikes. Initially intended to save the people of Benghazi, this soon morphed into a campaign to decapitate the regime, as the only way to end the conflict. It took until October for rebel forces to find and kill Gaddafi, with Obama able to declare that 'without putting a single US soldier on the ground, we achieved our objectives'. A White House adviser was quoted as saying that, in this case, Obama had been 'leading from behind'.

The Western media had portrayed the rebellion as another manifestation of the 'Arab spring', which, in Tripoli, to some degree it was. But the hard core of opposition fighters in Benghazi were organised Islamic militants who subsequently killed the US Ambassador there.

The US had made no promises about nation building in Libya; that was to be left to the Europeans, by whom no major or seriously concerted effort at nation building was ever made. Even if it had been, it is questionable how much could have been achieved in a nation divided between rival power centres in Tripoli and Benghazi. Obama contended subsequently that intervention had been worthwhile to avert a humanitarian disaster, but the outcome thereafter had been chaos (which he used a more graphic term to describe).

'THE RIGHT SIDE OF HISTORY'

Obama and his younger personal advisers, who had served with him in the campaign, reacted to events in the Middle East with a strongly reformist agenda. It seemed to them self-evident that the autocratic pro-Western monarchies could not survive without major democratisation. In his attempt to engage with the Muslim world on a very different basis to George W. Bush, in a speech in Cairo, Obama had declared that the Arab peoples wanted freedom of the press and greater liberty just as much as other peoples did. When demonstrations brought down the autocratic President of Tunisia and spread to other countries in the region, his political advisers welcomed these manifestations of the 'Arab Spring' and the newfound power of the 'Arab street'.

From January 2011, Hosni Mubarak, President of Egypt for the previous thirty years, was facing massive daily demonstrations in Cairo against the regime, featured nightly on CNN. The initial reaction of Hillary Clinton, still Secretary of State, and of Biden was to praise the stability that Mubarak had brought to the region.

But as it looked increasingly likely that Mubarak's days in power were numbered, Obama's younger and more 'idealistic' advisers on the NSC staff, Samantha Power and Ben Rhodes, a speechwriter who had become deputy national security advisor, wanted him to be seen as on the right side of history, appearing to believe that a regionwide uprising would sweep many of the other conservative Arab leaders away.

This approach was resisted by Gates, Hillary Clinton and Leon Panetta, who regarded themselves as the grown-ups in the room. They questioned whether Power and Rhodes knew anything about Egypt or the Middle East and regarded them as dangerously naive. But when Mubarak tried to damp down the protests by promising reforms, on 1 February Obama telephoned him to say that a transition 'must begin now', precipitating Mubarak's resignation. Obama hailed the demonstrators in Cairo's Tahrir Square as having 'bent the arc of history towards justice'.

The United States' allies in Saudi Arabia, Morocco and the Gulf states were appalled at the abrupt abandonment of a leader who, as Shimon Peres pointed out, had helped to keep peace in the region for the past three decades. Obama was told by Mohamed bin Zayed, de facto ruler of the United Arab Emirates, that his statement 'shows that the United States is not a partner we can rely on'. As Obama himself observed, this was not a plea for help; it was a warning.

For the manner of Mubarak's ouster inflicted lasting damage on America's relationships with all its key allies in the region. The Saudi and Gulf rulers reacted equally badly to the ensuing Iran nuclear deal, lifting US sanctions with no constraints on Iranian attacks on them, which they regarded as demonstrating a clear US 'tilt' towards Iran.

There was, in their view, a failure by Obama and the Western media to understand that what had happened in Cairo was not a spontaneous uprising by would-be Egyptian social democrats but one organised by the Muslim Brotherhood. When Mohamed Morsi became President of Egypt with the Muslim Brotherhood's support, he attempted immediately to give himself extra-constitutional powers. As protests erupted against him, in June 2013 the Egyptian military staged a coup, followed by a fierce crackdown, supported by more moderate religious leaders and, as several political figures put it, by all those who did not want to see their daughters ending up having to wear the chador.

The military takeover by General Abdel al-Sisi was welcomed by the Saudis and Gulf states, all of which regarded the Muslim Brotherhood as a terrorist organisation. Whether it is one or not, it is committed to the enforcement of Sharia law.

Within two years, on the urging of his new Secretary of State, John Kerry, and Defense Secretary, Chuck Hagel, Obama restored financial aid and arms supplies to Egypt, recognised again as a bulwark against extremism in the Middle East.

When, following the turbulence in Egypt, riots broke out among the majority Shia population of Bahrain, base of the US Fifth Fleet, Obama urged King Hamad to act with restraint. Gates and Hillary Clinton were despatched to deliver the same message. But King Abdullah of Saudi Arabia refused to see them. He had expressed directly to Obama his unhappiness at the US treatment of Mubarak. He was not prepared to see the Sunni monarchy in Bahrain overthrown by Shia demonstrators, whom the Saudis regarded as proxies for Iran.

Before Clinton even reached Bahrain, the armed forces of Saudi Arabia and other Gulf states intervened to quell the disturbances. When Obama called him to urge dialogue, King Abdullah said that he would never allow Shia rule in Bahrain: 'Never!'

With Obama back in realist mode, Gates and his national security advisor were despatched for meetings to seek to mend fences with King Abdullah.

The supposed 'tsunami' of the Arab Spring helped to trigger the overthrow of Gaddafi and made a lasting impact in Tunisia, but not elsewhere. Those in Washington who had hoped that the motivation might be a demand for Western-style liberal reforms, rather than revolution and radical Islamism, were left having to wait another generation to find out. The traditional monarchies, led by the House of Saud, had shown more staying power than anticipated. They undertook some measures of liberalisation, but on their own terms and with no intention of losing control.

What had changed, however, was their relationship with the United States. The only world leaders who celebrated when Trump took over from Obama were America's principal allies in the Middle East.

Obama was even more of a realist in his dealings with Israel. He had started with the high ambition of aiming to resolve the Arab–Israeli dispute. The Palestinians were excited to be told that he looked forward one day to welcoming them as members of the UN. He could not stand the Israeli Prime Minister, Benjamin Netanyahu, and he understood that by covering the West Bank and Jerusalem with new Jewish settlements, Netanyahu was bent on rendering a two-state solution impossible. But in the presidential election, Obama had won nearly 80 per cent of the Jewish vote and one third of his funding had come from the American Jewish community.

In Obama's first meeting with Netanyahu, he demanded a complete settlements freeze, securing only a partial and time-limited one. But his memoir, *A Promised Land*, shows him ever conscious of the political power of the pro-Israel lobbying organisations in the US and determined, therefore, to avoid any semblance of a confrontation with Israel. He vetoed a UN resolution declaring the settlements illegal. Having declared that he looked forward to Palestinian membership of the UN, as part of a two-state solution, he opposed any moves towards membership for them meanwhile.

It was not his fault that with Netanyahu in power in Israel and Hamas in control of Gaza, no progress was likely to be able to be made. The number of Israeli settlers on the West Bank was rising towards its present-day level of 450,000, with an additional 220,000 Israelis residing in East Jerusalem. By 2011, Obama had given up on promoting direct negotiations or trying to mediate between the parties. His Middle East negotiator, George Mitchell, quietly resigned.

'GERONIMO'

The search for Osama bin Laden was pursued obsessively by a dedicated CIA team from the time in December 2001 when he escaped through the Tora Bora mountain cave complex in Afghanistan across the border to Pakistan. The assumption was that he remained in Pakistan, with or without the assistance of elements within the ISI. All kinds of leads were pursued fruitlessly, until attention increasingly was focused on a courier with the pseudonym Abu Ahmed al-Kuwaiti. In August 2010 the courier was located in Abbottabad and reported to have visited a compound there with very high walls and other security, less than a mile from the Pakistan Military Academy. It was subjected to covert US surveillance.

The head of US Special Operations, Admiral William McRaven, was informed about the compound in January 2011. Obama was briefed on the options for attacking it at an NSC meeting in March

2011. He ruled out informing the Pakistan authorities. As it was not certain that bin Laden was in the compound, Gates was not sure that a commando raid without the knowledge of the Pakistanis was worth the risk.

At the next NSC meeting later that month, because of the likelihood of collateral damage from an air attack and lack of certainty that bin Laden would be known to have been killed, the idea of a bombing attack was put on hold in favour of a possible helicopter raid.

The raid was rehearsed at locations in the US where a mock-up of the compound had been built. In an NSC meeting on 19 April, Obama gave provisional approval for the raid. The US military were confident that they could reach the target undetected by the Pakistanis, but Obama accepted that they might then have to fight their way out. By 27 April, the Navy SEAL (special forces) team with its helicopters was in position at Jalalabad in Afghanistan, just across the border from Pakistan.

On the following day, the NSC approved the mission, with Biden dissenting ('I would say, "Don't go"'). Gates, having favoured a less risky drone missile strike, swung into support for it too. Having consulted McRaven again, the go-ahead was given at 08.20 Washington time on the 29th.

It then was delayed for twenty-four hours by bad weather, with Obama delivering a relaxed performance that evening at the White House correspondents' dinner, making fun of another guest – Donald Trump.

On 1 May at 3 p.m., Obama and his national security team assembled in the White House to watch the video of the raid, with Leon Panetta, head of the CIA, narrating what was happening.

The Navy SEALs arrived on two Black Hawk helicopters

modified to reduce their radar profile, with much heavier Chinook helicopters waiting in support. As the first helicopter hovered over the compound, its tail scraped the building and it came to rest against the wall, with the other helicopter landing just outside.

The SEALs stormed the building, breaching doors and walls with explosives. The courier was reported to have opened fire; he and his wife and brother were killed. Dodging knots of children on the stairs, on the second floor a SEAL encountered bin Laden, with his fifth wife, Amal, present too, cursing the intruders in Arabic. The SEAL shot bin Laden. Bin Laden's adult son Khalid also was killed.

The SEAL team leader radioed 'Geronimo' then, prompted by McRaven, 'Geronimo EKIA' (enemy killed in action). The raid was accomplished within the planned forty minutes. Three Kalashnikovs were recovered, one of them from bin Laden's room, plus a vast array of computer records, mobile phones, DVDs and a stock of opium.

Bin Laden's body was taken to a US aircraft carrier then, with Islamic funeral rites, was buried at sea. The chairman of the US joint chiefs of staff, Admiral Mullen, called his Pakistani counterpart, General Kayani, after the event, to inform him of the operation.

Obama had taken very big risks in authorising this mission, including accepting that if the SEALs were intercepted in Pakistan, they would have to be helped to fight their way out. He would not have wanted to be accused of having failed to try to dispose of bin Laden on this, the best opportunity to do so. But the raid could have gone badly wrong. The US military and all the other participants were impressed by his calm and decisive handling of this drama. At 11.35 p.m. he told Americans that bin Laden, responsible for the murder of thousands of innocent people, had been killed.

The US was not at war with Islam, but the war against al-Qaeda would continue. 'Justice has been done.'

*　　*　　*

This was the high point of success in Obama's overseas policy. In his second term, some of the tendencies that had caused problems earlier became more pronounced. With Gates and Clinton gone, Obama's senior advisers, John Kerry as Secretary of State and, especially, Chuck Hagel as Defense Secretary, risked being eclipsed as he relied even more on his campaign aides, with whom he felt most 'comfortable'. Ben Rhodes, an excellent speechwriter, was reincarnated as an expert on national security. Denis McDonough, formerly deputy national security advisor, became White House chief of staff.

'A LASTING STAIN ON HIS LEGACY'

Barack Obama, by this time, had developed a marked distaste for the US foreign policy establishment. He found it 'amusing that those who helped to authorize and engineer the biggest foreign policy disaster in our generation' (the Iraq War) should be criticising his policies. Ben Rhodes took to describing them as 'the Blob'. When discussing US involvement in international hot spots, in NSC meetings, Obama's favourite mantra had become 'Don't do stupid shit', by which he meant getting involved militarily in other people's wars.

Hillary Clinton, who had departed to run for President, had remained part of the foreign policy establishment and believed in the US as the 'indispensable nation', acidly observed that 'Don't do stupid shit' was 'not a sufficient guiding principle for the foreign policy of a great country'.

When it came to the civil war in Syria, Obama was determined not to get involved. He regarded it as a matter for the Europeans to deal with, if they wished to try to do so. But in August 2012, under pressure politically and in the media because of the threatened use of chemical weapons by the Syrian regime, Obama declared this would cross a 'red line' that would 'change my calculus' – a clear threat of military intervention.

In August 2013, the news broke of a devastating sarin gas attack, killing over a thousand people, carried out by the Assad regime on the outskirts of Damascus.

Britain and France committed to joining the US in air strikes in response. The entire senior US national security team, Secretary of State John Kerry, Defense Secretary Chuck Hagel, national security advisor Susan Rice, the US military chiefs and UN Ambassador Samantha Power all favoured military action. But Obama decided to consult Angela Merkel, who, given Germany's constitutional resistance to any action of this kind, he must have known would advise against. The White House chief of staff, Denis McDonough, also demurred. Some officials deserve to be remembered for what they did; others for what they didn't do. But McDonough was merely reflecting Obama's desire to back away from this problem.

In London, David Cameron took the unusual step of deciding to seek parliamentary approval before responding. This made no sense, as retaliation in these cases needed to be swift, before the targets disappeared. It also was unprecedented, as hitherto the practice always had been to take action, then justify it to Parliament, not the other way around.

The British government lost the vote, with the Labour leader, Ed Miliband, spearheading the opposition to any response, supported by a number of isolationist Conservatives. It was felt by many to have been a shameful day in the history of the House of Commons.

Obama, who had been hesitating anyway, thereupon decided to consult Congress, knowing, in Leon Panetta's view, that this was 'an almost certain way to scotch any action'. Visiting Moscow, he was told by Putin that Russia would help to solve the problem. Obama hastened to accept the Russian offer to take over and destroy Syria's chemical weapons, depicting this as a masterstroke from the US point of view.

'Terrible things happen across the globe, and it is beyond our means to right every wrong,' he declared, but when they could stop children being gassed, in a crime against humanity by the Syrian regime, 'I believe we should act'. But what he actually had done was to install Russia as, along with Iran, Assad's key military ally, consolidating their hold on Syria, which was important to them as giving Russia permanent access to the Syrian port of Tartus as their Mediterranean naval base.

The outcome, Leon Panetta felt, was a serious blow to America's credibility. 'When the President as Commander in Chief draws a red line, it is critical that he act if the line is crossed … By failing to respond, it sent the wrong message to the world.' Panetta's successor as Defense Secretary, Chuck Hagel, was appalled to be told by Obama on 30 August to cancel the planned retaliatory Tomahawk Cruise missile strike, Obama having, in Hagel's opinion, undermined his own credibility. Hillary Clinton was equally dismayed. François Hollande, President of France at the time, felt that the debacle sent a dangerous message to Putin, contributing to his conviction that he could get away, six months later, with his 2014 invasion of Ukraine, an opinion confirmed by former members of the Putin entourage, including the former Prime Minister, Mikhail Kasyanov.

Obama cannot have believed that Russia actually would destroy all of its ally's chemical weapons. Yet he claimed thereby to have 'solved' the problem, rather than having failed to do so. While a display was made of destroying an array of chemical weapons, the Assad regime continued regular chemical attacks, including with chlorine gas, for the five years thereafter, provoking no response, until Donald Trump retaliated for a brazen chemical attack in April 2018, following which they have stopped, with 'America First' Trump doing what the Nobel Peace Prize winner had failed to do. Obama's UN Ambassador, Samantha Power, concluded that his administration 'could not possibly be proud' of its performance in Syria. *Foreign Policy* magazine concluded that 'Syria will stain Obama's legacy forever'.

* * *

The Crimea, though part of Ukraine, was almost entirely Russian-speaking and contained the key Black Sea Russian naval base of Sebastopol. Putin's protégé Viktor Yanukovych had been elected President of Ukraine in 2010. But in 2013 massive demonstrations broke out against his corrupt, autocratic and pro-Russian rule following Yanukovych's rejection of an association agreement with the European Union in favour of an economic union with Russia. Having tried in vain to repress the revolt, in February 2014 he sought refuge in Russia. His ousting was the trigger for the Russian invasion of Ukraine.

For Putin forthwith invaded and occupied Crimea, then seized part of the industrial Donbas region in eastern Ukraine, provoking, as he had calculated, US and European sanctions in response, but not on a scale that could cripple the Russian economy. The invasion was carried out by Russian troops, in military uniform with the insignia removed, supporting and pretending to be local Russian-speaking secessionists, who proceeded to shoot down a Malaysian civil airliner.

What was most disquieting about all the lies told by the Russian Foreign Minister, Sergey Lavrov, about this incursion was that he must have realised that the Western powers, from the radio communications between Russian special forces and their commanders, knew that he was lying.

Equally concerning was the fact that the Obama administration chose to 'lead from behind'. The US and the Europeans implemented so-called 'scalpel' or targeted sanctions, which had limited effect on Russia and none at all on Putin. There was no appetite within the EU for tougher measures, in part due to the dependence on Russia for gas supplies. The tendency in Washington, as in Europe, was to accept what had happened as a fait accompli. France and Germany turned out subsequently to have continued weapons supplies to Russia despite the arms embargo.

Far from providing any leadership in this crisis, the importance of which it seriously underestimated, the Obama administration decided not to get further involved. It was left to the French and Germans to broker the Minsk agreements, which did result in a ceasefire but left the Russians demanding that the areas of the Donbas which they controlled must have veto powers over the foreign and defence policies of Ukraine. The US thereafter increased the supply of defensive military equipment to Ukraine, continued under Trump. But this was not an issue on which Obama was prepared to see the US leading or acting as the 'indispensable nation'. There was a failure to make clear the costs of further Russian aggression in Ukraine. Nor was any effort made by Donald Trump to do so.

*　　*　　*

The biggest headache by far on the international scene for the Obama administration was the possibility of Iran acquiring nuclear weapons. A civil nuclear programme had been under way in Iran since the 1950s. Western cooperation ceased after the 1979 Iranian revolution, following which Iran continued its nuclear programme on a clandestine basis. In 2003, the International Atomic Energy Agency launched an investigation after Iranian dissidents revealed undeclared nuclear activities being carried out in Iran at Natanz and Arak.

But that being the year in which George W. Bush invaded Iraq, the IAEA subsequently found it to be the moment at which Iran became more cautious about its nuclear programme. It was in October 2003 that the Iranian Supreme Leader, the Ayatollah Ali Khamenei, possibly concerned about potential US military action, posted on his website a fatwa against nuclear weapons, which he followed up by saying in 2010 that the use of weapons of mass destruction was haram (forbidden).

In 2006, the UN Security Council demanded that Iran should suspend all its uranium enrichment and reprocessing programmes. Between 2003 and 2009, Iran acquired several thousand uranium enriching centrifuges. In September 2009, US intelligence discovered the existence of a secret enrichment facility buried in a mountain near Qom. In 2011, the IAEA reported deep and growing concern about a possible military nuclear programme. While believing that, after 2003, Iran was engaging primarily in nuclear weapons research, the IAEA consistently stated that it was unable to conclude that Iran's nuclear programme was entirely peaceful. In 2010, the UN Security Council reinforced sanctions against Iran for continuing reprocessing and ballistic missile development.

Attempts to negotiate a nuclear agreement with Iran were led primarily not by the US but on behalf of the P5 group of countries, consisting of the five permanent members of the UN Security Council – the US, China, Russia, Britain and France – plus Germany. Medvedev was cooperating in the effort to contain Iran's nuclear ambitions. To keep the Russians happy, it was proposed that a large amount of Iran's uranium should be processed in Russia back to low grade.

The talks got nowhere until the election in 2013 of the moderate Hassan Rouhani as President of Iran. Rouhani was determined to secure relief from US and European sanctions, which were inflicting serious damage on the Iranian economy.

In August 2015, an agreement was reached with Iran, subject to verification by IAEA inspectors, in exchange for the lifting of economic sanctions. It reduced Iran's uranium stockpile and stock of centrifuges and placed limits on Iran's capabilities to enrich uranium, which was supposed to remain below 3.67 per cent. Obama said that the agreement, if implemented, 'will prevent Iran from obtaining a nuclear weapon'. It was claimed to have extended Iran's 'breakout time', i.e. the time it would take Iran to develop a nuclear weapon if it abandoned the agreement, to one year.

Iran asserted immediately that the agreement did not include any limitation on its development of ballistic missiles or arms supplies to its clients in the region – Hamas, Hezbollah, Iranian militias in Iraq, Syria and the Houthi rebels in Yemen. Far from suspending, Iran accelerated its ballistic missile programmes.

As the only way of preventing Iran becoming a nuclear power otherwise was likely to entail military action, the agreement received a near universal international welcome. It caused a major rift with the United States' traditional allies in the Middle East, as US sanctions were lifted against Iran in the absence of any undertakings that Iran would cease sponsoring attacks on Saudi Arabia and the United Arab Emirates. With the Republicans, who had won the midterm elections, and some Democrats opposed to the agreement, there was no majority for it in Congress and Obama had to scramble to get the thirty-four votes (out of 100) needed for a blocking minority to prevent it being overturned in the Senate.

OBAMA AND ISIS

The Islamic State of Iraq and Syria (ISIS) was founded by al-Zarqawi, with support from sections of the Sunni population in both countries. Asked about ISIS on 7 January 2014, Obama was dismissive about the threat posed by the militant Islamist group, comparing them to a 'junior varsity team', even though by this time ISIS had captured Fallujah. He did not want to have to send US forces back to Iraq to help deal with them.

This complacency was shattered by the capture by ISIS in June 2014 of Mosul, the second largest city in Iraq, vastly increasing their power base and financial resources. Obama turned down pleas from Prime Minister al-Maliki for air strikes against ISIS in the process of seizing Mosul. ISIS started posting videos of the beheading of hostages, including that in August 2014 of the American journalist James Foley, following an unsuccessful US attempt to rescue him.

In August, the administration decided to use air strikes limited to defending US personnel in Kurdish territory in northern Iraq, to protect the US consulate there. In September, Obama announced a shift to more general air strikes against ISIS, including against targets in Syria. The administration, however, did not want to get much more heavily involved, until al-Maliki, who was detested by the Sunni population, was replaced by a less divisive figure, Haider al-Abadi.

In February 2015, Chuck Hagel resigned as Defense Secretary. Dismayed by the fiasco over the 'red line' in Syria, he was frustrated at White House attempts to micro-manage defence policy. Pressing for a more effective policy against ISIS in Iraq and Syria, he had found Obama ready to authorise air and drone strikes but highly allergic to any US boots on the ground. So the military were unable to deploy special forces and forward air controllers, which would have rendered the air campaign more effective. Obama had eagerly embraced drone strikes, even more so than George W. Bush, as an antiseptic form of warfare, with no risk of US casualties. He did not want the US to be drawn into a new ground war.

Though numerous more air strikes were authorised, by the end of the Obama presidency in January 2017 there still was no plan to attempt to dislodge ISIS from their strongholds in Mosul and Raqqa in Syria.

THE TRANS-PACIFIC PARTNERSHIP

Like Clinton, who had secured congressional approval for NAFTA, Obama was a believer in freer trade. As the centrepiece of his and Hillary Clinton's 'pivot to Asia', in 2016 he committed the US to join the Trans-Pacific Partnership with eleven other countries in Asia-Pacific, including Canada and Australia but excluding, and to some degree aimed against, China.

The agreement was never ratified by Congress, as, although it removed obstacles to US exports to Asia, both Republicans and some Democrats feared that, after NAFTA, it would lead to an outsourcing of more US jobs. On taking office in 2017, Donald Trump withdrew the US from the agreement, which then was finalised under a new name by the other participants without American participation.

Obama's achievements in domestic policy were far more striking than any in overseas policy. Some of his own key advisers came to worry about his tendency to believe that as much could be achieved by words as by deeds. Yet he and the US military succeeded in wrestling with his major headache on taking office, the conflict in Afghanistan, where US force levels were down to a few thousand troops at the end of his term. 'No-drama Obama' would never have wanted to preside over a chaotic withdrawal of the kind that took place under Biden. Relations with the European allies were improved, but traditional US allies in the Arab world were alienated. He deserved full credit for authorising the extremely risky raid that killed bin Laden. The nuclear agreement with Iran, though flawed, was better than no agreement.

But the failure to uphold his 'red line' in Syria was damaging not only to his reputation but also vis-à-vis Putin. It was the fault of the Europeans, but also that of Obama, that the reactions to Putin's first invasion of Ukraine were so muted, with the Germans insisting on pressing ahead with the Nord Stream 2 pipeline even though this was bound to increase their already high dependence on Russian gas. But there was no display of American leadership either.

Obama subscribed to the vision of a world order based on free markets, democracy and human rights, underpinned by American influence. But he wanted that influence to be exerted rhetorically and by 'soft' rather than hard power (except for drone strikes).

George H. W. Bush liked Obama and admired his soaring rhetoric about an integrated society, overcoming racial differences. But Obama meant it when he said that he was opposed to the idea of America being regarded any longer as the 'indispensable nation' in dealing with world crises, and that retreat and its consequences were felt in Syria and Ukraine.

CHAPTER FIFTEEN

'AMERICA FIRST'

Donald Trump ran for office as a disrupter and governed as a disrupter. In doing so, he made no appeal to centrist voters. His appeal was to mainly white American voters revolting against the direction in which the country was heading. Against Hillary Clinton, he won in every category of white voters, regardless of income or educational qualifications.

In the primaries, he was successful in pillorying his more moderate competitors as Republicans in name only (RINOs). In the presidential election, George H. W. Bush voted for Hillary. George W. Bush did not vote for Trump either. John McCain and Mitt Romney, who eight and four years before had lost narrowly to Obama, were demeaned and insulted by him, and so was Jeb Bush.

Barbara Bush had not wanted Jeb to run for President, feeling that this made it look as if the Bush family thought they had some sort of blue-blooded right to govern. She also felt, correctly, that Jeb was too well mannered and gentlemanly to win a brawl with Trump. When Jeb declared that his mother was the strongest person he knew, Trump replied that she should have been running for President, rather than him. Apart from his, to them, appalling personality, Trump's belief never was in Republican orthodoxy – free trade and fiscal discipline – but in a populist version of the opposite.

In the front row, listening to Trump's inauguration speech, George W. Bush turned to his neighbour, Barack Obama. 'That was some weird shit,' he said. Barbara Bush declared that she was no longer part of the Republican Party.

Isolationism and protectionism are recessive genes in the US body politic, brought back to the surface by Trump, aided by the fact that there had been a large-scale outsourcing of formerly US blue-collar jobs. Car manufacturers took advantage of lower-cost production in Mexico. Consumer goods were made more cheaply in China. The US steel industry was a small fraction of its former size. Many US enterprises exploited the increased export opportunities due to globalisation, and American consumers also benefited. Highly skilled workers flourished in the technology sector. But in the manufacturing industries, a large number of others found their job opportunities and wages squeezed by cheaper production from overseas. Americans were ceasing to believe that their country was on the right track or that they would be better off than their forebears. An increasing number would agree, in the words of Yogi Berra, that 'the future ain't what it used to be'.

Of his economic policies, leaders of the US business community at the time tended to say that they did not like Trump's ego-driven pronouncements but they liked what he did, by which they meant lower individual and corporate taxes and less regulation. Trump was unconcerned about a ballooning budget deficit, which reached over $1 trillion in 2019. This, plus the close to zero borrowing rates maintained by the Federal Reserve Board, resulted in a US economy on steroids, with growth over 2 per cent per annum in his first three years and unemployment down to 3.5 per cent in 2019. This trajectory then was brutally reversed by the Covid pandemic, but for which he might well have been re-elected.

Trump's rhetorical excesses in the election campaign helped to ensure that much of the Republican foreign policy establishment were loath to work for him. The challenges of actually doing so proved insurmountable for most of his overseas policy advisers, who came and went through a rapidly revolving door. He prided himself on refusing to read briefing papers before important meetings and despised diplomacy, while hailing his own supposedly unparalleled negotiating skills. His public offer to 'buy Greenland' was greeted with incredulity by the Prime Minister of Denmark. In his pronouncements and a deluge of tweets, he continued, as in the campaign, to be belligerent, bullying, impatient, irresponsible and self-obsessed. There was, in the view of his Republican critics, no real commitment to the maintenance of the post-war liberal world order underpinned by the United States.

The traditionally good relations between Republican Presidents and the US military did not apply with Trump. He increased defence spending, but falling out with General Mattis, who was admired by his military colleagues, was damaging to him. The chairman of the joint chiefs of staff, General Mark Milley, felt obliged to warn his colleagues about the possibilities of extra-constitutional action by Trump when he lost his bid for re-election. He and the other military commanders were appalled by the 6 January 2021 attack on the Capitol encouraged by the President.

Trump's foreign policy was marked by his sense of grievance that, in his view, the United States was being taken advantage of not only by rivals like China but also by its allies, such as Germany, who relied on US protection while contributing little to their own defence. To this, there were added his personality traits of impulsiveness, unpredictability and belief in his erratic personal diplomacy. He was convinced that he was uniquely qualified to deal with tough, authoritarian leaders, lauding his personal relationships with Kim Jong-un of North Korea and President Xi of China, before berating them for failing to meet his expectations.

President Macron of France flattered Trump by inviting him to the 14 July parade in Paris, but they soon fell out thereafter. He remained constant in his distaste for Angela Merkel in Germany, as she did in hers for him. His erratic pronouncements, bluster and vanity led most Europeans to wonder how such a personality could have become President of the United States.

Trump never denounced Putin, for whom he kept professing admiration, claiming to have formed a 'bond' with him and that they would have a 'great relationship'. In 2017, he met Putin in Germany, then in July 2018 in Helsinki. In all, they met only five times, with interpreters only and with little disclosure of what was said. After the Helsinki meeting, Trump expressed scepticism about stories of attempted Russian interference in the US elections. The Mueller Inquiry cleared the Trump campaign of collusion with the Russians, and allegations by a former member of MI6 that Trump had been compromised on a visit to Moscow were discredited. But the unanimous view of the US intelligence agencies was that the Russians had made efforts to interfere in the US electoral process, just as they did in many other countries. In November 2018, a planned meeting between Trump and Putin at a conference in Buenos Aires was cancelled by the US side because of Russia's seizure of Ukrainian sailors and naval ships in the Sea of Azov.

While their exchanges were friendly, Trump never proved able to achieve much with Putin, though nor did Putin with him. The Russians did not believe that Trump would be able to roll back the sanctions imposed on Russia following their 2014 invasion of Ukraine because of congressional resistance and nor did Trump attempt to do so. Instead, while continuing to stress the importance of trying to 'get along with Putin', he increased US military aid to Ukraine.

He did so despite the disgraceful episode in 2019 when, in a telephone call to President Zelensky, Trump appeared to threaten that $400 million in American security aid might be withheld unless Zelensky helped to provide adverse information about Hunter Biden – who, very questionably, had been permitted by his father to accept a post with a Ukrainian energy company – as well as information about pressure from Biden in the Obama administration to remove a Ukrainian prosecutor who was failing to investigate corruption.

CRUSHING THE 'ISLAMIC STATE'

Though, under Obama, the US had responded to the threat posed by ISIS with drone and air strikes, supplying weapons to the Kurdish forces and offering additional training to Iraqi forces and winning back some territory, at the end of Obama's presidency, it could not yet be regarded as winning the war against ISIS. For at that point, ISIS remained in control of Mosul, Raqqa in Syria and vast areas of both countries.

Far more decisive results against ISIS were achieved when General James Mattis took over the campaign against them as Defense Secretary in the Trump administration, a key difference being the more effective deployment of US special forces and forward air controllers to assist the Kurdish and Iraqi ground forces, superseding Obama's concern to avoid the risk of casualties and any appearance of US ground forces being involved again in combat in Iraq.

In the ferocious street-by-street battles in Mosul, forward air controllers in the front lines proved indispensable in calling in very close-quarter US air strikes which had a decisive effect. By July 2017, Mosul had been liberated. The defeat of ISIS in its stronghold of Raqqa by the Kurdish Syrian Democratic Forces supported by US air strikes followed in October and by year end the ISIS 'caliphate' no longer controlled more than slivers of territory in Iraq and Syria.

Thanks to General Mattis, therefore, Trump could claim to have prosecuted the war against ISIS more effectively and decisively than Obama. But in another shameful episode, Trump then proceeded to show how unqualified he was to be Commander in Chief. In November 2018, he promised President Recep Erdoğan of Turkey, strongly hostile to the Kurds, that the US would cut off all military support to the Kurds in Syria, who had been America's key allies in defeating ISIS there. Mattis, not prepared to be complicit in US allies being abandoned in this way, resigned as Trump's Defense Secretary. The Pentagon subsequently contrived to continue some support for the Kurds.

In October 2019, the sinister Abu Bakr al-Baghdadi, leader ('caliph') of the Islamic State in Syria and Iraq, blew himself up during a raid by US commandos in the last remaining strip of territory controlled by ISIS in Syria.

* * *

Trump became the first Western leader to challenge head-on the unbalanced economic relationship with China, though most of the others have headed in the same direction since. For when China joined the World Trade Organization in 1999, no attempt was made to ensure that Western investors in China had anything like the same rights and opportunities as their Chinese counterparts. Nor were there any effective measures against massive subsidisation, technology theft and forced technology transfer, plus currency manipulation. The negative US trade deficit in goods with China went from $29 billion in 2000 to $419 billion in 2018. The overall US trade deficit in goods reached a record $916 billion in that year.

Proclaiming that 'I am a tariff man' and that 'trade wars are good and easy to win', Trump imposed high new tariffs on solar panels, steel and aluminium, aimed especially, but not only, against China. By 2019, Trump was paying $29 billion in subsidies to US farmers, around one third of total farm income. China was pressurised into undertaking to buy more US farm products, but its purchases fell well below what had been promised. China undertook to buy $200 billion more from the US in goods and services by 2021 than it had in 2017 but fell a long way short of doing so, leading Biden to keep the Trump tariffs in place.

Trump viewed China as the pre-eminent threat to US dominance, given the power of the state-owned enterprises, far lower environmental and labour standards, a rapid increase in military spending, expertise in cyber attacks and an increasingly aggressive attitude towards Taiwan and in the South China Sea. In this respect too, many other countries increasingly have been expressing the same concerns. He also blamed the Wuhan laboratory for the pandemic of what he called the 'Kung flu', a theory dismissed by the World Health Organization and many scientists, some with Chinese connections, though the possibility of an accident there cannot be discounted. He coupled this with assertions that he and President Xi Jinping had a 'great relationship', only to find Xi making promises on which China then failed to deliver.

In 2021, China held $1.1 trillion in US Treasury bonds, but the danger of China dramatically reducing its holding was and is slight, not only because US Treasuries continue to be regarded as a safe harbour but also because these purchases are an integral part of China's strategy to hold down the value of the renminbi.

The Trump tariffs increased costs to US consumers and did reduce the trade deficit with China from $419 billion in 2018 to $311 billion in 2020. But the overall US trade deficit in goods and services soared under Trump from $481 billion in 2016 to $679 billion in 2020. Where, however, Trump did succeed was in persuading the US body politic and most of America's allies to adopt a far more sceptical and challenging view of China than they had in the past.

Protectionism has always come with important costs, in terms of serious disruption to supply chains as well as the direct costs to consumers and the likelihood of triggering retaliation. In the near term, Trump won the political argument in favour of protectionist actions, but the US to date has derived little benefit from them.

China also was and is held responsible for repression of the Muslim Uyghur community in Western China and the suppression of democracy in Hong Kong.

What is missing from the present, generally adversarial, relationship is any semblance of the kind of strategic dialogue considered important by George H. W. Bush. This is liable to prove costly at a time when it is important to avoid driving China and Russia more closely together than they are already.

A key element in the prior discussions with the Chinese was how to restrain North Korea, which, having already developed several nuclear weapons, now was aggressively testing into the Pacific over Japan ballistic missiles with steadily increasing ranges, the apparent purpose of which was to develop and test a missile that could reach the West Coast of the US. In 2017, Trump declared that the US was prepared to inflict 'fire and fury' on North Korea if it continued these programmes, but that he was prepared to meet the North Korean leader, Kim Jong-un.

In the following year, Trump held the first ever high-level meeting with Kim Jong-un, in Singapore. The meeting was followed by a joint statement looking for better relations, a suspension of US–South Korea military exercises and possible denuclearisation of the Korean peninsula, leading Trump mysteriously to claim that 'there is no longer a nuclear threat from North Korea'. But 'denuclearisation of the peninsula', to the North Koreans, turned out to mean getting rid of any US nuclear weapons there, but not theirs.

In February 2019, a further summit was held in Vietnam, which failed to make any progress and was cut short due to North Korean insistence that the US should lift all sanctions forthwith, while Trump was boxed in by congressional insistence (and that of his predecessors) that sanctions would not be lifted without North Korea getting rid entirely of its nuclear weapons.

This it was extremely unlikely to agree to do, as it feared being subjected to a 'Gaddafi-style solution' being advocated by Trump's national security advisor, John Bolton, who was fired for also advocating a war with Iran. In June 2019, in a grandstanding performance, Trump crossed the De-Militarised Zone between the two Koreas, entering North Korea briefly in the company of Kim Jong-un, following which talks were resumed, again resulting only in deadlock and North Korea resuming missile testing.

* * *

In the US presidential campaign, Trump promised to build a high wall all along the 1,900-mile border with Mexico and, however improbably, that Mexico would pay for this. With 12 million illegal migrants estimated to be in the US, there was wide public support for tougher immigration policies, particularly on the southern border, though general scepticism about the feasibility, cost and efficacy of his proposed wall. Numerous measures were introduced to tighten immigration rules and reduce the acceptance of refugees. Most dramatic was the suspension of entry for several months for citizens of several predominantly Muslim countries. Subsequently, however, a majority of Americans have been dissatisfied with the laxer immigration policies pursued by the Biden administration, with chaotic scenes on the southern border.

Trump forthwith withdrew the US from the planned Trans-Pacific Partnership and launched an attack on the North American Free Trade Agreement, which he held responsible for a loss of American jobs, particularly in the automobile sector, to low-cost manufacturers in Mexico. As President, Trump negotiated with Mexico and Canada a revised version of NAFTA called the US–Mexico–Canada Agreement (USMCA), incorporating some additional protections for the US workforce, though the outcome preserved most of the benefits of the abolition of most of the barriers to trade and investment between the participants.

'NATO *IS* IMPORTANT AND THE RUSSIANS ARE *NOT* OUR FRIENDS'

Trump came into office questioning the value of NATO on the grounds that the US was devoting a far higher percentage of its gross domestic product to defence, while the contribution of Germany, which it was defending, was barely 1 per cent, and adoption of the euro, a much weaker currency than the Deutschmark, had helped Germany to achieve a massive trade surplus with the US.

But NATO had bipartisan support in Congress and the Republican Senate majority leader, Mitch McConnell, appeared on the steps of the Capitol to declare, 'NATO *is* important and the Russians are *not* our friends!'

Trump's warning about the weakness of European defence spending did bear some fruit, helped by increasingly aggressive Russian behaviour. When Trump attended the NATO summit in London in 2019, the NATO Secretary General, Jens Stoltenberg, congratulated him on the fact that the other NATO countries had committed to spending an additional $100 billion on defence, albeit with Germany continuing to lag a long way behind until the further Russian invasion of Ukraine triggered a large planned increase in the German defence budget.

Trump and the German Chancellor, Angela Merkel, notoriously did not get on. She found him bombastic; he resented the large German trade surplus. The other main bone of contention, not only with Trump but with every US administration, was German insistence on financing and completing the $12 billion Nord Stream 2 gas pipeline from Russia, the purpose of which, from Putin's point of view, was to bypass Ukraine and render Germany more than ever dependent on imports of Russian gas. This was a subject on which Trump and other US administrations were right and Angela Merkel emphatically wrong.

Nor was there any rapport with the aloof President of France, Emmanuel Macron, whom Trump called 'very, very nasty' for criticising the withdrawal of American troops from Syria. They fell out over US steel tariffs, French protectionism and Trump's threatened retaliation for France taxing US digital companies, plus not very realistic French plans for European defence separate from NATO. In November 2018, Macron, having described NATO as 'brain dead', declared that Europe must develop its own military capability to defend itself against Russia, China 'and even the United States'. Among the many justly derided statements of Donald Trump, it is difficult to find one much sillier than this. Apart from infuriating the Americans, the idea of Europe being able to defend itself without the US was dismissed by the German Defence Minister and all the East Europeans.

Trump did not have much time for the British Prime Minister, Theresa May, whom he regarded as weak. An ardent supporter of Britain detaching itself from the European Union, his favourite European leader was Boris Johnson, whom he regarded as a kindred spirit. He welcomed him enthusiastically when he became Prime Minister, describing him as a 'fantastic leader of the United Kingdom' and expressing support for a US–UK free trade agreement, causing Johnson initially to be regarded sceptically by Biden and his team when Trump lost the presidential election.

Trump rejected the scientific consensus on global warming, claiming that it was invented by the Chinese to penalise American industry. In the presidential election campaign, he promised to revitalise the US coal industry and to protect the US oil and gas industries. On taking office, in June 2017 he withdrew the US from the 2015 Paris Agreement on mitigating climate change, contending that the agreement would put the US economy at a 'permanent disadvantage' to countries like China and India, who were accepting no limits on their emissions, which, in the case of China, by this time were twice those of the US. It took three years to withdraw from the agreement and, helped by greater efficiencies in American industry, US emissions continued to fall during the Trump presidency. While Trump denied climate change, the Pentagon and US intelligence agencies continued to believe in it, as they made clear in their reports.

On his election, in February 2021 Biden signed immediately an executive order for the US to re-join the agreement, reinstating the $3 billion Obama had pledged towards the fund to help developing nations adapt. This was done by executive order to avoid problems in the Senate with those in both parties who wanted China and India to be bound also by some constraints on their emissions.

Most Americans support action to mitigate climate change, and large swathes of US industry, including the car manufacturers, have been adjusting to new limits on emissions. At the 2021 Glasgow climate change conference, Biden and his special envoy John Kerry promised to reduce US emissions by 50 per cent below 2005 levels by 2030. In the US, as elsewhere, energy consumers are not going to find it easy to accept the costs of achieving this worthwhile goal. Henceforth, it is going to be very difficult to persuade the US to agree to further binding targets unless China and India also can be prevailed on to do so.

*　　*　　*

The most dramatic move made by Trump in foreign policy was his decision in May 2018 to withdraw the US from the nuclear agreement with Iran, asserting that the 'horribly one-sided' deal placed, supposedly, only 'very weak' limits on Iran's nuclear activity and failed to deal with its ballistic missile programme, the funding of its 'terrorist proxies' Hezbollah and Hamas and subversion in Iraq and Yemen. His decision was deplored by the European allies, fearful that it would leave military action as the only alternative way to stop Iran developing a military nuclear capability.

On coming into office in 2017, the Trump administration had certified Iran's compliance with the agreement. But in the election campaign, he had criticised the agreement and the lifting of sanctions against Iran. Early in 2018, Israel released 100,000 files acquired by Mossad from Iran's secret nuclear archives. These revealed that Iran had lied about never having had a nuclear weapons programme, that the Fordow enrichment plant was a key component of it and that Iran was continuing nuclear weapons research. Israel had launched cyber attacks against Iranian nuclear institutions and in 2020 assassinated Iran's leading nuclear scientist.

There never had been a majority in Congress for the agreement, which was one-sided, as the US was required to lift sanctions while Iran was left free to continue its attacks on US allies in the Middle East – the United Arab Emirates and Saudi Arabia – both directly and via the Iranian-controlled Houthi rebels in Yemen, whom it had equipped with drones.

Nor was there any constraint on Iran continuing its efforts to kill US personnel in Iraq through attacks by the Iranian-backed militias there or on Iran supplying improvised electronic devices (roadside bombs) to the Taliban in Afghanistan. There followed a series of Iranian-sponsored attacks on the Ain al-Asad air base and Erbil airport in Iraq and on the al-Omar oil field and the al-Tanf base in Syria, aimed at the US personnel there. The agreement also did not prevent Iran from continuing to test ballistic missiles with a range sufficient to reach Israel.

Nevertheless, it did place constraints on the Iranian nuclear programme and reintroduced IAEA inspectors. Cancelling it increased the likelihood of military action, at any rate by Israel, becoming necessary at some point to prevent Iran becoming a military nuclear power.

In January 2020, Trump authorised a drone strike to kill General Qassem Soleimani, head of the Quds Force – the external wing of Iran's Islamic Revolutionary Guard Corps. As controller of the relationships with Syria, Hamas, Hezbollah, the Houthis in Yemen and the Iranian militias in Iraq, Soleimani was responsible for the campaign of destruction, destabilisation and inflammation of sectarian tensions aimed by Iran at asserting its dominance in the region. The Pentagon declared that the strike was ordered because Soleimani was 'actively developing plans' to attack US troops and officials.

Following the withdrawal of the US from the nuclear agreement, as predicted by Trump's critics, Iran rapidly accelerated its enrichment of uranium to 60 per cent, within reach of weapons grade, reducing the 'breakout time' it would take Iran to produce a nuclear weapon.

While the Trump presidency strained relations with the European allies, especially Germany, it re-established close relations with America's traditional allies in the Middle East. The US embassy in Israel was moved from Tel Aviv to Jerusalem. The Saudis and Gulf states were relieved by Trump's reversal of the perceived 'tilt' of Obama towards Iran. US diplomacy in the Middle East was spearheaded not by the State Department but by Trump's son-in-law, Jared Kushner. The traditional Arab leaders' dismay at Gaza now being under the control of Hamas, allied with Iran, led them no longer to give such priority to the Palestinian cause. In 2020, the United Arab Emirates, Morocco, Bahrain and Sudan followed Egypt and Jordan in normalising relations with Israel, with an especially close relationship developing with the UAE.

A BOTCHED NEGOTIATION WITH THE TALIBAN

The most toxic overseas legacy of Donald Trump was his agreement with the Taliban in Afghanistan. By the time he took office, the number of US troops in Afghanistan was down to 8,500, engaged mainly in training the Afghan forces, with further reductions thereafter. The combat role had been ended under Obama. General Mattis warned against a 'hasty withdrawal', but in 2019 Trump authorised his negotiator, Zalmay Khalilzad, himself of Afghan origin, to reach with the Taliban an agreement based on the withdrawal of US forces and no attacks on them meanwhile by the Taliban. The negotiation took place with no effective consultation with and no participation by the Afghan government and while the Taliban were continuing to launch full-scale attacks, including suicide bombings in Kabul.

In February 2020, Khalilzad signed an agreement with the Taliban in Qatar whereby all US and coalition forces would leave Afghanistan by May 2021; in exchange, the Taliban agreed not to let Afghanistan again become a haven for terrorists and to stop attacking US troops.

The Taliban also agreed to start peace talks with the Afghan government and to consider a ceasefire, promises they had no intention whatever of keeping. One of Khalilzad's numerous critics concluded that he was 'either delusional or cynical' in believing or pretending to believe that the Taliban would ever enter into genuine negotiations with the Afghan government, but he was influenced by the knowledge that Trump wanted to get out.

Trump shares the blame for the ensuing fiasco, though the primary responsibility rests squarely with Biden. The head of US Central Command, General Frank McKenzie, testified that the collapse of the Afghan forces' morale began when Trump agreed with the Taliban on the total withdrawal of US forces.

Some of the worst fears about Trump were not realised. He authorised General Mattis to crush the Islamic State and approved the killing of General Soleimani, but otherwise proved cautious about the use of military force. He had raised internationally a series of issues on which he had a point, which he then tested, at any rate oratorically, close to destruction. It was true that globalisation had resulted in a loss of American blue-collar jobs and/or a stagnation of wages. But his protectionist policies achieved very little. He was right to argue that the world needed to be tougher in dealing with China's trade policies, and other Western leaders followed to some degree in his wake, but he made no attempt to organise multilateral action to deal with this issue. He ignored science in his attitude to climate change. He was right that the allies were not doing enough for their own defence and to point out the dangers of increasing German dependence on Russian gas.

The agreement with Iran was indeed flawed in that US sanctions were lifted with no constraints on Iran attacking American allies, but he ignored the genuine constraints it placed on the Iranian nuclear programme. He was largely right about the futility of nation building in far-away countries with vastly different histories and societies but botched his negotiation to withdraw from Afghanistan.

Mark Esper, who succeeded General Mattis as Trump's Defense Secretary, described Trump as persistently wanting to withdraw all 28,500 US forces in South Korea, despite the threat from North Korea, because South Korea had a large trade surplus with the US and was not paying enough for their upkeep. (They did then increase their over $1 billion contribution a bit.) He abruptly ordered the withdrawal of 12,000 of the 34,000 US troops in Germany because of annoyance at the German refusal to cancel the Nord Stream 2 gas pipeline. Some were re-deployed to Poland.

Trump, at one point, wanted the army to send 250,000 men to guard the border with Mexico. He also wanted army involvement in dealing with the sometimes violent demonstrations associated with the Black Lives Matter movement, despite being told repeatedly that this was a matter for the National Guard. Esper was dismissed by Trump immediately after he lost the presidential election, presumably because Trump did not trust him to help contest the result.

More reassuring was the extent to which the system worked, in pushing back against Trump's demands. General Mattis resigned on a question of principle, but the Pentagon contrived not to cut off liaison with the Kurdish allies or to withdraw all US personnel with them in Syria. With Trump contesting the outcome of the presidential election, after the rioting at the Capitol, General Milley, chairman of the joint chiefs of staff, took care to ensure that the US military would not undertake any action not approved by the full chain of command. In his memoir, Esper concluded that Trump was not fit to serve as President because he was incapable of putting the interests of the country before his own interests.

Most commentaries on the Trump presidency describe it as 'America in retreat', which indeed it was, in particular in Afghanistan. But that did not apply to the Islamic State, dealt with more effectively by General Mattis than under Obama. And America, of Obama's own volition, was in deliberate retreat in his presidency, with his explicit disavowal of the notion of the 'indispensable nation'. Commentators on both the left and right in America noted the shared inclination of both Trump and Obama to limit the United States' role in the world. But words matter, not least in foreign policy. From that perspective, Obama was a far more acceptable spokesman for America than Trump vis-à-vis America's friends and allies, with the important exception of the traditional allies in the Middle East.

Trump did not end up undermining NATO. Nor did he make concessions to Putin. John Bolton was fired by him as national security advisor for being too bellicose. But withdrawal from the Iran and climate change agreements were major breaks with the international consensus and key partners. His protectionist policies were not successful but have endured under Biden. It was not his foreign policy but his personal style that proved fatal in the end to his re-election prospects.

CHAPTER SIXTEEN

'WE ARE NOT GOING TO DEFEND UKRAINE'

Joe Biden was chosen to be Obama's Vice-President in part because of his experience in foreign policy. In his 36-year tenure in the Senate, he served on the Foreign Relations Committee for decades, with two stints as its chairman. His expertise and judgement were not uncontested, as he voted against the war to liberate Kuwait but for the invasion of Iraq. Robert Gates, the respected former Defense Secretary under both George W. Bush and Obama, described Biden as having, in his opinion, 'been wrong on nearly every major foreign policy and national security issue over the past four decades'.

Biden also was famous for his gaffe-prone tendencies. Running against Obama in the Democratic primary election, he described his opponent as 'the first mainstream African American who is articulate and bright and clean and a nice-looking guy'. In the Democratic primaries to run for President against Donald Trump in the 2020 election, he struggled initially but benefited from the support of the black caucus, given his commitment to black American causes for many years. Above all, he owed the nomination to the polls showing that 'regular guy' Joe Biden could defeat Trump and more left-wing Democratic candidates could not.

Biden's key asset has been his likeability. He presented himself to the US electorate as the antithesis of the ego-driven Trump, and a moderate Democrat who would try to govern in a more bipartisan way, enabling him to defeat Trump by 7 million votes.

But in contrast to Clinton, who declared that 'the era of big government is over', Biden adopted the economic programme of the 'progressive' wing of the party. He was able to pass a badly needed bipartisan $1 trillion bill to revive America's flagging infrastructure, plus large-scale additional funding for the US electronic chip industry and for green energy. But his plans to spend a further $3.75 trillion on mainly social programmes were blocked by two of his own Senators.

EXITING AFGHANISTAN

In overseas affairs, he came into office contending that he would restore relations with America's allies, damaged under Trump. But in the hasty, botched withdrawal from Afghanistan, he did the opposite. There was no real consultation with any of the allies that had been helping the US in Afghanistan, none of whom supported an abrupt total withdrawal. The same applied to the US military. At the time, Biden claimed that there was no advice from the military against full US withdrawal in August 2021. Every senior US military commander subsequently testified in Congress that this was not the case.

Also untrue was Biden's contention that he had no option but to honour Trump's withdrawal agreement. In contravention of that agreement, the Taliban never severed or disavowed their relationship with al-Qaeda. The Interior Minister and No. 2 figure in the Taliban government today, Sirajuddin Haqqani, with a $10 million price on his head for his terrorist activities, including attacking the US embassy and bombing the Serena Hotel in Kabul, plus attempting to assassinate Hamid Karzai, was regarded as de facto leader of al-Qaeda in Afghanistan. In July 2022, bin Laden's deputy, Ayman al-Zawahiri, was found residing in the Taliban's VIP zone in Kabul and killed in a US drone strike. Also in contravention of the agreement, the Taliban rejected any negotiation with the Afghan government. There were good reasons, therefore, for the US not to follow through on the agreement until the Taliban did so. But Biden's objective was simply to get out.

The manner of the US exit then was handled as badly as it could possibly have been. It was decided to proceed at the height of the summer fighting season, amidst full-scale Taliban attacks across Afghanistan. The first step was to vacate overnight, without telling the Afghan forces, the crucial main US base at the Bagram airfield – a fatal blow to their morale – as they forthwith faced the loss of any US military help or logistic support. Chaotic scenes ensued, with the evacuation of as many as possible Afghans who had served with the US and coalition forces but, inevitably, a far larger number being left behind. Also left behind for the Taliban were $7 billion worth of US military equipment.

The bungled exit was celebrated by every jihadist on the planet. The Russians also withdrew from Afghanistan but, helped by geography, were able to take their equipment with them. Putin, a great believer in the power of the will, is reported to have concluded that Biden was weak, with consequences that have been playing out in Ukraine. Within the United States, those who were convinced that most Americans did not care about Afghanistan since have discovered that they do care about humiliation and a fiasco to which Trump contributed but from which Biden is still suffering.

THE TRIUMPH OF PROTECTIONISM

The United States used to be the leading world advocate of free or at any rate freer trade, believing that its industries would benefit from increased export opportunities, as many of them have done. This was a passion for George H. W. Bush, originator of the North American Free Trade Agreement. Bill Clinton and Obama both were free traders, as was Hillary Clinton, along with most post-war Republican leaders up to Donald Trump. But Obama found himself obliged to be extremely cautious about joining the Trans-Pacific Partnership (TPP). Hillary, as Secretary of State, campaigned vigorously for US membership, only to end up having to drop that cause in her campaign against Trump.

Biden, who is beholden to the large Democratic trade unions, has proved every bit as protectionist as Trump. He has maintained most of the Trump tariffs against China and has no interest in re-joining the TPP or in pursuing any other trade agreements, including with the UK. Unlike Bill Clinton, who took the US into NAFTA, and Obama, who wanted to join the TPP, the Biden administration does not have a trade policy, as it does not want to have to face the potential political fallout from having one. Until the United States recovers its interest in freer trade, there is going to be a damaging absence of leadership in world economic affairs.

ISRAEL AND THE SAUDIS

In July 2022, during a visit to Israel, in an effort to reassure the Israelis, who remained deeply sceptical about US efforts to revive the nuclear agreement with Iran, Biden declared that, if necessary, the US was prepared to use force to prevent the Iranians acquiring nuclear weapons, though only as a last resort.

In the course of the visit, he compared the plight of the Palestinians to Britain's 'attitude to Irish Catholics for four hundred years'. Biden's antecedents are as much English as Irish, but it is the Irish who have an organised political lobby in the United States.

During his presidential election campaign, Biden declared that the murder of the Saudi dissident Jamal Khashoggi, attributed by the US intelligence agencies to the de facto ruler, Mohammed bin Salman (MBS), showed that Saudi Arabia should be treated as a 'pariah'. Initially, he attempted to communicate with the ageing and ill King Salman, only to find that he had handed over all executive power. The Saudis and the United Arab Emirates regarded Biden as bent on reviving the nuclear agreement with Iran, with no protection for Saudi Arabia and the Gulf allies against continuing Iranian attacks. As the former Saudi head of intelligence and Ambassador to the US Prince Turki bin Faisal observed, the relationship was no longer one of trust.

When Biden wanted to urge the Saudis and United Arab Emirates to increase production to help reduce oil prices, they showed no interest in taking his calls. The US military sought to use their defence contacts to mitigate the lack of trust at the political level. Neither the Saudis nor the UAE joined in condemning the Russian invasion of Ukraine.

An attempted fence-building visit by Biden eventually was made in July 2022, with the President engaging in a 'fist bump' rather than a handshake with MBS and declaring that his main purpose was rather to meet the leaders of the Gulf Cooperation Council. This did not restore much warmth to the relationship but was intended to avoid further alienation, with the Saudis just as concerned as the Israelis that, in the last resort, the US should be prepared to use force against Iran.

'WE WILL DEFEND TAIWAN'

In March 2022, Joe Biden surprised many of his own advisers by declaring publicly that the United States would defend Taiwan if it were attacked by China. Hitherto, in accordance with the 'One China' policy, the US had relied on 'strategic ambiguity', not asserting that it would defend Taiwan, but not saying that it wouldn't either. Efforts were made to suggest that US policy hadn't changed. But in Japan, in May that year, Biden again stated publicly that the US would defend Taiwan against attack.

So, what changed the US position? The former Japanese Prime Minister Shinzo Abe spoke for pretty well all America's allies in Asia in urging the United States to make clear, in the face of increasingly threatening Chinese behaviour, that it would in fact defend Taiwan. It was feared that Putin's aggression in Ukraine might embolden the Chinese. Earlier, the Chinese had said that Biden would be 'flirting with fire' if he appeared to be supporting Taiwanese independence. Biden in turn accused China of 'flirting with danger' by flexing its military might at Taiwan. He endorsed the 'One China' policy but not any use of force by the Chinese government to achieve it.

The US foreign service professionals would have preferred him to stick to 'strategic ambiguity'. But for Biden to say this again was no accident. It was an explicit commitment, annoying the Chinese but intended to avoid any miscalculation by them. The respected head of the US Council of Foreign Relations and former White House aide Richard Haass was one of those who had argued that, given President Xi's increasingly aggressive attitude towards Taiwan and in the South China Sea, 'strategic ambiguity' had outlived its usefulness, especially following the Russian aggression in Ukraine.

As Biden ended his visit to Asia, North Korea responded with three further ballistic missile tests and four Chinese and Russian nuclear-capable aircraft conducted a joint exercise. The subsequent visit of the US Speaker of the House of Representatives to Taiwan triggered violent Chinese reactions.

Biden's attempt, meanwhile, to revive the nuclear agreement with Iran appears unlikely to succeed in the face of Iranian intransigence, opening the prospect of another potential crisis as Iran gets closer to a military nuclear threshold.

'WE ARE NOT GOING TO DEFEND UKRAINE'

In semi-isolation during the pandemic, Vladimir Putin wrote his long essay 'On the historical unity of Russians and Ukrainians', asserting that Russians and Ukrainians are one people, that Ukraine could not be sovereign except in association with Russia, that it did not need the Donbas and that its declaration of independence invalidated its claim to Crimea.

To justify his planning for the invasion of Ukraine, Putin focused on its potential accession to NATO. While during the presidency of George W. Bush, Ukraine had been assured that it could join NATO, admission would have required the consent of all NATO members, which was not likely to be forthcoming. The German Chancellor, Olaf Scholz, told Putin that the whole question was moot.

Putin also was continuing to demand the removal of defensive missile systems and all NATO forces from Poland and several other NATO countries, seeing it as his mission to re-incorporate in Russia countries which had been part of the Soviet Union and to bring former Warsaw Pact countries back within the Russian sphere of influence.

Notably missing from the exchanges in this crisis was any Kissinger-style secret diplomacy. It most likely also would have failed, given Putin's deliberate irrationality about Ukraine, but it should at least have been attempted.

The St Petersburg to Germany gas pipeline, Nord Stream 2, controlled by Gazprom but part financed by German companies, was conceived from the outset by Putin as a strategic project to bypass Ukraine and increase the already high dependence of Europe, especially Germany, on Russian gas supplies. But Biden's Secretary of State, Antony Blinken, helped to mobilise the European allies to join in threatening severe sanctions if Russia invaded Ukraine.

What Biden had made clear from the outset of the Putin-manufactured crisis was that the US and NATO would not intervene militarily to help to defend Ukraine. He did not feel that he could afford to create expectations that they might do so and he would not have had public support in the US if he had done. But, in Putin's calculations, this sealed the fate of Ukraine. In terms of deterrence and of what happened subsequently, it would have been wiser to make a less categorical statement than to promise what appeared to be no involvement by NATO.

In the run-up to the Russian invasion, the administration tried to use US intelligence about Russian troop movements and intentions to 'call out' Putin's plans to create a false crisis in the enclaves already occupied by Russia to justify an attempt to seize the whole of Ukraine, a vast nation of 44 million people who had voted overwhelmingly for independence.

WAS NATO ENLARGEMENT RESPONSIBLE FOR RUSSIAN AGGRESSION?

NATO enlargement should have been handled differently and certainly would have been by George H. W. Bush. George W. favoured pell-mell enlargement, the driving force for which was the fear of all the applicants that, otherwise, they might again be subjected to Russian domination, which they had good reason to fear. But for their membership of NATO, the Baltic states would have been the first victims of Putin's determination to 'reclaim Russian lands', restore 'historic Russia' and exercise continuing oversight over the former members of the Warsaw Pact.

Condoleezza Rice recorded that 'Moscow's patience finally snapped' with the invitations to Georgia and Ukraine to join NATO. This was foolhardy in the case of Georgia and half-hearted in the case of Ukraine, ignoring Angela Merkel's warnings. None of which can justify Putin's attempt to destroy Ukraine and erase it from the map of Europe, despite being told that Ukrainian accession to NATO was 'moot'.

Putin's justification for the invasion of countries with Russian minorities is a precise imitation of Hitler's pretexts for invading Czechoslovakia and Poland. In terms of a belief in their superior willpower, ruthlessness, ability to inspire fear and manner of dealing with opponents, the two have much in common beyond that.

Putin's objective, beyond seizing Ukraine, was to inflict on NATO and the West the kind of humiliation he felt Russia had suffered at the time of the break-up of the Soviet Union. When the invasion took place, Putin threatened 'consequences the like of which you have never seen' if NATO intervened.

When the Russians then invaded, the head of the German military criticised publicly his country's politicians for leaving his forces underfunded and unprepared, causing Germany to announce a dramatic increase in defence spending which, in time, will make a very important new contribution to European defence.

The White House initially continued to express concern to avoid 'provoking' Putin. Biden made clear that any attack on NATO territory would bring the alliance into the conflict, but beyond that and sanctions, the initial US response was cautious, emphasising the need to avoid a clash with Russia.

The invasion shocked Europe into an unprecedented display of unity and resolve in imposing really extensive economic sanctions against Russia, including its suspension from the SWIFT payments system and disinvestment by many major Western companies. Germany duly suspended Nord Stream 2. But the effect of sanctions to date has been largely offset by Russia continuing to earn vast sums from its oil and gas sales, including the diversion of sales to Asia. They should be more effective over time, as Russia now is facing a long-term loss of its gas exports to Europe. But Putin, in pursuit of his 'mission', is not going to be deterred by sanctions.

*   *   *

The risk-averse attitude of the US government was turned on its head when Putin's attempt to secure a quick victory and install a compliant quisling government through the seizure of Kyiv was defeated by Ukrainian resistance, helped by the supply by the US and others of large numbers of anti-tank and other defensive weapons. The skill and determination the Ukrainians showed in doing so impressed the US media and public opinion and changed the calculations of the Pentagon and the administration.

Ukraine, which had been expected to hold out for no more than a few weeks against the Russian invasion, now was thought likely to be able to do so for an extended period or, quite possibly, to achieve a stalemate. Scholz and Macron displayed a reluctance to burn their bridges with Putin, but hopes that he might be satisfied with Crimea and all or most of the Donbas region were based on a false assessment of him. His objective was to put an end to Ukraine's existence as a country.

By April 2022, the US had abandoned its prior reserve in favour of a far more adventurous policy, with the US and others, including especially Britain and Poland, supplying badly needed heavy weapons and artillery to Ukraine, though Germany delayed supplying armoured cars and tanks, while France supplied some artillery and, later, air defence systems.

Far from continuing to avoid 'provoking' Putin, Biden now declared him a war criminal (also a thug and a murderous dictator). Living up to his reputation as a 'gaffe machine', Biden declared in Poland that 'for God's sake, this man cannot remain in power'. The White House scrambled to declare that this did not mean what it said, as regime change was not US policy.

The US by now was committed to an entirely different, Pentagon-led, policy, having decided, as Secretary for Defense Lloyd Austin put it, 'on an effort to weaken the Russian military sufficiently to deter them from further aggression'.

This led the Russian leadership to conclude that they were now effectively at war with NATO, albeit on a proxy basis. The US Congress, on a bipartisan basis, rushed through tens of billions of dollars in military, financial and humanitarian assistance to Ukraine.

In a far from competent military performance, the Russians have been able to occupy more, though not all, of the Donbas, with Russian artillery reducing large areas to rubble, also seizing Kherson in the Dnieper estuary and Zaporizhzhya, including the main Ukrainian nuclear power plant there. But from September 2022 the Ukrainians recovered half of the new territory they had lost, including forcing the Russians to make a humiliating withdrawal from the city (though not the region) of Kherson on the west bank of the Dnieper River.

Putin's response was to call up 300,000 reservists and organise sham referendums on union with Russia in the Donbas and other regions Russia still had not been able entirely to occupy. These then were formally incorporated into Russia.

In response to Putin again 'waving the nuclear card', the US national security advisor Jake Sullivan declared that the Russians had been warned that if they used nuclear weapons, the US would react decisively, with 'catastrophic consequences' for Russia. The US and NATO would have the ability to use missiles and their superior air power to destroy the Russian military capacity in Ukraine. With President Xi of China also declaring that 'a nuclear war cannot be won and must never be fought', Putin has rowed back on his nuclear threats but has resorted instead to a systematic bombardment of the power infrastructure in Ukraine. His forces have intensified their efforts to occupy the remainder of the Donbas and continue to hold the territory they have seized north of the Azov Sea, giving them a land bridge to Crimea.

While giving wholehearted support to Ukraine, concerned to avoid escalation, the US has declined to 'encourage or enable' attacks on Russia proper, though the Ukrainians have launched some attacks with their own drones. A channel of communication has been reopened with the Putin regime. Ukraine's de facto allies will be cautious about efforts to recover Crimea, where, historically, there was more support for Russia.

* * *

As US Secretary of State Antony Blinken pointed out, Putin's objectives were not and never have been confined to annexing Ukraine.

They have been to humiliate the US and its allies and to undermine NATO, which remains his overriding objective.

Instead, his invasion of Ukraine to date has had the opposite effect. In 2019, President Macron declared that NATO, which in terms of deterrence has been the most successful alliance in history, was 'brain dead' and increasingly irrelevant, based presumably on his faith that Russia no longer posed a threat.

But the East Europeans, having suffered directly under Soviet occupation, never believed in that comforting theory. Unlike their Western counterparts, they did not regard Gorbachev and Yeltsin as likely to prove to be the template for the future in Russia. They thought it more likely that the Russians would revert to their traditional desire for a 'strong leader' who, almost by definition, would pose a threat to others. Hence their disregard for Macron's ideas about a European defence system separate from the United States (to be led by France).

The principal effect of Putin's invasion of Ukraine has been to revitalise NATO and challenge the notion that the United States can afford to abdicate its role as the 'indispensable nation' in dealing with major world crises. US forces in Europe have been increased to 100,000. Nothing short of this display of Russian aggression would have brought the traditionally neutralist Finland and Sweden to apply to join NATO, despite Russian threats that they would face consequences, 'including military', if they did so. Far from being deterred by Putin's threats, they have regarded these as reinforcing the case for them to join the alliance.

The Ukrainians have been creating their own legend of heroic resistance. Ukraine will be hard put to recover all the territory seized by Russia, but Putin has failed in his attempt to erase Ukraine from the map of Europe. The outcome in the end is likely to be determined by the military facts on the ground. It is a vital Western interest to ensure that Putin's aggression is stopped in Ukraine, deterring him from his ambition of also annexing the Baltic states.

CHAPTER SEVENTEEN

A NEW COLD WAR IN A
BIPOLAR WORLD?

'THERE IS EVIL IN THIS WORLD'
– BARACK OBAMA

The British intelligence services at first were reluctant to believe that the poisonings of Putin's opponents by agents of the Russian intelligence services were authorised by the Russian President. The first spectacular case was the attempted poisoning in 2004 of Viktor Yushchenko, the pro-Western candidate in the Ukrainian presidential election. Yushchenko barely survived but won the election. There followed the poisonings of Alexander Litvinenko, the Skripals and Alexei Navalny and the shooting in the back in a Moscow street of Boris Nemtsov, former Deputy Prime Minister under Yeltsin and Putin's principal adversary at the time. Another Deputy Prime Minister under Yeltsin, Anatoly Chubais, having resigned from the Putin government over the invasion of Ukraine, hastily left the country.

This study is a reminder of a time when a great President helped to manage the series of crises accompanying the break-up of the Soviet Union, including seeking to avoid any apparent humiliation of Russia in the process. Before him, Henry Kissinger, with his upbringing in the 1930s, saw it as his task to try to conjure away the danger of clashes between the major powers, to considerable effect in terms of détente with the Soviet Union and the normalisation of relations with China. Both were believers in techniques of personal and secret diplomacy which have been missing in the present crisis. However reluctantly, we now find ourselves back in the George Kennan era of containment, certainly so long as Putin remains in power.

The United States always liked to regard itself as a 'reluctant sheriff' in intervening against hostile or aggressive regimes around the world, though for decades the reluctance was not evident in its interventions in Latin America. The invasion of Iraq has become the classic template for a war that did not need to be fought and Afghanistan an illustration of the difficulties of the once popular but since largely discredited theory of nation building. Globalisation, previously hailed, as at some point it will be again, for the economic benefits it has spread around the world, has fallen out of favour too. Freer trade and the very notion of any new trade agreements have been abandoned completely by the Biden administration.

But the idea that the United States can safely disengage from its post-Second World War role in the world, just as it was gaining favour, has been turned on its head by Vladimir Putin. The willingness to continue to display leadership in dealing with international crises depends on Americans being convinced that it is in their interests to do so. Putin has reminded them that it is. The West now finds itself engaged in a new Cold War with Russia, while the trade conflicts and general toughening of the US attitude, plus the reactions to increasing Chinese aggressiveness in Asia, have pushed Russia and China closer together than they have been before.

That is not an entirely natural alliance, given the tensions in the past on their vast common frontier and their different economic interests. China received a clear warning from the US that if it assisted the Russian offensive in Ukraine, it could find itself subject to the same sanctions as Russia, causing the Chinese hastily to declare that Chinese policy would be guided by Chinese interests. Though China too is an expansionist power and must continue to be deterred from attacking Taiwan, Biden has assured President Xi that the US is looking for 'competition, not confrontation' in the relationship with China. A sustained attempt will need to be made to re-establish a more effective dialogue with its leadership, as was achieved, in no less challenging times, by Henry Kissinger and George H. W. Bush.

Russia will try to claim some form of victory but will emerge from the war in Ukraine with its economy damaged, the reputation of its armed forces dented and a host of forces more effectively arrayed against it. Putin's claim that he could occupy six European capitals in forty-eight hours would be laughed at today, but the problem is not just Putin but the nature of the Russian state and an atavistic desire to dominate its neighbours.

The consequences of Putin's unnecessary war in Ukraine, which posed no conceivable threat to Russia, will take decades to play out. It would be nice to hope that this will galvanise the Europeans into doing more to help secure their own defence. If they wish seriously to develop their defence capability, the only effective framework within which to do so will be NATO, not some separate entity with neither the power nor the collective will to make a difference.

At some point there will be an at any rate temporary end to the fighting in Ukraine, most probably on unpleasant terms. This is a moment in world history when the tectonic plates will prove to have shifted. Overcoming their own differences, the US and its allies again will need to show sufficient resolve to make further aggression an unattractive option for Russia and, potentially, China while seeking to avert a drift towards a bipolar world.

But what if Donald Trump manages to return to the White House? Given his lack of appeal to centrist voters, complicity in the storming of the Capitol and failures in the US midterm elections, that is a very big if. There would be another period of chaos in US foreign policy. He might try to seek an accommodation with Putin over Ukraine, only to find that Congress will not lift sanctions. His disruptive behaviour is unlikely to prove the norm for the US in the future, given its failure to date to deliver any perceivable benefits. The Republican Party will have a better chance of remaining competitive by reverting to the inclusive politics of George H. W. and George W. Bush than by persisting with the deliberate divisiveness of Donald Trump. If they wish to enhance their chances of winning the next presidential election, they would need to nominate the Florida Governor, Ron DeSantis, or another candidate with a better chance of doing so than Trump.

Barack Obama may be right that the US will not want to continue indefinitely assuming the burdens it has in the past. Americans will want it to be more selective about doing so. But the Biden undertakings to support Ukraine against the Russian invasion, to do whatever is necessary to prevent Iran becoming a nuclear power and to defend Taiwan against China have bipartisan support. As George H. W. Bush forecast, neither these nor other world crises can be successfully managed without the United States being willing to continue to act as the 'indispensable nation' in leading the effort to do so.

INDEX